MANHATTAN PASSIONS

DISCARDED
From Nashville Public Library

Books by Ron Rosenbaum

Manhattan Passions: True Tales of Power, Wealth, and Excess

Rebirth of the Salesman: Tales of the Song and Dance 70s

Murder at Elaine's

Manhattan Passions

True Tales of Power, Wealth, and Excess

Ron Rosenbaum

BTB
BEECH TREE BOOKS
WILLIAM MORROW
New York

Copyright © 1987 by Ron Rosenbaum

These stories have appeared in slightly different form in
Manhattan, inc.

All rights reserved. No part of this book may be reproduced or
utilized in any form or by any means, electronic or mechanical,
including photocopying, recording or by any information storage
and retrieval system, without permission in writing from the
Publisher. Inquiries should be addressed to Permissions Department, Beech Tree Books, William Morrow and Company, Inc.,
105 Madison Ave., New York, N.Y. 10016.

Library of Congress Cataloging-in-Publication Data

Rosenbaum, Ron.
Manhattan passions.
1. New York (N.Y.)—Social life and customs.
2. Manhattan (New York, N.Y.)—Social life and customs.
3. Interviews—New York (N.Y.) 4. Celebrities—New
York (N.Y.)   I. Title.
F125.R67   1987   974.7'1   86-17351
ISBN 0-688-06612-7

Printed in the United States of America

First Edition

1 2 3 4 5 6 7 8 9 10

BOOK DESIGN BY JOHN BELLACOSA

BIB

The word "book" is said to derive from *boka,* or beech.
The beech tree has been the patron tree of writers since ancient times and
represents the flowering of literature and knowledge.

For Jane Amsterdam

87-17243

Acknowledgments

I'd like to thank my editor, Jim Landis, for his belief in this book and for the thoughtful and perceptive suggestions that improved it. I'm also grateful to his colleagues at Beech Tree Books, Jane Meara, Dennis Combs, and Bruce Giffords, for their help and attentiveness.

Among the many talented people Jane Amsterdam brought to *Manhattan, inc.* who made working on these stories such a pleasure, I'm particularly grateful to the brilliant art director Nancy Butkus, whose visual imagination and verbal wit are unsurpassed. And to managing editor Duncan Stalker, whose editorial suggestions were always on target and whose amazing good nature matches his discernment. I'm also thankful to assistant editors Adrienne Simmons and Pat Singer for the care with which they worked on my manuscripts.

My agent Kathy Robbins, smart, cheerful, and dedicated, has been a continuing source of excellent advice and inspiration.

And finally I'd like to thank some people whose intelligence, sense of humor, kindness, and presence in my life have, in many and various ways, been particularly important to me while I've been working on this book: Betsy Carter, Jan Drews, Mike Drosnin, Liz Hecht, and my sister, Ruth Rosenbaum.

Contents

———— ● ————

INTRODUCTION

———— 🍎 ————

"Swimming in Money"

I didn't quite grasp it at first, the full emblematic significance of the mirrored ceiling over Donald Trump's desk. At the time I was too preoccupied assessing Trump's improbable dream of negotiating a nuclear arms deal with the Soviets to do more than note the curious presence of a golden mirror over Trump's head.

Now I'd seen mirrored ceilings before. For strictly journalistic reasons that are too complex to explain here, I'd more than once found myself in the high-roller "comp suites" of certain casino-hotels. But the mirrored ceilings in these bowers of bliss were invariably located directly over the satin-sheeted bed or the heart-shaped tub. I'd never seen a mirrored ceiling over a desktop before.

And the mirrored ceiling over Donald Trump's desk was no standard-issue blank for that matter. It was composed of golden squares of mirror-finished precious metal alloy. The awe-inspiring effect was to suspend Trump's desk, his phone set, and Trump himself upside down in a digitalized golden shimmer on the ceiling.

Seeing Trump hovering up there in that golden realm overhead made me think of those grade-school American history texts that would scoff at the immigrants' deluded dream that the streets of New York were paved with gold. Little did the dusty pedants who wrote those books realize that the immigrants' dream was just not grandiose enough: Manhattan in the eighties is a city whose *ceilings* are paved with gold.

I dwell on Trump's mirrored ceiling because I've come to think of it as the most characteristic emblem of this particular era in the life of the Imperial City. If an age declares its ruling passions in the transactions it chooses to eroticize, then the passions of Manhattan in the eighties are best embodied in the golden mirror over the dealmaker's desk.

This is a fascinating inversion of the erotic dynamic of Victorian pornography described by Steven Marcus in *The Other Victorians*. Marcus noted that the secret sexual fantasies of that age were often expressed in metaphors from the economic realm. "Up until the end of the nineteenth century," the distinguished Columbia scholar tells us, "the chief English colloquial word for the orgasm was 'to spend.' "

In our era by contrast, wealth itself has become erotic and it seems more common for people to seek orgasm *by* spending. Consider for instance one of the rash of yuppie jokes that may provide future scholars with folkloric corroboration of this peculiar erotic phenomenon of eighties:

Q. What is the favorite sexual position of the New York yuppie?

A. Facing Bloomingdale's.

But—to return to Trump's golden mirror—I would like to address myself to a question that occurred to me as I leaned across his desk to adjust my tape recorder and glanced up at my head intruding into the golden realm above: What am I doing in this picture?

There's an moment early on in *The Great Gatsby* when Nick Carraway—a first-time guest at one of Gatsby's epic weekend parties—stumbles upon "the owl-eyed gentleman" in Gatsby's library. The owl-eyed gent is just struggling to his senses from a week-long stupor that seems to have begun at the previous weekend's party. He seems deeply disturbed about something, as if he's just awakened from a sinister sorcerer's spell, or perhaps suspects he's a soul newly arrived in hell.

"Who brought you?" he cries out to Nick. "Or did you just come? I was *brought.*" The distinction seems important to him.

And so, in reply to the question "What am I doing in this picture?" I can truthfully say I was brought. In fact, I practically had to be dragged kicking and screaming. But in retrospect, I'm grateful. I might have missed the whole Gatsbyesque carnival of the era if I hadn't been brought. And so if you'll bear with me I'd like to explain how that happened and introduce you to the woman who brought me. Which will require beginning with the Blue Blazer of Shame.

The place is Christ Cella, a clubby midtown Manhattan steakhouse. It is the spring of 1984, the year *Newsweek* will subsequently call the Year of the Yuppie, and all the tables but one, it seems, are occupied by dark-suited corporate VP types wearing earnest looks and those telltale gold ties that had suddenly bloomed that year around the necks of dress-for-success types in Manhattan.

But off on the periphery of the upstairs dining room is a table occupied by two anomalous types: an attractive woman in a stylish silk blouse and an uncomfortable-looking guy in an ill-fitting blue blazer.

Do you know those really terrible-looking generic "sports jackets" stuffy restaurants keep on hand in their coatrooms for customers foolish enough to arrive without the required attire? Actually, you probably don't know them, not the way I do; I've worn more than my share of these lint-flecked beauties.

Usually it's a threadbare blue blazer with an ancient *foie gras* stain on the sleeve. Or a somber black number of an appalling gloominess that suggests previous tenure in a casket. The Sports Jacket of the Living Dead.

But regardless of size or style, they all seem to have been tailored internally to bind the arms in such a way that the wearer will feel the discomfort of a prisoner in the public stocks.

Of course that's what these jackets are: not helpful amenities but punishment garments, designed to identify the wearer as a social transgressor as surely as if they had been dyed with the big black-and-white stripes of a chain gang prisoner or emblazoned with a scarlet letter.

Well, that was me at Christ Cella encased in the punitive confines of the house blue blazer. And that was Jane Amsterdam sitting across from me, trying to talk me out of an incredibly misguided notion I had.

Let me explain the context. Jane had just left *The Washington Post*'s Investigative Unit—"the SWAT Team" as it was known in the investigative reporting trade—to return to New York to edit a new magazine, something she said would be called *Manhattan, inc.* She'd invited me to lunch to discuss my writing for it and I'd made the mistake of showing up in an old college warm-up jacket, a miscalculation that probably betrayed my misgivings about the nature of the venture. As SWAT Team deputy editor, Jane had been working with Bob Woodward on investigatory enterprises that were supposed to be at the cutting edge of newspaper journalism. As I tore into the tasty sirloin and cottage fries, I wondered aloud to Jane why she'd left to start this *Manhattan, inc.* thing.

Wake up and smell the coffee brewing, Ron, she said, although not exactly in those words. She spoke of how the attention of the SWAT Team had shifted from the public sector scandals of the seventies to the behavior of the potentates of the resurgent private sector, the CEOs of Mobil and General Dynamics, for instance. She pointed to the way David McClintick's *Indecent Exposure* had made the boardroom backstabbing at Columbia Pictures seem more dramatic than most of the studio's on-screen melodramas. Look at the way the clash of takeover titans was becoming a national spectator sport. Look at the way the country had been captivated by the Agee-Cunningham romance as it played itself out amidst the chivalric imagery of white knights and poison pills, the elevation of the CEO to romantic hero status. For better or worse, the whole decade was being defined by a new cast of characters with a new set of values and they were all congregating in Manhattan—the raiders, the fast tycoons, the shadowy new Gatsbys of the roaring eighties all jockeying for position in the fluid new hierarchies of wealth and status. This should be exciting to you as a writer, Jane told me, because it's a realm that's previously been written about mainly by bottom-line-minded business magazines. This is where the good stories are, Ron, she concluded.

I wasn't interested.

My mind was on a different decade, I explained to Jane. I'd spent the past year immersed in research for a novel set mainly in Berlin in the thirties. It was, to say the least, a different mind-set from that of Manhattan in the eighties.

And besides, the stories I liked most tended to be about outsiders rather than insiders. About transgressors of one peculiar sort or another. I'd written about "phone phreak" outlaws and double agents for *Esquire*, about Weather Underground fugitives for *New Times*, about moles and heretical SAC majors for *Harper's*, about self-proclaimed "dental faith healers" for *Rolling Stone* (*"God's out there tonight, fillin' teeth"*).

I preferred stories about people with grand obsessions and poetic delusions, cancer-cure visionaries, doomed romantics who died in strange circumstances. The only time I'd written regularly about people in power was when I'd covered the White House for *The Village Voice* during the final year of Watergate—but they were all transgressors there.

I tried to be polite with Jane Amsterdam. I told her I was sure she'd be successful with her magazine (in fact, *Manhattan, inc.* was to win the National Magazine Award for general excellence on the basis of Jane's first four issues alone). But I didn't want to be part of it. I didn't want to have to take power people and power lunches seriously. Nonetheless, I told Jane magnanimously (this is painful to recall), I *would* be willing to write about lunch.

About lunch? she asked.

Yes, about lunch, I explained. About food. I'll do a restaurant column for you. I'll review the restaurants where the power people eat their power lunches but I'll write about the lunch, not the power.

"You want to write about velvety sauces?" she asked incredulously.

I explained to her I'd always secretly harbored a (not uncommon) lonely-writer fantasy: Wouldn't it be great to have a restaurant column, take tons of friends out for fantastic meals, and write it all off with a few deft remarks about "fiery mélanges of flavor" and the like?

I'll always be grateful to Jane Amsterdam for understanding how truly bad my restaurant review idea was and yet still caring enough about me to think of an ingenious way to deflect me ever so gently from this course of madness.

"Uh, Ron, what you're saying is, you want to go to these power-lunch places and write about the lunch while ignoring the people?"

"I wouldn't ignore the people entirely," I said with a demented reasonableness. "Maybe I could incorporate some overheard conversation, capture the flavor of the place . . ."

"Well," said Jane, judiciously maintaining a straight face while gazing at the Blue Blazer of Shame (and undoubtedly wondering how I'd ever even get seated in any of these places), "it's true that some of the best scenes in *Indecent Exposure* took place at Côte Basque when the Columbia Pictures execs would lunch with the Allen and Company bankers. Maybe you could go to lunch with someone like Herb Allen at Côte Basque and—"

"No," I said. "I don't want to *talk* to these people. I don't want to talk to Herb Allen." I was adamant on this point. I would be willing, I said, to work something about Herb Allen into a discussion of the food but—

"What if you took a tape recorder to lunch with some of these characters?" Jane suggested, sensing compromise. "Listen to them talk while you eat, do conversational portraits of them."

"People with power never tell the truth about themselves," I objected.

"That doesn't mean they won't reveal themselves," she said. "You're interested in obsessions. Take them to lunch, tune in to their obsessions." The obsessions of insiders, she suggested, could be just as revealing as those of outsiders, and just as close to the surface.

And so we reached a tentative agreement. But the struggle wasn't over, at least in my mind. In the beginning, I was still determined to write about lunch rather than power. In my first outing, the one with Ed Koch, I was able to sustain this delusion because the mayor's food obsessions turned out to be an unexpectedly revealing mirror of his political personality. His description of his hungry fat cells seething with frustrated rage at the demands of self-restraint was a perfect reflection of—and perhaps explanation for—his intemperate political style. Viewed in that light it's not surprising that the mayor's initial reaction to the suicide attempt of cash-hungry politico Donald Manes was to ascribe it to the despair of a dieter in the throes of a liquid protein regimen.

And the late Roy Cohn's bizarre tuna fish fetish (he forced the celebrated chefs of Le Cirque to mix Bumble Bee and Hellmann's for him) was a perfect example of the way he manipulated the peculiarities of his lifestyle in service of his carefully crafted image as the Ultimate Insider.

But after that early encounter with Cohn, descriptions of food begin to disappear from these pieces and lunch itself exists mainly as an excuse, a setting, for a conversational portrait—and sometimes disappears even as an excuse, as with Mario Cuomo, with whom I shared only an ascetic cup of coffee sufficiently bitter to mortify the flesh.

But Jane Amsterdam turned out to be right about the obsessions of insiders. It may have something to do with the fact that I'm a bit of an obsessive type myself and so I tend to bring out, tune in to the obsessive side of others. The Ancient Mariners of the world have always singled me out to tell their troubled tales to. It may also have something to do with the relatively unguarded circumstances of the lunch setting; it was after all an age in which the ritual of the public lunch replaced the private therapy group as the prime stage for the self-expressive dramas of the ruling spirits of the age.

Whatever the reason, some of my favorite moments in these stories are the ones that see the emergence of some sort of telltale obsession or passion—a talking seal, the fourth-century heresy of Pelagius, Kaddafi's pilot, hungry fat cells, an automatic bathroom door latch, to name a few.

But something more than the form changed in the course of these conversations. Something about my own attitude toward the people and times changed, too. The more I looked up from the memoirs of the thirties I was reading and paid attention to the ruling obsession of the eighties, the more I began to develop a Bad Attitude toward it all.

It was a time when a certain sort of individual would lean across a table in a loud Cajun café and fix you with a look people used to fix their friends with when they were on the verge of announcing they'd taken *est* or accepted Reverend Moon as their savior. They'd wipe the margarita foam from their lips and tell you they'd discovered that the truly important thing for their personal growth at this point in their lives was to make a huge pile of money, *"After all,"* they'd say, as if the following three-word formula explained and excused it all, *"it's the eighties."*

The fascinating thing about those who blossomed into full *"it's the eighties"* consciousness, was that it wasn't enough for them to boast of their own liberation from inhibitions about the shameless pursuit of wealth. It was also necessary for them to denounce all those who failed to attain their clarity of conscience about the lust for a life of Marcos-style excess.

There's a perfect illustration of this latter phenomenon in the savage reaction of the city's rich and social to my story about the Rohatyns.

When the Rohatyns dared suggest to me that the whole socialite charity mechanism was failing to address the life-and-death urgencies of the city's poor, and when I characterized this as "The Shame of the Super Rich," there were screams of vengeful outrage up and down Park Avenue. *"Haute* Manhattan was buzzing with one question last week," reported *Newsweek.* "If you can't trust a senior partner at Lazard Frères to keep his mouth shut about things like this, who can you trust? . . . In any case the reaction from wealthy institutions was immediate rejection."

But the rejection of the Rohatyns was more than institutional. It turned very personal.

W, the faithful chronicle of the city's rich and social, filled a two-page spread with snide, sometimes vicious, often anonymous attacks against the embattled couple. The rich and social rose up in fury to trash the Rohatyns— questioning their motives, their personal generosity, practically questioning their sanity. "I think they've really lost it on this," sniffed one anonymous socialite.

What was fascinating about this furor was that not one of the angry socialites had a single word to say about the situation of the poor. Nor could they *conceive* of the possibility that the Rohatyns might have been motivated—in however naïve and muddled a way—by the slightest iota of genuine concern for the suffering of the poor. Such a possibility didn't seem to cross their minds.

Now while I was aware of the ironies of people in the Rohatyns' position expressing concern for the poor and while my concluding paragraphs make explicit my own feelings about the nature of the Rohatyns' naïveté, nonetheless, I was shocked by the incredibly heartless reaction of the rich and social. The only suffering they seemed to awaken to from this controversy was their own.

"Working for these charities is slogging," moaned Pat Buckley to *W*.

How harsh and tormenting could that slogging get? "Pat Buckley deserves a medal of honor" for her heroic toil, an awed Estée Lauder told *W*.

Undoubtedly she does, but there seems to be a lack of perspective among the rich and social about the relative levels of suffering, a narrowing of the world to their own golden-mirrored fantasy realm in which everyone is rich.

Here again, a comparison to the realm of Victorian pornography is instructive.

"The world of pornography" in that era, Professor Marcus reminds us, "is a world of plenty. In it all men are infinitely rich in substance, all men are limitlessly endowed with the universal fluid currency. . . . Just as in the myth Zeus descends upon Danaë in a shower of gold, so in pornography the world is bathed, flooded"—you get the picture.

It's a picture that bears some resemblance in its imagery of fluid excess to the one Felix Rohatyn conjured up when he tried to capture the flush feeling of the rich and social: "People in our world are swimming in money."

Now Gibbon wisely cautions against the tendency "for the inferior ranks of mankind to claim a merit for the contempt of that pomp and pleasure which fortune has placed beyond their reach."

And so while I don't claim a merit for it, nonetheless I can't deny that my attitude toward these people began to make itself manifest in certain of these stories and also in certain of the actual encounters—most notably my lunch with Malcolm Forbes, who evicted me abruptly from his wine cellar in response to what I suppose was a deliberately provocative question. And also in my fascination with the almost perversely contrarian anti-materialist passions of Mario Cuomo.

My problem with figures like Forbes, I think, was the failure of their dreams to live up to the romantic splendor of Gatsby's. Gatsby, you recall, created his entire grandiose West Egg artifice just to arrange a meeting with the woman across the way, the one who lived in the place with the green light whose glow became the focus of all his yearnings.

But it became evident to me that the green light the Gatsbys of the eighties yearned for was merely the color of money.

THE SHAME OF THE SUPER RICH

———— ✦ ————

Meet Felix and Elizabeth Rohatyn: Society Dissidents

They don't want to come right out and say it. It's just too shocking. And what's more, it involves their friends, their set. Felix and Elizabeth Rohatyn are talking about the collective moral behavior of the richest, most powerful, most social people in Manhattan. They're talking about the dirty little secret of the city's super rich.

And so every time they come face-to-face with the full implications of what they're saying, they try to make disclaimers.

"We don't want to be making moral judgments," Felix Rohatyn says.

"We don't want to be in the position of attacking people," Elizabeth Rohatyn says.

"I don't want to sound socialist or leftist," Felix says.

But they are, she is, and he does.

They're saying something very radical about the values of Manhattan society, about human nature, about the shame of the city's rich.

And the fact that it's coming from them, the fact that I'm hearing these sentiments in the elegant living room of the Rohatyn's co-op at Park and Seventy-third, makes it all the more shocking.

Because if I were sitting in a drafty Lower East Side loft listening to a "socialist or leftist" tell me the rich in New York won't abandon their ceaseless pursuit of glamour to attend to the agony of the poor sleeping on their grates— well, that would be one thing. If a "socialist or leftist" were to tell me the whole busy glittering mechanism of the socialite charity world merely disguised a shocking neglect of the real needs of the poor—perhaps I'd be skeptical.

But it's quite another thing, isn't it, to hear such things here in the Rohatyn's living room, here amid porcelain and damask, to the accompaniment of sherry and biscuits—to hear it from socialites, not socialists.

Because if anyone knows, they know. The Rohatyns are situated in the very eye of the pyramid of power, status, and money in this town. There's Felix, of course—senior partner at Lazard Frères, chairman of the Municipal Assistance Corporation, the man many credit with saving the city during the fiscal crisis, a man with X-ray eyes for the real profile of public and private wealth in New York. And there's Elizabeth, with her patrician sensitivity to the nuances that distinguish the glamorous from the non-glamorous charity, with her ability born of years of socialite fund-raising work to distinguish the generous from the non-generous giver. She knows who's been naughty and nice.

And O ye rich and social, they've got your number. They know how "generous" you've been. They know you'll shell out six figures to rub shoulders with Brooke Astor at a Literary Lions dinner, or twice as much to be courted by smooth-tongued curators at a Met gala with Jackie O. But you won't have the time, you can't spare a dime, if the cause involves the non-chic sick, the poor of unglamorous races, and no Blue-Chip Board Personalities.

They've got your number. They've seen it and they don't like it and they're upset enough to speak out. Meet Felix and Elizabeth Rohatyn, Society Dissidents.

Already they're beginning to feel the heat from the socialite mafia for breaking ranks, for saying, in effect, that the black-tie and ball-gown costumes of the charity balls are nothing more than the emperor's new set of clothes.

It began last fall when an alert *Times* reporter, Kathleen Teltsch, noted some pointed criticism Felix made of the private-sector charity world in a speech to the City Club. Although the *Times* buried her story in the back of the Sunday paper, the socialite mafia took note of the critical comments from both Felix and Elizabeth therein. Tongues began wagging behind their backs all over town, the general tenor of those tongues being: What are they doing rocking our boat?

I ask Elizabeth Rohatyn what her socialite friends told her to her face. She claims many of them were supportive: "They said they were pleased that two people have stood up and said much of what they're thinking about."

"But sweetheart," says Felix, "I think in fairness that what was equally important is how many people in our circle of friends who are involved in these things *didn't* really speak to you. It's a very *eloquent* silence."

"It's a pregnant silence," she says.

They know they're isolated, exposed, way out in front on this. Because they know just how shocking the bottom line of their critique is.

"When will this story be coming out?" Felix asks me at the close of our conversation as I'm packing up my tape recorder.

"Six weeks or so," I say.

"We'll just have to plan to be out of town then, dear," she says.

The crusade began as an afterthought, an accident, or so Felix says. Of course, they'd talked about it a lot, agonized over it privately, but they hadn't gone public until Felix added those few fateful words to his City Club speech.

"Elizabeth had been concerned about this as a result of her work with the Lenox Hill Neighborhood Association," Felix explains. "I happened to mention it, stick it in at the end of a speech I gave that dealt mostly with mass-transit financing. And I put it in because of a speech Pat Moynihan made about the division between rich and poor in the city. Pat had given a rather despairing speech about the gulf existing, about how it was going to get wider, and really there was no way to deal with it. I was trying to be a little less despairing and talked about a couple things that might be done to help the poor in the light of federal cutbacks. And one was the capacity of wealthy, glamorous New Yorkers to make a difference. But to do so there would have to be a shift in emphasis from the glamorous people being involved with glamorous institutions, to try to divert this energy and this wealth to less glamorous institutions."

He didn't plan to turn his remarks into a crusade. It happened more by accident, he says. "This was not an Elizabeth and Felix joint effort to attract anybody's attention. It's just that we were both troubled and it's clear something out there is not right, and Elizabeth was in my office at Lazard one day when this reporter from the *Times* called me to talk about my speech. It happened Elizabeth was doing . . ." He turns to his wife.

"It was family planning," she says.

"Oh yeah, that was a real fiasco," Felix says.

"Why was it a fiasco?" I ask.

"That wasn't a fiasco," Elizabeth says, glancing pointedly at Felix. "I had been asked to get together a group of New Yorkers who cared about family planning because the governor thought it would be helpful. So I said sure, I'd get Victor and Betsy Gotbaum, I'd get Pat and Thornton Bradshaw, I'd get this one and that one. And so the morning comes when we all arrive to do this thing and Betsy gets there and I get there and Pat Bradshaw gets there, and Thornton couldn't come because he had a board meeting that came up and Victor couldn't come because he had something going on, so Felix found himself in this room full of women dealing with this issue of family planning."

"I said I'd be happy to cooperate if it's just print media," says Felix. "But all of a sudden in troop all of these television cameras and my partners are wondering what the hell is going on here. And I'm trying to explain to them that this is a Planned Parenthood—"

"Family planning, darling," says Elizabeth.

"Family planning, okay. But this is how it all happened, because the reporter was calling and I put her on with Elizabeth, and that's how this all started."

One of the fascinating things about Elizabeth's quotes in the *Times* story was that she seemed to direct some of her fire at her own husband for not doing anything about the problems he was speaking out on.

"Now wasn't there some implicit criticism of your husband in your comments?" I ask Elizabeth.

"It was rather explicit," says Felix, laughing.

"It was not criticism *of* him," Elizabeth says, "it was criticism of an *idea* he had."

"Which was?"

"It's that Felix felt that one way to make it equitable would be to ask the big institutions who bring in enormous amounts of money to agree to give five percent of their raised monies to sister and brother institutions such as a small dance group in Harlem. . . ."

"I still think it's a good idea," says Felix, somewhat disconsolately.

"And he still thinks it's a good idea. I said, '*No way!*' I've been a fund-raiser for years and years and years and you work hard to raise that money. If someone came to me and said, 'Well, I'd like to take part of what you raised and give it to somebody else,' I'd say, 'Forget it, you can't have anything. . . .' "

What we're listening to here is what seems like a long-running debate between the two of them about how best to get the vast, money-churning engine of the private charity world back on the tracks. It's really a debate between two views of human nature and it all comes down to who gets to squeeze the man from Squeedunk.

"There's a finite amount of money that individuals and corporations will give," Felix explains. "The more spectacular, glamorous institutions—their development departments have become a business. They've become a business like government and what they do is begin to think of ways of raising money regardless of . . . well, there is a tendency to say, 'Here is Mr. XYZ, who's got a billion dollars and is just moving into the city of New York from Squeedunk. And what project can we figure to bring him so that he gives us ten million dollars and we'll put his name on the door?' And whether the project is really related to the purposes of the institution or not is only the secondary thing."

Felix sees these development departments as sorcerer's apprentices gone wild. "They are sort of self-perpetuating money-raisers. It becomes a vacuum cleaner for glamorous money, and the question becomes whether the marketing arm can figure out a way to convince Mr. XYZ, who's just moved into the city with a billion dollars, to get on the cover of *Manhattan, inc.* by contributing ten million dollars to this institution."

"Darling!" exclaims Elizabeth.

"I wonder who you might be referring to?" I ask.

"Off-the-record time," she says, pointing to the recorder.

We have an off-the-record discussion about a certain Squeedunkian who has achieved new heights of civic respectability and top dinner invites in part by making huge donations to the most glamorous and social of charities. It is clear that Felix and Elizabeth, who have participated in the squeezing of a few Squeedunkians in their time, are not sure what to make of this new behemoth on the glamorous charity circuit.

When we go back on the record, Felix is talking about the "indecent" excess on the charity banquet circuit. There was one night in particular that really tore it for him.

"I was recently asked to attend one of these things. They dragged me on because I was chairman of MAC or whatever, and it was a very elegant affair at the grand ballroom of one of the hotels—black tie, splendid-looking ladies, wonderful flowers. I'm sure the tables were extremely expensive. In the middle of this they bring out these little black children because the program was aimed at helping poor black children. Which is a perfectly good cause. But there were these little kids floating around in extraordinary opulence in midtown Manhattan with photographers, and I just thought this was wrong. It was just in very poor taste to have these kids there."

The parade of poor kids made him question the whole process: "I asked myself, you know, is there any other way to raise the money for the programs that merit being supported than to get people to go to these functions in order to see and be seen by the rich and powerful in the city?"

He was tired, in other words, or being used as a status object, as a social-climbing peak to increase the draw of occasions that required a parade of the poor to open the wallets of the rich.

"But darling," says Elizabeth, "these are what the people

who go to them *buy*. It used to be that people wanted to go to Mrs. Belmont's and Mrs. Hoopdedoo's and Mrs. Whatever's, and those private parties and entities don't exist anymore. That whole kind of social movement has moved into the *bought party*. And so if Mr. and Mrs. So-and-so want to pay five thousand dollars to go to a party so they can say that they sat at the same table with Mr. and Mrs. X and their picture is going to be in *W*—well you can't really fault that."

"You're saying that's sort of human nature," I suggest. "That people are always—"

"Social climbing has always been that," she says. "Trollope wrote about it, Dickens wrote about it, Edith Wharton wrote about it. I mean it's always been the same thing."

"I just feel that we've crossed some lines in terms of excess," Felix says.

I turn to Elizabeth. "And what you're saying is that it's not bad to harness the energy of social climbing for a good cause. But do you think there've been lines that have been crossed?"

"Well, it just *has* gotten too opulent. The dynamics of it is that you say to yourself, okay, we've got to raise x money. Let's just let the ticket price rise to a thousand-dollar fee. Okay, if you're going to do that, my gosh, we have to give them a really good dinner, we have to have some really good music, we have to have a spectacular person for the entertainment, we have to have magnificent flowers, we have to give each woman a present to take home to remember that she came to this wonderful thing. That's where I think it gets out of line. I mean, wait a minute, isn't this to take *in* money and not to give out money? You know, let's not have party favors. I think that's defeating the purpose."

Let's not have party favors. It may not sound like a revolutionary manifesto. But detach yourself from the dynamics of party giving and consider the psychosocial reality that gives rise to such a plea.

"People in our world are swimming in money," Felix remarks at one point. They're swimming in money, but in order to get the city's rich to give a lousy thousand dollars to the poor who are drowning in front of their eyes you have to parade little black kids in front of them *and* give them party favors. I've read all of Dickens, and most of Edith Wharton, but I can't recall coming across anything quite so monstrous. Perhaps I should read more Trollope.

But the Rohatyns are a practical couple, less interested in condemning this state of mind than in finding a solution to the current scandalous state of affairs.

"What you're suggesting," I say to Elizabeth, "is that you want to harness the energy of social climbing by getting the real draws, the objects of social climbers, to shift their attention to nonglamorous charities which then—"

"That's surely what they did with the Citizens Committee for New York. Because we were in a crisis, it attracted across the board all kinds of fantastic New Yorkers to save the city's cultural institutions. I would like to see the same enthusiasm re-enthuse the whole level of the smaller, struggling agencies, the ones providing services to people in need—because that's the crisis now, rather than the big institutions that—"

"You see," Felix interrupts, "I think that's as hopeless an exercise as you think my suggestion is of leaving the powerful, wealthy, glitzy people in the city to support the big, glitzy institutions as long as these institutions are willing to take five or ten percent off the top by adopting neighborhood associations."

Felix lacks faith in Elizabeth's plan to get the peaks of the social-climbing world to put the squeeze on the Squeedunkians for more genuinely needy causes.

"Trying to get these very powerful, glamorous people to get interested in little, unglamorous—"

"You don't have to get involved," Elizabeth says. "What turns people on is sort of who you would be associated with if you did x, y, and z. Anybody who's coming to New York or living in New York or involved in New York would like to know those Blue-Chip Board Personalities."

Ah, the Blue-Chip Board Personalities. The elbows Squeedunkian elbows yearn to rub. You Blue-Chip Board Personalities, you Everests and Annapurnas of the social-climbing world—you know who you are—Elizabeth Rohatyn has a message for you: She wants to raise your consciousness, and thereby raise the consciousness of the rest of the rich from the top down. And she promises no heavy lifting.

"If you wanted to help a small agency," she says to a hypothetical Blue-Chip Board Personality, "it's not that you would have to get in there and roll up your sleeves and work and do a nine-to-five job or whatever," she assures them. "If you could find one that matched up with your interest and simply be sort of an assister or a door opener. . . ."

An assister or door opener: in other words, "Hello, Mrs. XYZ. I'm Mrs. Blue-Chip Board Personality, and normally I don't speak to people so newly arrived from Squeedunk, but I've got an *exquisite* little charitable agency that's hardly been discovered, and you and I are going to work *magic* with it, so I've asked its development director to speak to you personally about your commitment."

Sad to think that the survival of so many of the poor in this city must now depend on the tortuous rituals of squeezing rich social climbers, but such, it seems, is New York in the eighties.

Who exactly is suffering from the current system? I ask Elizabeth. Which are the less glamorous organizations the

Blue-Chip Board Personalities are neglecting?

"I think there are things like illiteracy programs. I think there are drug programs. There are teenage pregnancy programs. . . ."

Felix is feeling a little uncomfortable with the implications of what they've been saying. He's not comfortable in the role of Society Dissident.

"But again I must say we had no intention . . . First of all, this was not an Elizabeth and Felix joint effort to attract anybody's attention," he tells me. "You know we're talking about institutions and people that are . . . that we are *involved* in, that lots of our friends are, that we support, and we're not trying to—"

"You're raising questions . . ." I suggest.

"Yeah, we're uncomfortable. . . ."

"I'm a trustee of the New York Public Library, you know," says Elizabeth, "and we have monumental problems and a spectacular development department and . . ."

"And I was on the board of the Philharmonic until last year when I went on the board of Carnegie Hall, where I thought there were more things I could do," Felix says. "It's just that we were both troubled, and it's clear that there is something out there that is not right because if that weren't so we wouldn't have gotten the response we got."

"It raises an interesting philosophical question, doesn't it?" I suggest. "In a mixed economy like ours, how much should the private side be doing in the face of federal cutbacks to the poor? Has the response been adequate? Has the private sector really pulled its weight in making up for—"

"It can't ever make up," says Elizabeth.

"The private side can't make it up," says Felix.

"That's one think I realized in talking to Victor Gotbaum," says Elizabeth. "He said he read what I'd said in the paper and he said, 'Elizabeth, what the problem is, is that the government should be doing a lot of the funding of the kind of things you're talking about on the neighborhood community level. And they're not. And the private sector doesn't have the experience nor the desire to take on all that.' "

"Yes," says Felix, "but that *really* raises the philosophical issue, where does the concept of charity . . . If the government is the only source of help to indigent and poor people, and if rich people's charities only go to very fancy, glamorous institutions, you know that's not right. Maybe that's human nature. But then if the government cuts back on help to the poor people, uneducated people, or teenage mothers, and there is a need, and you do have large institutions raising large sums of money from wealthy, glamorous people, shouldn't we try to channel some of the existing big pipeline to at least the small institutions? . . ."

Rechannel the existing pipeline. A quintessentially Felix-type solution, the vision not of a social architect so much as a social maintenance man, a fixer-upper: To achieve social justice one need not redesign the machinery of society, just reconnect the pipes.

"Is it so inconceivable to think that when some big, fancy ball is given at a huge price that one can say, well, five percent of his money or ten percent of his money is going to be devoted to an adopted institution? I don't think that's so crazy," he says to Elizabeth. "I know you do."

"I only think it's crazy because I don't think the institutions are going to go for it."

"I read some figures in preparing for this that surprised me," I tell the Rohatyns. "I guess what I'm beginning to wonder is—you see all this flurry of strenuous activity in the charity ball world and you think the rich must be generous, but could it be the rich are really Scrooge-like?"

"What I object to," says Felix, "is that a lot of the giving is sort of tied in to the glitz. And again, I don't want to make moral judgments, but I do have a question in my mind about the nature of the giving and the way these larger glamorous institutions—it's like IBM getting a larger and larger share of the computer market. The larger institutions get a larger share of what's given and—"

"But isn't that the inevitable tendency of free markets, toward consolidation?"

"Well, it may be. Which is why free markets have to be controlled to some extent. It may be a socialist or leftist view, but I still believe, whereas Elizabeth wants to change—"

"Change the consciousness," she supplies.

"I'm much more prepared to stay within the system," says Felix, "and say, 'Fine. Wealthy, glamorous people and large corporations are always going to give to the largest institutions.' But I'm asking the institutions themselves to say this is a tough world we're living in and why shouldn't the charitable institutions adhere to the philosophy of tithing to other small programs in real need? . . ."

"What about the phantom-ball solution?" I suggest helpfully. I'd read that one solution to the party-favor glitz problem of charity benefits was to announce a fancy ball but don't actually give it, just have people send a check for what it would have cost *if* the ball had been held, thereby saving all those expenses. And most people wouldn't miss hearing Lester Lanin for the three-billionth time.

"That doesn't work," Elizabeth tells me.

"Why not?"

"First, there's a huge segment of people who *enjoy* doing that. They want to do it, to go see their friends; they want to do it to wear their new ball gowns or show off their new hairdo. . . ."

"I think there are more women than men who like to do that," says Felix.

"Well you can't say that," snaps Elizabeth. "You don't know that. I think it's a sexist remark. I don't think you can really say that."

"I don't know. The men I see at a lot of these things, they're all exhausted. . . . They're saying to each other, 'My God, what are we doing here?' "

"Maybe the men could make phantom appearances—pay double not to go," I suggest.

Elizabeth talks about the disappointing experience of a friend of hers who tried the phantom-ball solution.

"One year she had a big reception and she raised two hundred thousand dollars. And then she wrote a very clever letter, you know, about the wonderful pleasure of staying home and being in your own place and not having the wear and tear of buying a ball gown and everything else, so please there will be no benefit this year, and please just send in your contribution. And she got forty thousand dollars instead of two hundred thousand dollars which the ball generated."

"Elizabeth had a good idea as an alternative to the testimonial dinner," Felix says, "which was not to have a dinner but to have the recipient of the award—because a lot of people like to receive these awards and get up and think they're speaking to the General Assembly of the UN—give them three minutes on *Good Morning America* or *The Today Show* with a vast audience and ask people to make a contribution to the charity giving the award to Mr. XYZ for being the Man of the Year."

"Then skip the hours of testimonials to them," I say.

"And skip the hours of . . . I thought that was a pretty good idea."

"It was fantastic," Elizabeth says. "Actually I thought of this years ago when Barbara Walters was on *The Today Show*. And I mentioned it to a few CEOs at that time and they didn't think it was a good idea at all."

"W ny?" I ask.

"I :hink they liked to make their speech," Felix says.

"E xactly," says Elizabeth. "I deduced that they liked the exhi:aration of being there in front of the Waldorf-Astoria packed to the gills."

O ye vain CEOs. O ye Men of the Year, ye Lifetime of Service honorees . . . listen and weep, for your number is up, ye who demand hours of testimonials to your generosity, ye for whom three minutes of *Good Morning America* is not enough. . . . Listening to the Rohatyns dissect the real psychology of the city's rich is enough to drive one to take up the cry of the prophet and wail: *Alas, Babylon.*

But let's get practical here. After all, we're talking with Felix Rohatyn, the man who rescued the city from bankruptcy. He should be able to figure out how to rescue the private charity world from moral bankruptcy.

"I think there could be a mix of answers," he says. "One is yours," he says, nodding to Elizabeth, "to raise the consciousness of the movers and the shakers in the city to get involved in some more nitty-gritty programs. The other is my idea that there are some institutions," he says, looking warily at Elizabeth, "*some* institutions that would not think this adoption system is such a terrible idea. And then there's the third idea which would be much more controversial."

"What's that?"

"It would be to calibrate the amount of state and local support a charity agency raises to the money it raises from the outside. Now, how do you calibrate reduced government support and channel it to institutions that raise less money? . . ."

"Isn't what you're suggesting a kind of Big MAC solution for the charity world, create an institution that would allocate scarce resources and—"

"Well, I don't know. That would involve such a control over a process that's very diffuse right now."

"I guess someone would have to pick which organizations are needy."

"That's the trouble, you see," says Felix. "What we did with the city was say that you have so much money to spend, now you set your own priorities within this sum of money. At which point the political leadership has to make the allocation. . . ."

"Maybe you could have someone saying what's really urgent, as an advisory—"

"What I wanted to do years ago," says Elizabeth, "was a little business which would compile a sort of Moody's rating for all the eleemosynary institutions out there."

"That was a good idea. Why didn't you do it?" asks Felix.

"I'll tell you why," she says. "I was quickly told by some lawyer—he said you'll have a lot of lawsuits, madam, because the agencies that were not able to raise money because they had a B rating in my book would sue me for having, you know . . ."

"Nobody gets sued," says Felix adamantly. "Listen, that's something I know about. You can't sue a rating agency. Moody's downgraded MAC bonds ten years ago. I was on the ceiling and thinking of suing them until wiser heads prevailed. But you know," he says to Elizabeth, "you could have a rating book where you don't have to put A, B, C, D; you just show the ratio of overhead to actual expenditure."

"Yes, but everybody's so sophisticated now," says Elizabeth, who is nothing if not a realist when it comes to assessing the true state of the charity racket. "They're so sophisticated now they'd just cook the books."

"You mean," says Felix—this sounds new to him—"by just taking off the—"

"Oh, you know, they do this and that and the other and so the figures—"

"Like municipal accountants," says Felix.

"Yeah. So you wouldn't get anywhere," says Elizabeth.

"Look," says Felix, sounding a bit discomfited by this last cook-the-books exchange. "This is something Elizabeth knows. It's clearly not something I know a hell of a lot about. I'm uncomfortable with it. I'm not sure that it was such a great idea for us to all of a sudden find ourselves publicly in this debate. You know Elizabeth was asked, we were asked, to go on television. But we didn't do it. We didn't do it. But you know when you're hitting a nerve very, very quickly after some public statement because it comes back to you. And clearly there are a lot of troubled people."

The discussion turns to deeper questions of human nature and why people give at all, and Felix tells the story of their friend from the Little Sisters of Jesus.

"We have a friend who's a saint, a friend of Elizabeth who's involved in this organization called the Little Sisters of Jesus. And she's a French nun who really lived in the Ethiopian camps and worked in a South African chocolate factory, and her order lives among the poor. They don't just distribute money but they feel that the way they can help is by actually living with poor people. The most wonderful thing was when they were raising money Elizabeth would take her around, and you'd have this nun with blue eyes wearing this sort of burlap robe with sandals and Elizabeth in her biggest hat and her shortest dress and very high heels going to hit up corporate presidents for donations."

Felix sounds affectionately bemused by this approach.

"You know, I have no problem. We all give for a mixture of ego and the desire to be recognized and have people grateful and the desire to feel good. . . ."

But the Rohatyns are not feeling good. Not about what is happening in the city. They are feeling deep pessimism.

"The number of people who are in dire circumstances is increasing," says Elizabeth. "And today's problems coming into the agencies are the kinds of problems that are unattractive to deal with. People don't want to think about teenage pregnancies. They don't want to think about AIDS. They don't want to think about the sick and lonely persons and their problems."

If only the poor had more attractive problems, perhaps the rich would notice. And then there are the problems that are *too* attractive. "At the Literary Lions dinner for the library," Elizabeth points out, "there are only a certain number of tables and a limited number of people who can buy a table. And there's a waiting list of people who want to come to that function because they've read about it. It's attractive. Jackie Onassis comes to it. But they're not waiting out there to help the family-planning problem."

"We're not passing any moral judgments," says Felix for about the fourth time. "We may be wrong. But things are bad out there. Old people, poor people, sick people, indigent people are not glamorous. The facilities for these things are not attractive places. You're not going to have your corporate functions there. . . ."

His pessimism about the widening gulf between the rich and poor and the failure of the rich to notice or care leads him to a deeper pessimism about democracy itself.

"I just don't believe a democracy can function well, can even survive, when you have this fabulous wealth and extraordinary misery side by side." Perhaps he's thinking of Europe in the thirties; what he witnessed growing up there. "You can have fabulous wealth here and misery in Ethiopia and the systems never touch each other," he says. "But you can't have wealth and misery side by side here. Either something's wrong with the system or the system has got to change."

As I left the Rohatyns and took a cab down Park Avenue, I was trying to recall something I'd read recently about the rich, something Sir Thomas More said. . . . Felix had told me that he shared an admiration for the sixteenth-century statesman and martyr with Governor Cuomo. The two of them talked, he said, about what they'd learned from More's attempt to mingle statecraft and spiritual idealism.

When I got home to my Bleecker Street sublet, I found what I'd been looking for. It was in the collected essays of Christopher Hill, the Oxford literary historian.

"The rich were getting richer, and the poor poorer," Hill writes of the decades preceding the Puritan Revolution. "It may well be that Sir Thomas More was right to see all commonwealths as conspiracies of the rich to oppress the poor. . . ."

If this is true, then perhaps Felix is a bit naïve. There's nothing "wrong with the system." The system works, alas, just the way it's always been meant to work.

THE MODEL VANISHES

—— • ——

In Which a Beautiful Ford Model Makes an Appearance. And a Disappearance.

I don't know about you, but I know that *my* attitude toward New York models has always been guided by the spiritual meditations of the sixteenth-century poet Edmund Spenser. No poet worried more copiously about reconciling the delusive but undeniable appeal of sensory beauty with the proper object of the soul's yearning: Heavenly Beauty, the Beauty of Moral Goodness and Divine Grace, which has nothing to do with worldly beauty.

Or does it? In his "Hymne of Heavenly Beautie," his last word—well, his last three hundred lines—on the subject, Spenser makes the case that the contemplation of wordly beauty is not to be totally scorned, because the longings it inspires can ultimately stir the hearts of men to seek the Higher Form of beauty, to "lift themselves up hyer,

And learne to love with zealous humble dewty
Th'eternall fountaine of that heavenly beauty.

This has certainly been true in my case, and so dinner with the Ford family of Ford Models, and Khadija, their astonishingly beautiful "star quality" discovery, was for me an occasion to inspire searching contemplation of the relationship between the beauty of this world and that of the world beyond it. And—speaking of other worlds—before we sit down to dinner with the Fords and the exotic Khadija in the dining room of their town house, let me throw out a theory about the nature of New York models developed by a friend of mine whose boundless interest in the subject has recently led him to a mystical explanation for their otherwordly beauty. Let's call it the "Beautiful Space Visitors" or "Chariots of the Models" theory.

"They *are* more than human," he insists. "A Higher Form of Being. Descendants, probably, of a race of incredibly cute aliens. Beautiful Space Visitors. Born to families scattered all over the earth, these women of unearthly beauty and telltale Higher Cheekbones awaken to their destiny shortly after their Sweet Sixteen parties and from the scattered corners of the globe begin to gravitate inexorably to New York City. There they cloud the minds of men until, at a certain age (rumored to be twenty-seven), they suddenly are transponded back to their home planet, unless they're locked into a long-term cosmetics contract."

What he says has a certain metaphoric if not scientific validity. And so, metaphorically, you can think of the Fords' brownstone on East Seventy-eighth Street as the Mother Ship. From the far-flung realms of the earth, the most beautiful of the Beautiful Visitors come to New York to take shelter in the Mother Ship where Eileen and Jerry Ford groom and prepare them for their mission on earth.

Over the years many embryonic superstar models have

made the Ford town house their first home in New York. Suzy Parker, Jerry Hall, Renée Simonsen, all have slept here under the watchful eye of Eileen Ford, all have become not merely Ford models but Ford family.

And this month they have another Beautiful Visitor living with them, a model for whom the Fords are planning an equally lustrous future.

Her name is Khadija, and she's come all the way from Kenya after having conquered Paris with her appearance in the St. Laurent show last fall. That triumph was, in fact, her first modeling job. She's only been in New York for ten days now, and the Fords are giving her the full treatment. Assignments with superstar photographers. Spreads in the most sophisticated and prestigious fashion magazines. And a carefully sheltered, one might even say *guarded*, home life, which includes a 10 P.M. curfew on phone calls. Anyone who calls Khadija after that is told to hang up.

"Jerry Hall said in her book that she'd gone to Paris and had been living her own life and then she came here and she had to be home every night at ten," Eileen recalls at the dinner table. "She said it was awful: She had to get up every morning and do yoga with me for an hour at seven."

"Well," says Khadija.

"Well, what's new, right?" says Eileen. "Not much."

"The two of you exercise together?"

"Yes," says Eileen. "We do it normally at six-thirty."

"It's a new way of life," says Khadija, sounding not too thrilled about it.

"We were talking about Khadija's busy week," Eileen tells me. "She's already worked twice with *The New York Times* with Eric Boman, who's a very good photographer. Then she had *Harper's Bazaar* with Scavullo. Something tomorrow. Then she's working Saturday and Sunday in Southampton for *Glamour*. Monday again for *Harper's Bazaar* or *Glamour*. All great photographers, good clients."

"How did you find each other?" I ask.

"I know how I found her," Eileen says tartly. "She didn't exactly find me. I found her. She had been in the news-paper— in *Women's Wear Daily*—from the show at St. Laurent, so from that moment on it was a matter of tracking her down, which I did with great skill. I assumed she'd like to come and look at New York and see if she'd like it, which she did, and so she's here. But she has never been allowed alone in Paris. They took very good care of her at St. Lau-rent. They provided her with living quarters and a chaperon and so we had to be very careful. She doesn't know anything about city living, so she stays with us and we take her around."

"What was it about Khadija that you saw when you saw the *Woman's Wear* photo?"

"She looked like a star," Eileen declares. "She really did have star quality because if you look that great in the news-paper picture—she *had* to be very good. And she is."

"Tell me a little more about star quality," I ask Eileen.

"First of all, taste your smoked salmon," her daughter Lacey prompts.

"Aren't you going to eat?" Eileen demands.

I dutifully eat some of my smoked salmon.

"Now, star quality?" I ask again.

"I don't like it," Eileen declares. It appears she's talking about the smoked salmon.

"Some of it is good, Eileen," says her husband, Jerry.

"I don't believe in eating many smoked things," says Eileen.

"You're right, it's bad for you," says Lacey.

By this time—for better or worse—I've finished my smoked salmon, and Eileen returns to the subject of star quality in models.

"Star quality is hard to verbalize," Eileen says, "because it's something that's just *there*. I think it's sort of born into somebody. If you had two people who looked exactly alike, one might be a star and one might not. Why would two people who are equally lovely not always succeed in the same way? That's because there's just an inner fire, I think, in that person that shows itself to a camera. And when you see that picture, you respond to it, you react to it, instantly. They were laughing at me in the office today. I had seen a picture I really love—I still get excited after all these years. And when I saw that picture of Khadija, she wasn't wearing anything that special and she just looked right at the camera and the camera looked right at her and there was a spark."

"I must say, Khadija," says Lacey Ford, who runs the Fords' *Face of the '80s* worldwide model-recruiting TV pageants, "the other day when we did a piece for a new TV program with the new Ford stars, and when I saw you put on the clothes, you were just—the other girls were beautiful, but when you put the clothes on, you had such an attitude that it really was a very powerful thing to watch. Everybody. The cameramen. They were freaking out suddenly."

"It's chemistry," says Eileen.

"Can Khadija have some water?" says Jerry to one of the servants who's collecting our smoked-salmon plates.

"How many other models were in this program that Khadija stole the show from?" I ask Lacey.

"Five. But five of our new *stars*, not just five models. Five girls who are—"

"Top models," says Jerry.

Who are they?

"Oh no," protests Jerry. "Names of number two? No way."

"Somebody asked me," says Eileen, " 'How much does Christie Brinkley make?' What a terrible thing to ask. You can't say how much a model makes."

"Why not?"

"It's a direct invitation to the IRS, who then want to prove me right."

"Did you fly to Paris to meet Khadija?" I ask Eileen.

"No. I just called her on the phone. She came here," says Eileen.

"I was very flattered," says Khadija. "I'd heard of her when I was growing up."

"In Kenya you heard about Eileen Ford?"

"Oh yes. We get all the American programs in Kenya. *Brady Bunch. The A-Team.* Lucille Ball. I don't know, *Three Stooges*, everything."

"So you knew of Eileen, but how did St. Laurent discover you originally? Were you living in Paris?"

"No. I was living in Kenya, but I was in London for the Miss World contest and a photographer told me to stop over in Paris from London. I was curious more than anything. And I was taken to meet St. Laurent and that was that. I went back to Kenya and he sent me a ticket and said come over. He arranged everything. So I went back to Paris and here I am."

"What did St. Laurent say when he first saw you?"

"He waves his hands when he's excited. He's very shy to strangers and I couldn't be more strange. They taught me the basic *haute couture* movement, which is totally different from other shows. In the other shows you can move freely, but in *haute couture* you have to be very straight. He told me, 'I don't want you walking like a stereotype model. I want you to walk like a Kenyan girl. Remember how you walked in the streets of Kenya.' "

"Do you want some water?" Eileen asks Khadija.

She tinkles her little silver serving bell.

"Could Khadija have some water, please?" she asks, renewing the request Jerry made earlier.

Khadija talks about the difficulty of making the transition from the streets of Kenya to the streets of New York City.

Cab drivers do strange things in her presence.

"The one yesterday. He was weird. The man was telling me all very rude things, telling me all about his wife and what happened. I said, 'Please let me off.' And he called me names after a while."

Walking hasn't proved a better alternative.

"I wouldn't mind walking," says Khadija, "if somebody didn't try to pull my hair."

Who tried to pull your hair?

"I met these three guys and one of them pulled my hair. That was yesterday too. It was a bad day. I had lots of makeup on my face. They probably thought I was having a good time on the street."

"They were just admiring you," says Lacey.

"Just an expression of their desires," says Eileen.

"Maybe they were drunk," says Khadija.

"Eileen, do you have a master plan for Khadija?"

"Yes, and it's falling into place so quickly. What would you say, Jer?"

"She's in the first stage of—" Jerry begins.

"Our master plan is to get her very solid business first," Eileen says.

"And then to help her become as well known as she should be, and hopefully to achieve the kind of thing that Brinkley and those people achieve," says Jerry.

"It's step by step," says Eileen.

"It's a development process," says Jerry.

"And making the right choices," says Eileen.

"What are some of the choices you've had to make?" I ask.

"The important things are what we won't do," says Jerry. "I can think of lots of examples of that. I had a call today for some of my younger models for an acne preparation. It's not—there's nothing wrong with it, a lot of our models would be very happy to have it, but for certain people it's just the wrong thing to be involved with. It's not compatible with the top end of the fragrance and beauty business."

"There's, well let's call it a cheaper cosmetic line that I won't mention," says Lacey. "And they wanted to pay a fortune for some of our better models and we turned it down because we felt it would be just damaging to their future income in terms of other things they'd be likely to get in the same area."

"You know, in this business it's easy for somebody to come along and offer twenty-five thousand dollars for a single ad," says Jerry, "and it's a lot of money for one day's work, and why not? But it isn't much money in terms of what it can mean to that individual model over a period of time. . . ."

The talk turns to the effect of the beauty of models on the hearts of men. Is it possible that the otherworldly beauty of models—ever present in image, yet inaccessible in reality —causes sorrow and dissatisfaction in the minds of men whose choice is limited to women of this world?

"I don't know about that," says Jerry. "I don't think men get interested until models get out of the women's magazines. The only models you hear men talk about are the ones in *Sports Illustrated.* . . ."

Well, what about Mick Jagger, Bruce Springsteen, Billy Joel, men like that, no mere *Sports Illustrated* readers?

"Well, if they live in New York and happen to follow it very closely," he concedes, "there are bachelors who think that's chic. . . ."

"Aren't the two of you known for going to great lengths to protect your models from these New York men obsessed with models?"

"Yes, but there are limits on that," says Jerry. "We don't live with them all."

"The world of playboys is pretty European. I remember when I was young," says Eileen, who is sixty-two, "and you would read about Pitiño giving somebody a bracelet of emeralds and Shipwreck Kelly going out with Brenda Diana Duff Frazier and it was very glamorous and women got presents. They don't exist today. You don't have the milieu here for that. . . ."

"But there are playboys," says Jerry. "I wouldn't even call them playboys, but they're guys who—"

"They're not glamorous," says Eileen firmly.

"—hang around the business trying to meet models."

"But those are creeps," says Eileen.

"The answer is, yes we do try, but—"

"We're not always successful. But I have a fair batting average."

"And also these young women—they're independent. It's not our—we don't own them."

"But when they're living here—" says Eileen.

"Except when they live here, Khadija," says Jerry.

"What do the two of you say to models who are tempted by offers from other model agencies? What do you say you can offer them that they wouldn't get elsewhere?"

"Security," says Khadija, unprompted.

"You say it," prompts Eileen.

"I would say I would rather be here than anywhere else, because it's safe," says Khadija. "You get personal attention and you're totally—you feel at home. If you break the rules, it's like home. And when you feel bold enough, if you feel you're bright enough to walk out and live on your own—"

"They push you out," says Jerry.

"Time to leave the nest," says Eileen. "Lacey, what would you say?"

Almost as if on cue, a phone rings, interrupting this discussion of security.

"That's yours?" Jerry says reproachfully to Khadija. It's a few minutes after ten o'clock.

Khadija runs off to deal with the postcurfew phone call.

She's back in a flash, smiling like the kid who got her hand caught in the cookie jar.

"Did you disconnect it?" Eileen demands.

"No. I said, 'This is Khadija,' and she said, 'I guess it's the wrong number. . . .' "

"Well, don't forget what I said about the time you normally hang up," says Eileen reprovingly.

Meanwhile, Lacey continues describing what she thinks is the competitive edge the Ford agency has over its rivals.

"We run as hard as if we were the hungriest people in town," she says. "We've always been strong in recruiting, but you can't just recruit. Once you get a model you have to know what to do with her. And you have to know how to do it quickly and really move things along, and I don't think anybody could have as smooth running a machine as we do."

"Our bookers have been in the business longer than any other bookers in any operation," says Jerry. "We have more bookers per model than any other agency. We have nineteen bookers. Nobody else has that ratio. We have the momentum of being us."

Of being us?

"Because we are who we are, models tend to come to us first. And because of that clients tend to come to us first. So it's all part of the momentum. We certainly have the best accounting setup. When models work with us and call up two years later and want to know every penny they earned and every expense—they get it. The other agencies do that now, but they didn't always. It's catch-up. And try that in any place in Europe."

"Try and find out what you made," says Eileen.

"Models come back from Europe just shaking their heads. You have that secretive thing about money because people over there don't pay taxes, and on top of that you have an incomprehensible accounting system."

"I know what we have that we can give people better

than anybody else," says Eileen. "And that's Jerry. It's true. He's a great innovator in this business. There has never been a need for a union in our business because Jerry has been so innovative in finding ways of making money for models. When we started in the business, for instance, a model didn't get paid for a fitting. A weather-permit booking would be booked and held indefinitely, and if it rains for a week, the model didn't make a cent. Jerry did not tolerate that for long. They got paid if it rains. Then when it seemed that models were being really under contract by association with a product and were not being paid for exclusivity, Jerry said if you're gonna use them more than a certain number of times, you have to sign a contract and make them exclusive with you. Jerry changed the whole tenor of the business. The girls have good security for their money and he finds good financial advice for them. We don't attempt to manage their money. When it comes time to find a movie person for them, we do that. So I think there's that, and the fact that we are a family does sort of give you a sense of continuity. Also, we fight very hard for these models, we really do. I have heard everything in the world said about me, but nobody has ever said I didn't fight for the models."

Toward the end of dinner—a tasty lobster stew followed by a zesty mango mousse—we somehow get into a long conversation about beautiful exotic birds, savage wild birds, the curiosities of nature and civilization, interspecies communication, and the transmigration of souls.

It begins with Khadija telling the story of witnessing a rogue bluejay attack the Fords' house cat in the garden in back of their brownstone.

Then Eileen tells a story about a golden eagle who'd escaped three times from the London Zoo. It's loose again, wildly swooping down and attacking dogs and people on the streets.

"I don't like birds very much," says Khadija. She tells a story about a school friend of hers in Kenya who was attacked by a falcon. "They get attracted by the sight of wounds and red flesh," she says. And her friend had a burn from chemistry class.

"I was there," says Khadija. "I saw my friend scream and she had this big huge hole here. . . . I've never liked birds since then. I was thirteen."

Eileen then proceeds to tell a story about Caroline Granger, one of her top models, who walks around with a golden cockatoo on her hand.

"You'll see it in the office one day," Eileen tells Khadija.

"It's a beautiful bird," says Lacey. "It's intelligent. I just saw the strangest piece—on a vulture. This bird had fallen in love with its owner and apparently they can't get it to lay eggs unless he's around. He would come up and he would stroke this vulture on her neck. . . ."

"Then it would—" Khadija begins.

"It's a very rare bird so they're very concerned about her relationship with him."

"But you know the more you think about it," says Khadija, her voice taking on a more thoughtful far-off tone, "when you get rare animals that are very sensitive, you start to believe in bits and pieces of Buddhism, like where they say you are born again. Because not all animals are intelligent. But some of them can be so intelligent. You wonder . . ."

When she speaks this way, about special souls in the bodies of rare birds, it almost sounds as if she's speaking in an allusive way about what it's like to be a Beautiful Visitor.

"I heard about a talking seal here in America," she continues, fascinated with the interspecies contact theme. She says she read in *Reader's Digest* about a family that trained a seal to "talk," that is, imitate the sounds of the human voice. But then, says Khadija, "the family had to move and they couldn't afford to keep it, so they left it behind. And people passed by its pool and they heard somebody's voice talking, and only the seal was around. And the family had taught the seal to sing, and sometimes in the middle of the night you'd hear the seal singing that song."

"Does the seal have an agent?" Jerry asks. And everybody laughs. Except Khadija. There's something about this abandoned-seal story that appeals to her. As soon as she read about it, she says, she wanted to go see the seal.

"I really wanted to hear it sing," she says. "If you're lucky and you pass by it and it's very quiet, it goes, *'Who's there? Who's there? Hello, hello, who is there?'*"

Listening to Khadija singing the lament of the lonely seal, one can hear both tenderness and loneliness in her voice. I am reminded suddenly of the sweet, sad heroines of Jean Rhys novels, Caribbean-born women who find themselves lonely and abandoned in the corrupt civilization of England, haunted by the loss of the beautiful island realm they've left behind.

Trying to brighten the mood, I bring up my favorite exotic animal story. About Koko, the "talking" gorilla, the one who communicates by sign language with her keepers. About how Koko adopted a pet cat who died and how she "told" her keepers she wanted to adopt a new kitten.

"In America everything is possible," says Khadija, laughing.

But immediately she turns serious again and her thoughts turn to Kenya.

"Talking gorillas, my God!" says Khadija. "My grandmother would probably think it was the end of the world."

Khadija's grandmother is a traditional Kenyan inclined to see signs of the end of the world in many things.

"If you took my grandmother to Norway and at midnight the sun came out—she'd believe it's the end, because there's a saying that it's doomsday when you see the midnight sun."

"I think if your grandmother had to spend the summer up there," suggests Eileen, the jaded traveler, "she'd believe it anyway."

"My grandmother," says Khadija with that far-off Beautiful Visitor tone. "I cannot imagine my grandmother in New York."

"Are they worried about your being here?" I ask.

"They're worried," she says. "It's like I have broken a rule. They are very religious and very traditional. My sister is engaged to someone she doesn't really know. An arranged marriage."

"Would you have an arranged marriage if you had stayed there?"

"I turned one down. I was always different. For some reason I was always different."

I think of the Beautiful Visitor theory.

"Why do you think that was?" I ask Khadija.

"It was partly the education I got. They took me to a Western school. I did not know who I was then and I was sort of lost between their world and this world," she says. "And now I've made a choice."

Mystifying Postscript

Where's Khadija? Not long after I concluded this piece with Khadija's declaration that "I've made a choice," something happened to raise a question as to just what that choice might be.

I got the news when I arrived at the Ford town house for the photo shoot two weeks after the dinner. The Fords were there. But Khadija was missing, and no one seemed to know just where she might be found.

One member of the Ford household thought she'd gone to Paris and would be back within a week for a *Vogue* shoot. Another thought she'd gone to Kenya and wouldn't be back until August at the earliest. Another wasn't sure where she was but was confident she'd be back "momentarily."

Eileen Ford pronounced herself "aggrieved." She seemed to treat Khadija's unexpected flight from *her* world with the same gravity with which Khadija's grandmother had viewed the departure from hers: A Rule had been broken and the end of the world seemed near.

Where did Khadija go and why did she leave so much mystery behind? Did she flee the confinement and the curfew of the Mother Ship for the high life of Paris? For the home life of Kenya? Had she been transponded back to the home planet of the Beautiful Visitors? Spirited away by a rival model agency, caught up in the high-stakes game of international intrigue, a pawn in the hands of the intelligence agencies who—no, they already made that movie.

Actually, I have my own theory about the nature of Khadija's hegira. I think she went to wherever it is that the lonely seal is harbored. So that, at least once, when the abandoned beast bellowed out its haunting cry of *"Hello. Hello. Who's there? Who's there?"* there would be *someone* there. Someone who would listen—and understand. A Beautiful Visitor.

ALL POWER, NO LUNCH

Roy Cohn Brings His Own to Le Cirque

"That's Barbara Walters over there," Roy Cohn tells me, pointing helpfully to the *other* corner table along the front wall of Le Cirque. The second-best corner table. Roy's got the best, the one with the wide-angle view of the mirrored, flowered, high-powered array of Le Cirque at lunch.

I've just arrived—a little late—and as I settle into the turquoise banquette to the left of Roy, he fills me in on what's been going on at this lunchtime playhouse for all of those people you read about in "Suzy Says."

It seems, Roy tells me, that Barbara Walters is interested in seeing if her old friend Roy can help persuade Archbishop O'Connor to sit down with her. Alice Mason, who's at the banquette on the left, has leaned over to ask Roy's help in getting Claus von Bülow to come to one of her parties this fall. Archbishop O'Connor. Claus von Bülow. An odd pairing to be sure, but just two more of that many and varied tribe who constitute the Friends of Roy Cohn.

Could there be a bit of poetic justice, well, poetic *resonance* here in Roy Cohn's helping the newly presumed-innocent Claus to get back into the social swing of things with the Le Cirque crowd? After all, there was a time when Roy himself was about as unwelcome as Claus in certain circles of what he likes to call "the stuffed shirt establishment."

That was back in the sixties, when Roy himself faced three separate federal indictments for conspiracy, bribery, and fraud, and it looked like the brash Bad Boy of the McCarthy era was about to get taken to the federal woodshed for a while.

But it didn't happen that way. Roy won three acquittals, and in the years that followed, the onetime Bad Boy has risen to almost elder-statesman status in the Reagan conservative establishment. He's a regular figure at the best tables at "21" and Le Cirque, a power broker among Permanent Government types in both political parties. His widely publicized birthday bashes draw a fusion of the powerful, rich, and famous. So many local judges attended a party for him on the twenty-fifth anniversary of his admission to the New York bar that the *New York Times* editorial page questioned the propriety of all those judicial figures nibbling on Roy Cohn's anniversary cake. (Roy tells me that he thinks *Times* editorial-page editor Max Frankel, the official voice of the "stuffed shirt establishment," has it in for him.)

Of course it wasn't easy: It took Roy about ten years after his last acquittal to go from Mr. Outside to Mr. Inside. It seems to have taken Claus less then ten weeks. Perhaps this difference can be attributed to Claus's blue-blood demeanor. Complete respectability—which for Roy seems to mean the approval of the *Times* editorial page—still eludes

Roy. Perhaps because he continues to delight in being, in one way or another, outrageous. This is the man, after all, who just recently called Mr. Justice Respectability, Felix Frankfurter, "a $50,000 political pimp." This is the man who speaks with relish of the scorched-earth policy he pursued in concluding one bitter divorce case, in which he represented the husband:

"We got an order evicting her from the apartment, but she wouldn't go," Roy tells me, "so we just pulled up moving trucks, broke down the door, moved everything out of the apartment. But she wouldn't go. She got into the bathroom and locked herself in. [Her lawyer] called me and said, 'What are you gonna do about her?' and I said, 'I don't know, in a couple of weeks we'll send somebody around to pick up the bones.' "

Roy waves to Barbara Walters in her corner. Barbara waves back.

"When I used to go out with Barbara," Roy tells me a bit later, "we used to argue extensively about one thing."

What thing?

"Jewish dinner parties," Roy says. "The kind where I'd be seated between two women and all they wanted to talk about was what Joe McCarthy was really like and were the Rosenbergs guilty.

"It took Barbara a long time to realize how important she was," says Roy, a man who has never suffered from this disability. "When she finally did realize it, she realized she didn't have to go to them anymore."

At lunch today Roy has more congenial company. Sitting across the corner from us is old friend and sometime client Paul Hughes, chairman of one of Revlon's international divisions.

"Paul and I go back a long time," Roy says. "To when we owned the heavyweight championship together."

The heavyweight championship. This is an aspect of Roy's

varied career I hadn't been aware of. But before he gets to explain, it's time to order.

Paul orders the salmon. I choose the rabbit stew. Roy orders tuna fish salad "my way."

Tuna fish salad at Le Cirque?

"I only have tuna fish salad wherever I go," he explains. "And I only like Hellmann's mayonnaise, so I make sure to keep a jar of Hellmann's in the kitchen back there. Remember when we were in Majorca," he reminisces with Paul, "and we had everybody flying the tuna fish in for me?"

"When did you start this tuna fish thing?" I ask Roy.

"I've been doing it for about twenty-five years."

"Is it some kind of health thing?"

"No, I just like it. I like American lunches," he says.

Not all restaurants cater as assiduously to Roy's tuna fish thing as Le Cirque; "21" does. They keep a jar of Hellmann's for him there. "But there's another restaurant that I like, Paone, which is patronized by William F. Buckley and Meade Esposito—at Paone's they won't make tuna fish specially for me," Roy complains. "There I have to bring it in."

"So do you just sit down and unwrap your takeout tuna?"

"At first, yes," he says. "But now they unwrap it for me."

Roy's other food obsession, he says, is iced tea. "At some point I got the compulsion to carry a glass of iced tea around everywhere. I leave the house in the morning at eight o'clock; people think it's Scotch."

So he arrives at Le Cirque with his own iced tea, and he eats the Bumble Bee brand tuna they bring in for him with the Hellmann's he supplies. It occurs to me that Roy has refined the notion of the power lunch to a new level of purity at Le Cirque: all power, no lunch.

Now about that heavyweight championship business. It is a part of Roy's fascinating post-McCarthy odyssey I'd never heard of. I know that after the senator's decline in the mid-fifties, Roy had been taken up as adviser and confidant by various flamboyant tycoons such as Lewis Rosenstiel of Schenley, and Charles Revson—fearsome self-made tyrants with McCarthy-like temperaments, known for bullying subordinates. I knew that in the early sixties he had gotten involved with some high-flying financial speculators who were in on the first flush of takeover fever during the go-go years. There was a short-lived attempt to take over Lionel Corporation (the toy train company) and turn it into a defense-contracting electronics conglomerate.

Then in the mid-sixties the indictments came down. The result, Roy has always claimed, of a "get Roy Cohn vendetta" ordered by then attorney general Robert Kennedy. A claim that seemed to be substantiated several years ago when former assistant U.S. attorney Irving Younger confessed in *Commentary* that he had been ordered to "get" Roy Cohn and that he'd used questionable methods to do it.

I knew that throughout this turmoil Cohn had continued to build on his reputation as a high-priced, highly effective hired gun for big-stakes legal shootouts. That he'd won acquittals for various alleged underworld figures like Tony Salerno. That he was, as Bill Murray might say, "a real party animal," a constant fixture of the high life and the night life of the city: afternoon lawn parties with Buckley conservatives on their Connecticut estates and late-night parties with the Studio 54 demimonde.

I remember coming upon Roy Cohn while I was covering the 1980 Reagan inaugural ball. There he was in black tie, seated in a Washington hotel ballroom with his law partner, Tom Bolan, and Senator-to-be D'Amato (who named Bolan to his screening panel for federal judgeships). Donny Osmond or somebody squeaky clean was bubbling away at the mike. That first week in the White House, Reagan's inner circle of aides would give a private dinner party for Roy in appreciation of his advice and counsel during the campaign. Mr. Outsider had become Mr. Insider. And yet he looked bored. He looked like he missed the days when he would stroll into the Stork Club and pick up the heavyweight championship of the world for a song. For a lark. For the hell of it.

Roy and Paul speak fondly of that heavyweight champion escapade. It's a long tale involving a Runyonesque character by the name of Humbert (Hard Luck) Fugazy.

"So we go to Hard Luck Fugazy," Paul recalls, "and I say to Hard Luck, 'Roy and I have got a chance to buy [Floyd] Patterson's contract for five thousand dollars,' and Hard Luck says, 'Do it,' so . . ."

"The parties for these fights were great," Roy says. "All black tie. We had Gary Cooper, Liz Taylor. Used to be a big social event," he recalls wistfully. "What a great time we had with it."

The conversation shifts from the heavyweight bout to a little legal sparring match Roy has been engaged in on behalf of Donald Trump.

"There's this guy . . . a businessman named Julius Trump," says Roy. "No relation. Now as long as he stays Julius Trump . . . fine. But he's got this thing he calls the Trump Group and he's making a buyout offer on some discount chain, Pay 'n Save, something like that. So Donald Trump sees the ads Julius is taking out for this Trump Group and he hits the ceiling. 'He's trying to pretend he's *me*,' he says, and he tells me to get an injunction. I go to court tomorrow."

Roy's also going to bat for George Steinbrenner in his embittered litigation with his outfielder over Steinbrenner's financial pledges to the David M. Winfield Foundation.

"I want to see the books," says Roy. "I'm concerned about how much of it is actually going to charity," he says, with the air of an injured altruist.

Roy seems to enjoy playing the hired gun called in to tackle the tough ones for lone-wolf tycoons tired of timid establishment law firms.

Onassis, for instance. Roy tells me the story of the time Ari called him to consult about instituting divorce proceedings against Jackie.

"It started over this totally different thing," says Roy of his involvement in the putative divorce action. "It started over this popparuzzi [sic] business."

The "popparuzzi" business was Mrs. Onassis' invasion-of-privacy suit against photographer Ron Galella. According to Roy, "Ari didn't want her to bring the case, right as she might have been—all she was doing was giving this guy millions of dollars of free publicity. Now Onassis was a pretty shrewd guy, so he said to her, 'You want to do it, I can't tell you not to do it, but I'm out of it.' Till the lawyer's bill came. A big fat bill came. And he went berserk. At that point, Johnny Meyer, a good mutual friend of all of us who used to work for Howard Hughes, called me and said . . ."

The noise level in Le Cirque drowns out Roy's voice on my tape at this point. He's saying something about his advice to Onassis. " '. . . Use my name, then go back to them and say you'll have to go to court to collect. I'm sure you'll get a good price that way.' It was the next time I spoke to him that it came up," Roy says, referring to Ari's divorce intentions. "There would have been a New York aspect to it because of all his properties here, and he wanted to know if I would be available. *The New York Times* found some memo from one of his people to him about it. And the basis was two things. The money, her spending. And also she seemed never to be where he was all the time. Of course he died before he took any action. . . ."

Roy's karma with the Kennedy family certainly has been turbulent over the years, hasn't it? I ask him if it is true that it could all be traced back to a fistfight he and Bobby

Kennedy got into when the two of them were counsels for the McCarthy committee.

Roy says it goes back to *before* the fistfight, to the very first moment they met in the committee's Senate office. Bobby had wanted the chief counsel post that Roy got, even though, says Roy, "Bobby didn't have any experience. *I did.* I had prosecuted the Rosenbergs. So when I got to the office I'd never met Bobby, but he started looking me over, sizing me up and—"

At this point there's a curious interruption. A very well dressed, stately woman glides over to Roy's table. She smiles and waves at Roy with standard Le Cirque effusiveness but seems to have something on her mind.

"When will you release my one hundred fifty?" she asks Roy.

"That is not up to me," Roy says in a tone that suggests he's made this point at least once before. "That's up to [a law firm] and my co-executor."

"But with *your power*," she says sweetly, with a hint of iron beneath the honey.

"But I have to find a *sound basis* for exercising my power," Roy says. "Have your lawyer file a claim," he says with finality.

"Couldn't you come over for cocktails and explain all this to me?" she persists with that surface sweetness.

"Just call me," says Roy.

"I can call you?" she asks.

"Call me," Roy repeats.

At this point Roy and Paul get sidetracked into an anecdote about Henry Kissinger being photographed next to "a couple of very well-endowed women at an international conference." There is considerable chuckling before Roy returns to the year 1953 and Bobby Kennedy "sizing him up."

"Yeah, so he's sizing me up and he says, 'Morton Downey

thinks you're the greatest guy in the world. Other friends of ours don't trust you.' And I say, 'So what am I supposed to do—am I being *graded* on trust or something? Am I supposed to make a defense? I'm prepared to state Morton Downey's right.' "

Not long afterward, Roy says, a woman told him that she received a message for Joe McCarthy from "someone in the Kennedy family" while she was in the Senate beauty parlor. The message was "He'll never do anything to hurt Joe McCarthy, but he's gonna get Roy Cohn."

"I never knew why," Roy says, all injured innocence. "I don't know if it was our different backgrounds, milieus, religions. I don't know," he says.

Well, what about the fistfight?

It began, Roy says, over Bobby's behavior while Roy was giving testimony during the Army-McCarthy hearings.

"Bobby is sitting directly behind the three Democratic senators, staring at me. He has this real *evil* grin, and every time his eyes meet mine he breaks into this grin, and it really started getting to me. He was feeding them questions for me, asking questions like crazy—and that was the immediate thing. We ran into each other afterward. I said something to him. He said something to me and he started screaming at me, and I started screaming at him, the bastard. Then I said, 'Come on, let's step outside,' and Senator Mundt, who was horrified, followed us out."

Who won?

"Well, Mundt stopped it before it really started. For which I'm glad, because although I'm not lacking in self-confidence, I don't go climbing mountains or go rafting on rivers," he says, mentioning Kennedy family pursuits. "Bobby got terrible mail on the fight," Roy says. "Mothers all felt sorry for me."

There's a fascinating postscript to this inspiring tale of dedicated public servants: Roy's story of the final face-off between himself and Bobby, almost fifteen years later.

But before we get to that, I'd like to describe Roy's tuna salad, which arrives about now along with Paul's salmon and my rabbit stew. Do you know those women's magazines by supermarket checkout counters that are always featuring cover stories on "How to Turn Plain Old Tuna Salad into a *Fantastic Tuna Fiesta*"? Well, some dutiful soul back there in the kitchen of Le Cirque has opened a can of Bumble Bee, gotten Roy's jar of Hellmann's down off the shelf, gone to work with some bits of exotic greens here, a few shallots there, and turned plain old tuna salad into a *Fantastic Tuna Fiesta*! I couldn't help wondering: When Richard Nixon comes here, as he does more than occasionally, do they do some fabulous thing with cottage cheese and catsup for him?

But to return to the Final Showdown between Cohn and Kennedy. The place was Orsini's restaurant. The Le Cirque of its era.

"I went there with ——— and a couple of girls," Roy reports. "We're sitting at a table and Bobby Kennedy comes in with Margot Fonteyn. They put him at the next table. Well, we stop talking. They never started talking."

The Kennedy and Cohn tables sat there in silence until, Roy says, "I get up and go over and say, 'Look, this is ridiculous. We're gonna ruin your evening and you're gonna ruin our evening. Why doesn't one of us move?"

What a great New York moment. Roy Cohn and Bobby Kennedy facing each other down with dire threats of ruined dinners hanging in the air.

But then, according to Roy, "Bobby said, 'You're absolutely right. Since you were here first, we'll move.' So he moved, and that was the very last time I saw him."

"When was that?" I ask Roy.

"Shortly before his death."

He sounds regretful, a fighter mourning the loss of a

particularly hard-punching sparring partner. Still, is it just my imagination, or could the inclusion of Margot Fonteyn in the anecdote be construed as what they used to call, in the McCarthy era, an innuendo? One final jab at Bobby?

So here's Roy Cohn sitting in splendor at Le Cirque. He's gotten what he wants out of life; there's no one out to get him anymore. He's got a Connecticut estate, a Manhattan town house, a lavish lifestyle; he's a power broker respected and feared by the Big Boys. I remind Roy of a quote in a story about his re-ascendance that ran in the *Times* several years ago, in which he said he's still fighting "the stuffed shirt establishment." Doesn't he feel like he's part of the establishment now?

"Oh no," he says quickly. "I'm not part of the establishment. God forbid. I can't stand those people. I dislike them as much as they dislike me. See, I don't like to be the only Jew. I'm not impressed by the fact I could get into X Club; I don't want to get into X Club if they don't approve of Jews and so forth.

"There's nothing abut the establishment I like," Roy continues. "I don't like golf; I don't like Saturday afternoon cocktail parties with the three martinis at the club; there's nothing in my profession the establishment has to offer. The establishment law firms look down on matrimonial cases, they look down on criminal cases—everything I find exciting and challenging. It comes up a lot over my representation of so-called underworld figures," Roys says.

He assures me, "They never tell me anything about the underworld, so I don't know if that's what they are, although some I might deduce. But I've met a couple of them I respect, that I just *like*. One of them's Tony Salerno, who's supposed to be the big sports gambler."

Roy got Tony Salerno off on income tax charges. He says he likes Salerno "as much as any person in the world. He's refined. A quiet, peaceful person. He's a sports gambler."

Roy has a lot to say on the subject. It seems to be a sore point.

"People say to me, 'Why do you choose to represent them?' And I say, 'I'm not their *consigliere* or whatever you call it.'" Roy makes a big distinction between what he does and what is done by "real mob lawyers," a class of attorneys he has no great respect for.

"I have enough of a varied practice that I can't get tagged as a mob lawyer. I don't like mob lawyers. I can't stand them. Know why? They have only one thing to sell. Loyalty. They're very loyal. There's only one problem. They lose practically every case."

Roy says that certain people occasionally ask his opinion of this mob lawyer or that, often describing the mouthpiece in question as "a stand-up guy."

"I say, 'You're damn right, he's a stand-up guy. Do you plan to use him as a witness? Oh. You plan to use him as a lawyer. Well, when you find out when he last won a case, tell me about it.'"

Mob lawyers are that incompetent? I ask Roy.

"Yeah," he says. "Now Carmine Galante, Nicholas Rattenni—they had the sense to go to a nonmob lawyer. Namely myself."

I think it's about this time I first take notice of the wallpaper at Le Cirque. It's kind of peculiar: Our corner, anyway, is dominated by a fanciful scene of chimps—or are they orangutans?—dressed up in the beribboned and ruffled costumes of milkmaids. Specifically, the sort of elaborate, expensive mock-milkmaid garb adopted by Marie Antoinette and her ladies-in-waiting when they played at being peasants in the gardens of the Petit Trianon.

Somehow this image of expensively attired primates seems a particularly apposite one when Roy begins to launch into his epic tales of divorce wars among the filthy rich.

I wish I had the space to record here all his tales of unholy matrimony, tycoons and fortune hunters, some of them rivaling in their lurid appeal the ones Truman Capote retold in his notorious "La Côte Basque, 1965." And like those stories—in their own way—these are morality tales. Le Cirque 1984 is a spiritual descendant of Côte Basque 1965, or if you prefer, Petit Trianon 1789.

In fact, if Capote was the Proust of Côte Basque, you could call Roy Cohn the Homer of Le Cirque. The man is an inexhaustible storyteller. And if he is the Homer of Le Cirque (okay, I said *if*), the story of his most bitter divorce case—the epic battle over the Rosenstiel divorce—is Roy Cohn's *Iliad*.

By the time Roy really gets into the Rosenstiel story, we've been at Le Cirque almost three hours. The place is entirely empty except for the three of us at Roy's corner table. Roy has spent the last hour rhapsodizing over the virtues of Ronald Reagan and gossiping about White House intrigues. How so-and-so screwed himself out of the Treasury post. How, as Roy put it, David Rockefeller sent Henry Kissinger to Gerald Ford to convince him to make a last-minute run for the presidency in 1980. How Kissinger and Alan Greenspan went to the convention in Detroit and tried to persuade Reagan to adopt the bizarre plan whereby Ford would accept the vice-presidential nomination with assurances he would be some sort of "co-president." (These Kissinger stories sound like a Trilateral Commission conspiracy theorist's fantasy, but Roy says he knows they're true.) How Reagan campaign aides discovered Roy's name on Geraldine Ferraro's congressional campaign contribution list and revoked his credentials at the Dallas convention this August—as a joke. (Ferraro "comes to my birthday parties," Roy says.) How there's only one Democrat who frightens him: Mario Cuomo. ("He's tough," Roy says, respectfully. "I saw one thing he did that *scared* me. When he was debating Lew Lehrman, Cuomo gets up, goes over to Lehrman, grabs him by the wrist, and holds it up so people can see this expensive watch Lehrman's wearing. Then he asks the audience, 'Now, how many of you can afford a watch this expensive?' Wow," Roy concludes, "if I were Reagan, I'd stay a million miles away from anywhere Cuomo is.")

Great stories, but nothing compared with the Rosenstiel divorce wars, in which Roy went head to head with Louis Nizer, who was representing Susie Rosenstiel, the fourth wife of Roy's client, liquor tycoon Lew Rosenstiel.

Just the mention of Suzy Rosenstiel reanimates Roy. His eyes light up as he describes the way he and Nizer went at it, springing secret injunctions here, pulling surprise judgments in obscure jurisdictions there.

"Susie," Roy says, "My God. We were in Connecticut, Florida, New York, Mexico on that one."

"Susie," says Paul, "I see her sometimes. . . ."

"She's in Paris," Roy says in an almost awestruck whisper. "You know who ran into her? You know, the guy who sits at that table over there. I ran into him in Monte Carlo a few weeks ago, and he was telling me he ran into her in Paris," he recalls. "Look at the repercussions of that case —Senator Javits's brother was suspended from the bar."

The problem, Roy says, was some tricky abrogation of an annulment decree of a previous marriage.

"That's where I came in," Roy says.

"Well what was it about this legendary woman?" I ask Roy. "Was she incredibly beautiful?"

"No, it wasn't that," he says. "Lew Rosenstiel was a very susceptible guy when he met her. His crushing marriage was to the present Mrs. Walter Annenberg, Lee Annenberg. She [divorced] Lew [and married] Walter Annenberg and he never really got over that."

He proceeds to tell the fascinating tale of how the future Mrs. Rosenstiel wooed the susceptible tycoon.

"The story's told, and I can't prove this," Roy says, "that Susie found out when—you see, Lew would go to Europe once a year and meet the liquor trust, the DCL heads. And they never signed a written contract like on his franchise deal with Dewar's; there would always be a raising of a finger, that would be the deal." Roy raises his index finger to illustrate. "He'd get off the boat, and they'd have lunch in some hotel, they'd shut the doors, they'd make the deal, they'd all raise their fingers, and then he'd go home."

Well, according to Roy, Susie just happened to book passage on the *Queen Elizabeth* when the lovelorn liquor tycoon was on board for one of those finger-raising trips. "And then, you know, she's walking around the deck and then she sits down next to him. He loved cards. So she played cards with him and the one who lost would take the other for dinner in the Verandah Grill. So she lost, she took him to dinner in the Verandah Grill, and they came back and she moved in, and that was that."

There's something about this tale that fascinates me. It's not the evocatively Art Deco courtship story. No, it's the part about the liquor trust and the raising of the fingers behind closed doors.

Roy Cohn seems to me someone who early in life was initiated into the intimate rituals of unspoken power enacted behind closed doors. The vision of life that he has developed from knowing too well the way the world works—you could call it cynical. You could call it realistic. You would probably not call it idealistic. In its awareness of the corruption of human nature, of the dark springs of human motives, you might best call it *conservative*.

These tales of Rosenstiel prompt Roy and Paul to lament the passing of the Revson and Rosenstiel breed of self-made tycoons.

"That was an age of giants," Roy says.

Paul agrees. It sounds as if they miss the high-powered,

heady excitement of those days, when they were on the outside nipping at the heels of respectability with the lone-wolf tycoons. One gets the feeling that Roy Cohn is finding his renaissance of respectability a bit boring. Yes, his life is a Fantastic Tuna Fiesta, but part of him—the part that's attracted to the raffish and the Runyonesque, the "sports gamblers" and the demimonde—misses the old days, misses the thrill of combat.

Probably even misses Bobby Kennedy.

As I leave the four o'clock dimness of Le Cirque and all these tales of the way the world really works, it suddenly occurs to me: I miss Bobby, too.

ONE MORE THING TO HATE ABOUT CALIFORNIA

———— ◗ ————

In Which Adman Jay Chiat Discloses the Secrets of Authentic Attitude

You're in a bar. Guy comes in, sits down. Hip urban beer-drinker type. Picks up a bottle on the bar, glances at the label. Frowns and says: "I hate California."

Doesn't stop there. Proceeds to launch into stream of anti-California invective:

"*Have a nice day,*" he mimics, mockingly, in a cretinous simper.

"*Surf's up,*" he says with a brain-fried smile.

"I mean their idea of culture is yogurt," he snickers.

"Formal dinner parties mean you wear socks. Blondes everywhere, pink tofu? Excuse me? Soy burgers? I really hate it," he concludes with a heartfelt sneer.

"I even hate what they drink," he adds, picking up the bottle, which—we now see for the first time—is labeled "California Cooler."

"What'll you have buddy?" the bartender asks him.

The guy nods sheepishly at the bottle.

"One of those," he says.

The camera pulls back and the announcer delivers the voice-over punch line, which also appears on the screen:

CALIFORNIA COOLER: ONE MORE THING TO HATE ABOUT CALIFORNIA.

It's a memorable commercial, one of those that makes watching network TV marginally worthwhile (it's scheduled to break nationally this spring). It's smart, it's funny. You have to admire the marketing cleverness with which it addresses a difficult problem: how to sell a flavored-wine drink to beer drinkers. You have to appreciate the way it captures that elusive grail of all beer-drinker ads: Authentic Attitude. What the Löwenbräu "here's to good friends" guys missed because they were a little too creepily self-conscious about their precious camaraderie. What the Stroh's guys are striving for but don't quite attain because their humor is just a little too complacently cutesy.

But more than that, it's one of those commercials that captures something evanescent but real going on in contemporary culture, captures the bicoastal split in our national consciousness, the continuing dialogue between the pleasure principle (California permissiveness, the suggestion of the polymorphous perverse embodied in "pink tofu") and the reality principle (East Coast urban wise guy, work ethic "realism"). Captures it authentically, and then cleverly, sneakily, seductively figures out a way to reach out and touch the secret, sheepish California impulse hidden within the urban beer-drinker's soul.

"One more thing to hate about California" is the kind of line that has made Chiat/Day Inc., the bicoastal, California-based ad agency that created it, the hottest "creative" agency on both coasts. It's the kind of campaign that—along with those for Apple and Nike and Pizza Hut—has got the ad trade papers doing big features on a California-led "creative revival." It's the kind of thing that's made agency head Jay Chiat himself "one more thing to hate about California" in the mind of Madison Avenue.

The day before my lunch with Chiat (pronounced *Shy*-at), I'd gotten some coincidental confirmation that he really *was* on the mind of Madison Avenue. In the lobby of the Pan Am Building, I ran into a guy I'd known at Yale, who's since become vice-president/creative director at a major Madison Avenue agency. This is a very charming, very preppy guy—heir to the John O'Hara–era adman tradition. Not one, in other words, to fall for every new ad fad.

But he took Chiat quite seriously. "He's making the rest of us look bad," he declared. "Absolutely. It's going to take us a while to get up to speed with the kind of work they've been doing."

What's interesting about the kind of work they've been doing is how often a Chiat/Day ad campaign has turned out to be not just a headliner in the ad trades but a mainstream media event in its own right.

First there was the spectacular "1984" TV spot for Apple. The one that ran only once nationally (during the Super Bowl), but which instantly became the most talked-about TV commercial in years (okay, until "Where's the Beef?"). If you didn't catch it when it ran, you probably saw clips of it on *The Today Show* or *Entertainment Tonight*. Once you've seen it, you can't forget director Ridley Scott's haunting, heart-stirring sixty-second epic about regimentation and freedom. It's set in an evil, blue-tinted Orwellian society in which mindless, zomboid, blue-tinted worker drones worship a fearsome, blue-tinted Big Brother haranguing them from a huge screen about "the beauty of

oneness" and the creation of a "garden of ideological purity."
We cut from close-ups of the mindless, robotic, chanting
faces to quick glimpses of the only non-blue-tinted figure:
a full-colored, full-blooded, California golden-girl Olympian
striding to the rescue in running shorts, bearing some kind
of sledgehammer, radiating *intensely* healthy vibes, re-
leasing the sledgehammer with a wild, deep, sensual primal
cry, and succeeding in blowing up Big Brother's giant televised face.

Truly an amazing ad. It was another one that worked by
stirring up the tension between repression and release within
us all and then manipulated that tension on behalf of a
shrewd marketing strategy: Without mentioning arch-rival
IBM (known on the Street, of course, as Big Blue), the ad
managed to reposition the Apple challenge to IBM as a
crusade—individual freedom against encroaching Blue
Meanie totalitarian uniformity.

Not since Doyle Dane Bernbach positioned Avis as "number two, but trying harder" has an ad packaged a corporate
challenge more appealingly. Nor—despite Apple and Chiat's
denials that the blue-tinted Big Brotherites had *any* relation to Big Blue IBM—has any ad construed the opposition
in such a profoundly villainous way.

And then there was the Nike campaign that broke right
before the Olympics. Another crowd-pleasing coup. First
there was the irresistible transformation of Randy Newman's "I Love L.A." rock video into a slick Nike commercial
without once mentioning Nike.

But even more stirring, more groundbreaking, were the
spots that captured Authentic Athletic Attitude, the Soul
of Sweat, in grunting, heaving, sweat-dripping close-ups
of Moses Malone knocking himself out crashing the boards.
What was particularly brilliant about these ads was the
way they repositioned Authentic Athletic Attitude on the
value spectrum: They pictured the athletic impulse not as

the kind of frivolous California self-indulgence you'd do in designer jogging attire, but as work ethic self-improvement. "We haven't forgotten why they're called sweats" was the tag line. It proved that Chiat/Day could play both sides of the California split.

Chiat himself, who now lives in New York and commutes bicoastally, has increasingly become a beneficiary of the growing star system on Madison Avenue. Looking Southern California cool with silver hair and aviator shades, his picture until recently had been a familiar fixture next to the column he wrote for *Adweek*.

Chiat seemed to be riding the wave of the future. Until "Lemmings."

Was it a fiasco? Was it a triumph? They're still arguing that in the trades, although the consensus seems to have been negative.

Well, the ad was negative. It was one of the most profoundly negative ads ever run. One of the most powerfully negative pieces of *film* ever run, in fact. I might be wrong, but I think it certainly was a breakthrough of some sort in being the first ad to depict the mass suicide of middle managers. Still, I loved it for its outrageously vicious antiauthoritarian spirit. Designed to be a can-you-top-that successor to the "1984" Apple commercial, "Lemmings" ran during 1985's Super Bowl.

The scene is a bleak heath only King Lear could love. The sound: a deadly, mournful, slowed-down chant, which on closer hearing turns out to be "Heigh-ho, Heigh-ho, It's Off to Work We Go," the cheerful Disney work-ethic tune turned into a funeral dirge.

What we see are long chains of look-alike executive types in look-alike dark suits. Wearing black blindfolds, they march lockstep up the heath to the edge of the cliff. And then, one by one, they blindly plunge to their death in the abyss below.

The mood is, shall we say, not exactly upbeat. This is not That Pepsi Feeling or That Toyota Feeling. This is That Jonestown Feeling.

Oh yes, there is a hint of hope at the end—we'll get into that later. But the overall tone of the ad is more than merely negative. It almost seems *hostile*. As if to say to all those decision-making office computer purchasers out there: *If you blindly continue to choose IBM over Apple, you spineless zombies, you deserve to die.*

The ad was so extreme it not only provoked bad reviews in the ad trades, it almost led Apple itself to disavow it. Was "Lemmings" a turning point in the rise of Chiat/Day? Has the California Crusade been turned back? I'd heard that the agency had been invited to make a presentation for one of the most lucrative and desirable accounts ever to come up for bids. Miller was junking the long-running "Miller Time" campaign and looking for an agency to recharacterize its Miller High Life brand. I'd heard that Chiat had hired Robert Altman to direct their agency's presentation TV spot for High Life. And that something had gone wrong.

The first thing I asked Chiat when we sat down to lunch—at the restaurant called America—was what had become of the Altman Miller opus.

"We had done," he says, "what in effect was a paid spec pitch for Miller High Life. It was a kind of slice-of-life thing. We did a situation where people were talking to each other about kind of serious things, like their jobs, quitting to go into business for themselves, divorce, marriages, things that had to do with real life instead of beer talk. It was much more *aspirational* than the kind of thing where everybody at the bar is having a good time partying. This was up, but serious."

Sounds a bit like "The Stroh's Guys Go to Esalen." Or, come to think of it, Robert Altman"s *California Split*.

"Right," says Chiat. "Altman's technique gave you the

kind of voyeur aspect of looking in on these people as they had these rather intimate, overheard conservations."

What was the marketing thinking behind this approach? I ask Chiat.

"We actually did what we thought was some valid market research. The beer was getting killed by Budweiser in the markets, and we had to give it a positioning that was just different from what other beers had. I guess in the beer business you would call it "belonging positioning." Beer is more of a wardrobe, just as cigarettes are. It represents your selection of who you are, and who you think you are as a person. Well, there was a market out there that was concerned with serious parts of life rather than just partying. . . ."

Don't you love the way ad guys talk? Beer as a wardrobe. Aspirational positioning. I ask Chiat what happened with the Altman spot.

"I think what happened was he became more of a commercial director than a film director, and we didn't have what we went after. We didn't quite get what we wanted and we tried to reshoot it, but because there are certain rules about making pitches, we couldn't. My feeling is we just failed, missed it, blew it. Big opportunity."

Chiat used "belonging positioning" to give the Nike brand a new identity. The problem the agency faced coming into the account was that "Nike had what we thought was a powerful brand, but it was being footballed by retailers."

"Footballed?"

"Discounted by retailers. JC Penney's and people like that do their own ads that just feature Nikes on sale, so Nike had no brand identity. Now this was a moment in time when we felt that designer logos had had their day in athletic wear."

You remember that moment in time, too, don't you? We all felt it.

"And so the strategy we decided on," Chiat continues,

"was authenticity. People who were really athletes or presumed themselves to be really athletes would not wear Ralph Lauren brand to go out and play touch football. So by doing these naturalistic commercials, that—well, the Moses Malone ads, those never even identified the athlete. It was deliberate. It kind of said, 'If you don't know who it is, then you're probably not for the brand. You're not into authenticity.' "

It is time to order. I love the huge America-size menu at America, which features all kinds of authentic regional American goodies—hush puppies, po' boys, Fluffernutter sandwiches, and the like. The strategy of authenticity seems to have worked well for America, which is always crowded and noisy. Could this be the *year* of authenticity?

Chiat orders *huevos rancheros* and I order black bean cakes and *fajitas*.

I ask him to tell me how it was a Bronx-born boy came to be Mr. California Cool adman.

"I was there," Chiat says. Stationed in the Air Force in Sacramento. He got a job, when discharged, handling recruitment advertising for an Air Force contractor. Got fired, and found a job with a small ad agency in Orange County.

"I never did anything distinguished for them," he says. "I didn't know enough about advertising, but I had a certain work ethic and subconscious need for excellence. So I used to look at all the advertising coming out of New York, particularly the annuals published by the New York ad clubs. And at that moment in the mid-sixties, Doyle Dane Bernbach was just doing all that great work. Avis. Volkswagen. Polaroid. I guess without knowing it I began studying at the feet of all these brilliant writers and art directors who were doing all that great work then, and I tried to emulate them. And since most fresh ideas are just restructuring of old ideas, you could pretty well steal. You start by stealing, and as it evolves, try to give it a twist so that it's not really stolen."

"What happened to that sixties creative revolution?" I ask Chiat. "Why did it die out? Why is there a creative revolution now after so long?"

"I'm not sure there *is* a creative revolution now," he says. "In the sixties, I think, the economy was really good and you had some talented people, and when things are good, people are more courageous. In the seventies, the economy turned. You now had agencies that were more sizable and therefore more concerned with the status quo. You started having agencies going public. You started to have agencies acquiring other agencies. They bought PR companies and direct-mail companies and started to think of themselves as a business rather than this kind of eclectic art form and craft, which it is. Clients started to feel the pressure of the economy and say, 'We don't have time to be clever or cute.' I think in the eighties you started to get a recovery. Plus you have the growth of new disciplines and businesses that didn't exist before—high-tech companies, computers—which have been founded by entrepreneurs, who by temperament have more acceptance of new ideas. They haven't come up the corporate ladder and had their souls stripped out. Plus the fact, I think, the seventies weren't *successful* with all the dull garbagy advertising they did."

"Souls stripped out." That's strong stuff. Sounds like the scathing critiques of conformist, fearful, mass-minded, manipulating admen you read in angry fifties novels—*The Man in the Gray Flannel Suit* and the like.

Or is it a California-based disapproval of narrow, New York careerist admen who wouldn't know from human potential if it came up to them and said, "Have a nice day"?

I ask Chiat if he thinks there a distinctively California sensibility to Chiat/Day's work.

At first he says, "No. I really don't think so." But then he immediately goes into a long disquisition on California–New York differences that suggests there is something characteristically Left Coast about his agency.

"I think what there might be is maybe less arrogance, more politeness. Less abrasiveness. California I think *is* really different. . . . I think people in the supermarkets are politer—I don't think it's the case that New York is more intentionally rude. They just protect themselves more. You don't have to do that in California because there's no body contact in California. You get out of your house, you get into your car, you drive to work, and you don't have any physical relationships with people you don't know. That makes a big difference. As a result of that there's less fear and more eye contact. Maybe that comes through."

Chiat is a big eye-contact guy himself. One thing *I* hate about Californians, particularly the ones who go for eye contact as a kind of "strategy of authenticity" is that my eye sockets get cramped from the unaccustomed constant eye-contact task. I'm always afraid if I drop my gaze from theirs for an instant, it will seem like I've got something to hide. A couple of hours of constant eye contact and I'm longing for the guilty, darting gaze of the New York street-psycho.

How does this eye-contact ease affect California versus Madison Avenue advertising consciousness? I ask.

"I think by the way the system works here in New York, people are less trusting," Chiat says, beginning to allow his Californianism to flower here, "and that relates even at work. Advertising is a very collaborative process, so if you don't trust your colleagues, you're going to have to really be schizophrenic. And in New York, there's more need to take credit for things because everyone is grabbing for the credit, whereas I think our attitude, which has to be somewhat California-based, has been 'Hey, everyone is on the skyline. Everyone will get credit, everyone will be noticed.' As a result, I think people trust each other a little more. I think they'll ask colleagues what they think about something and maybe get some help. Whereas if you're afraid that you're going to lose credit for the ideas, you're not going to share anything. I mean, even our office has an open plan. There are no walls, because we're trying to get an energy level so it contributes to people almost osmotically feeling what's going on."

Hey, everyone's on the skyline.

Trust. Sharing. Openness.

Energy level. Osmotic feelings.

Hey, I'm beginning to feel kind of osmotically Californian myself.

Have a nice day.

I ask Chiat if New York admen have to overcome a little culture shock in adjusting to Chiat/Day's California culture.

"It seems it takes a minimum of six months," he says.

Let's talk about trust. I ask Chiat about rumors that there'd been a breach between his agency and Apple over the "1984" ad. Did Apple have any doubts?

"Oh yeah. It's a hard commercial not to have doubts about."

"What were they?"

"Whether it would offend people, whether it was really positive. Apple has a very positive cultural view of itself. They had the same doubts about the current commercial. The difference is, after '1984' was done, the Apple people liked it. After 'Lemmings' was done, they *still* didn't like it."

"Why don't they like it?"

"They don't see hope in 'Lemmings,' and we do. I think it's a subjective difference of opinion. I think the beauty of it is that, in spite of that, they ran it. An incredibly courageous thing to do. When the chief executive officer, the chairman of the board, and the marketing manager universally do not like the commercial and still allow it to run—well, we had a meeting that went until midnight the night before the decision was made to run it. We said, 'We all feel this way at the agency, that it should run, and we understand that you don't *like* it, but that's not a logical reason.' They are just so terrific that they said, 'If you have so much passion for it, then we have to believe in you.' "

The moment of hope in "Lemmings," in case you missed it, was that evanescent glimpse of just one of the blind-folded, dark-suited zombies stopping at the brink of step-ping off the cliff and pausing to lift his blindfold. He looks at his situation instead of plunging blindly into the abyss. The others keep marching relentlessly toward mass suicide.

Is that hope enough? I ask Chiat.

"That's hope for me," he says, "because all people are individuals and most of us make the mistake of following safety blindly. The spot was an allegory. I think it was a powerful one. To us it's marketing. We cannot recapture IBM's franchise. What we almost have to do is wait for these kids who are using Apples in grade school to grow up, and that's a long time to wait. Now we have the Mac-intosh office, which we think is based on Apple's concept of small work groups in large companies, and we've just got to crash through and say, 'Hey, if you're an individual, *this* is what you want to do. Don't follow blindly.' "

Chiat still feels good about the whole "Lemmings" cam-paign.

"The brilliant thing to me in that was the newspaper ad that we ran the day of the Super Bowl, and that was [Apple chairman] Steve Jobs's idea. We were having dinner two nights before at La Tulipe and we were talking about it. We knew that the ad was running in the fourth quarter and we said, 'What if the game's a rout?' So Steve had an idea for us to take full-page ads in big Sunday papers that just said, 'Today, fourth quarter, Super Bowl,' with just the Apple logo. I called it in to Greg Helm, the account super-visor, and I said, 'See if those guys can beat it,' and of course they did beat it. They wrote a better ad: 'If you have to go to the bathroom during the fourth quarter, you'll be sorry,' with just the Apple logo."

Now that he's shifted his residence to New York and the agency's New York office is billing about $50 million (out of a bicoastal total of $300 million), Chiat is beginning to go after New York-type accounts.

"We're doing new work that will be on TV for Drexel Burnham," he tells me. "It separates them from the other investment banking houses. What we do actually visually in the ad is turn Wall Street upside down. This is what they've been doing with their deals and their junk bonds —they invent money in effect, if you want to strip it down to its basics."

But the new campaign he's most excited about is the repositioning of Bazooka bubble gum.

"This is one of those great brands that never really advertised much, so we positioned it as 'the hard stuff.' Whereas there are all these soft, tacky, fake bubble gums, well, we got these guys for the Bazooka spot—one of them is a wrestler with a nineteen-inch neck, and the other guy's a kind of Gene Wilder–looking guy. And they start chewing the gum. You know how hard it is to get started, so when they come down on it, you hear an ignition trying to catch, until all of a sudden they get the gum going and you hear [he makes roaring engine sounds]. And the slogan is 'Are you man enough to chew the hard stuff?' We'll probably be thrown off the air with this."

Note here in this humble bubble-gum ad concept what seems to me the characteristic Chiat/Day selling technique: incorporating a self-indulgent pleasure into a work ethic framework. Getting pleasure from this bubble gum requires hard work and dedication. It's not for everyone. From its bicoastal perspective, Chiat/Day has come up with the perfect strategy for selling tender pleasures in a tough-minded time: Make them seem like things you have to *earn*.

The waiter comes over to inquire why my plate still looks so full of *fajitas*, tortillas, and bean cakes.

"It's very big," I explain. "It sure is a big plate."

Chiat is a regular at America. His New York headquarters is just three blocks away. He says America attracts a big daytime lower–Park Avenue ad agency crowd that fills its huge space.

"Everything here is like America," he says. "Bigger than real."

Apple chairman Steve Jobs shows up at this point and sits down with us. He and Chiat have some unspecified plans for that afternoon. Jobs and Chiat, both newly arrived bicoastal residents of New York, both bachelors, seem to like to hang out personally as well as professionally.

They make an interesting pair.

Chiat, fifty-three, is low-key, kind of deadpan, and laid-back California cool. Jobs, thirty, still radiates the frenetic energy and high-wire drive that created the $1.5 billion Apple empire out of a tiny garage operation manufacturing "blue box" phone-freak devices. Jobs still has some of the nervous, manic restlessness of the computer hacker whose mind is always going a mile a minute. No eye contact at all.

"I ran into Gloria Steinem on the way over here," Jobs reports. "On the street with her new boyfriend. I was with [investment banker] Bob Towbin. And I said to her, 'You're going to do a commercial for us.' She says, 'Yeah.' She was real excited about it."

"Which commercial is this?" I ask.

"We're doing a commercial for Apple based on the song 'Girls Just Want to Have Fun,' " says Chiat. "It's women in business. It's Gloria and serious women. One of them is a shot of the Supreme Court going into their chambers."

"With 'Girls Just Want to Have Fun' in the background?"

"Isn't that a great song? They're playing it against Women Doing Serious Things. We tried to get Sally Ride, but I don't know whether NASA would okay it. But it's a kind of tribute to women—teachers, execs, women taken seriously."

Jobs takes his vegetables seriously, in a very California way. This is causing a bit of bicoastal misunderstanding with the waiter.

"I'd love the fresh vegetable appetizer," Jobs tells him. "Seasonal fresh vegetables, right?"

"The *crudités?*" the waiter asks.

"That's just raw vegetables, right? Do you have any plain cheese?"

"Just plain cheese?" the waiter asks.

"Yeah," says Jobs. "Like you get in a mozzarella and tomato salad."

"How about a tomato and mozzarella salad?" the waiter suggests.

"Can't you give me two slices of plain cheese and some vinegar or whatever sauce you put on the mozzarella?"

It takes a while, but they finally come to some sort of understanding.

Jobs and Chiat, though, it turns out, are still at odds over the now notorious "Lemmings" ad. I get the two of them to talk about their sometimes stormy agency-client relationship.

"You're definitely the best agency that we've ever talked to," Jobs says to Chiat. "But we all care about it so much that sometimes it gets really tense. And we don't ever think about parting company . . . but we know each other's hot buttons."

"It's highly volatile," says Chiat.

"Because we just want to do great work," says Jobs.

"So as a result of that, everything gets questioned twice as much as it would. Actually," Chiat says, deadpanning, "I would think Bazooka bubble gum is really *our* best client. Nothing personal, Steve."

"So what are your feelings about 'Lemmings' now that the smoke has cleared?" I ask Jobs.

"I can answer that on several levels," he begins. "I don't think it was as good a commercial artistically as '1984.' 'Eighty-four' was an epic; in my book, 'Lemmings' was a myth. I don't think it produced as widespread awareness as '84,' and I don't think that it left the residual taste in people's mouths that we really, long term, can afford to leave that often."

"Actually, I don't agree with any of that," says Chiat.

"Is the difference between the two of you over 'Lemmings,' " I ask, playing Esalen therapist, "really about the question of hope?"

"Yeah," says Jobs. "There's no hope in it. But I'm glad we ran it, and the reason is because, see, Apple's not like Disney or any other company like that. We don't know who we are really. We're struggling to find the boundaries of who we are. And if we're so safe all the time that we're afraid to run things like that . . . well, Apple's benefited more from running 'Lemmings' in that we learned that we're *not* that. And that was good to learn."

Are you following this? I could explain it, this California Corporate Existentialism, but—oh forget it.

Jobs then comes out with a shocker for Chiat: He wants to run a *retraction* of "Lemmings."

"Mike Murray [Apple's marketing director] had a great idea," Jobs says. "A lot of people were put off by 'Lemmings,' a lot of school districts and things like that where we sell lots of computers. Mike Murray thought about taking a *Wall Street Journal* ad and apologizing for it, saying we went a little too far with it, but Apple is the kind of company that has to push boundaries, that has to try to speak from a different mouth then just the normal IBM corporate voice. I think it [the retraction] is a great idea."

Chiat looks a little taken aback by this. But he recovers well and deadpans, "Well, the fact that we didn't run it ["Lemmings"] on the teen-suicide special *should* say something to the school districts. . . ." At this point he excuses himself to go to the men's room.

"He's a really great person," says Jobs in Chiat's absence. "He doesn't have to be doing what he's doing. He's got plenty of resources and other things at his disposal. He's doing it because he loves doing it."

Doing?

"Advertising—he really wants to do great advertising. He really wants Apple and the few other select companies he works for to succeed. And all the companies he works for, most of them have messages that are hard to communicate, Apple probably being the hardest."

Jobs and I chat about the fate of various phone freaks until Chiat returns. Returns with a counterbrainstorm to Jobs's retraction idea.

"You know how we were talking earlier, Ron, about getting ideas while running?" (Both Chiat and I had confessed to using this technique for writing.) "Well, the men's room—that's another place where you can get really good ideas. Like the one I just thought of."

Which is?

"I had this idea," he tells Jobs, "that if you go ahead and run that ad where you apologize for 'Lemmings,' the agency will buy the *adjoining* page with a retraction of the apology. Saying we don't agree."

"That's not a bad idea," says Jobs.

The adman and client have a funny bickering-couple kind of relationship.

When I tell Chiat how much I like his "One More Thing to Hate About California" premise, Jobs acts jealous:

"How come you didn't come up with a line like that for us?"

"Apple is too big to *just* have a line," Chiat says diplomatically. Then adds a zinger: "You *had* a good line once. You didn't like it: 'Soon there will be two kinds of people.

Ones who use computers and ones who use Apples.' I think *that* was a good line."

"In its *time*," says Jobs a bit uncharitably. "I think that's already done."

"In its *time!*" says Chiat a bit indignantly. "It only ran for two weeks. Like most things we do with Apple. 'In its time,' " he mutters. "Catch the second."

"The biggest thing about working with Jay," says Jobs, getting more serious now, "is that we don't look at them as our ad agency. We look at them as really part of our marketing department, strategic marketing—how do we position our products, what market segments are we going after, what are our team messages, not only to the consumer but to the dealers. So we involve them in everything, just everything. And they always tell us when they think we're full of shit, too, which helps a lot because they're usually right."

But still, down to the bitter end he will not concede Chiat was right about running "Lemmings."

"Ron said he saw hope in 'Lemmings' without me prompting him," Chiat tells Jobs.

"The guy lifting the blindfold wasn't hope enough for you?" I ask Jobs.

"Steve always hated that guy," Chiat says as they get up to go. "He thought he was a wimp."

THE SANDINISTA IN THE WINE CELLAR

———— ❥ ————

Investigative Lunching with Malcolm Forbes

Malcolm Forbes didn't exactly walk out on me. After all, we were having lunch in *his* place: the wine cellar in the basement of Forbes's Fifth Avenue town house headquarters. And he didn't exactly throw me out. I'd call it the modified, civilized bum's rush: Suddenly, abruptly, in response to a certain question, he stood up and—before I could finish my coffee—told me that the hospitality had come to an end.

You probably want to know what the Offending Question was—and I'll get to that in due course—but perhaps it might be wise to begin with something Forbes showed me before lunch. Because it turned out to be a portent, a prefiguring of the trouble to come.

It happened as Forbes was leading me from his baronial office up to his baronial drawing room, where we were to have drinks before descending to his baronial wine cellar for lunch.

As we came to a landing on an interior staircase, Forbes gestured to some paintings and drawings lying on a table there. Recent acquisitions, he said, for the vast, illustrious Forbes art collection.

One of them caught Forbes's attention: a framed ten-by-fourteen satirical drawing. He picked it up to show me.

"Long before your time," says Forbes, "there was this famous episode with Diego Rivera and John D. Rockefeller."

You've probably heard about that episode: The famous Mexican painter was commissioned to do a mural for Rockefeller Center. Rivera, no fan of the U.S. role in Latin America, incorporated a heroic-looking figure of Lenin in the mural. Which caused John D. to see Red, and to order the offending image expunged from his wall.

In the drawing Forbes shows me, we see a shocked John D. contemplating the face of Lenin. And we see Lenin (who seems to be buried beneath a muralistic jumble of factories and forges) looking pretty shocked to see John D.

"This is by a very famous—can't think of his name, it's a South American guy, a Mexican," says Forbes. "Very famous, but it isn't Rivera himself. I couldn't resist buying it; a famous artist did it, it's a satire of the episode. Look at the horrified look on Rockefeller's face."

"And here's Lenin peering out from underneath the capitalist tools," I point out.

Forbes, contemporary America's Capitalist Tool in Chief, chuckles indulgently at John D.'s provincialism.

"The irony is," says Forbes, "that Nelson and all the rest of them became very liberal in their thinking. . . ."

Liberal? Yes, up to a point. Later, back out on the street after asking the Offending Question and being instantly shown the door, I'd think back on this little moment on the stairwell: It should have been a warning.

But meanwhile we're up in Forbes's baronial drawing room having drinks and getting into the intricacies of investigative yachting. Actually, I'm the only one drinking; I ask for a beer and a steward brings me a hefty glass, then withdraws a few yards from where Forbes and I are seated. The steward remains àt attention, silently observing the descent of the beer line in my glass throughout this prelunch chat. It's a bit disconcerting having a silent witness who's treated as if he weren't there, but it seems a standard practice; later an equally silent steward attended us in the wine cellar downstairs.

It was Forbes who brought up the subject of yachting. He told me he spent part of the morning conferring with his sons on the guest lists for his annual ballooning jaunt at his château in Normandy and for his July 4 cruise on the yacht *Highlander*.

The *Highlander*, a 126-foot, 276-ton motor yacht, was, you might recall, the subject of an epic battle between Forbes and the IRS, which disallowed Forbes's claim that yachting expenses were part of his magazine's function.

This still seems to be a bit of a sore point with Forbes, because mention of the *Highlander* sends him into a long, slightly defensive-sounding explanation of how central his *Highlander* cruises are to the uniqueness of the *Forbes* brand of business journalism.

"The bedrock of what differs *Forbes* from our competition," he says, "is the ongoing intensive effort to appraise the caliber of the man running the company. My father [*Forbes* founder B. C. Forbes] used to say he never bought a balance sheet when he bought stock in a company. He bought his appraisal of the capabilities of the guy in charge. You can't evaluate the man at the wheel if you don't know the man. I'm not talking about sparring across the desk. If you haven't broken bread together, sailed on the *High-*

lander all day with them—these things and having them one on one here to lunch with me—"

"Investigative lunching?"

"What we're trying to do is get the *feel* of the guy. It's not so much investigative as—trying to appraise tangibly the intangible factor. What kind of person is this that's going to make the decisions for GM for the next five or six years?"

He may not like to call it investigative yachting, but to hear Forbes tell it, the yachting experience is a powerful investigative tool, central to the ongoing Forbesian appraisal of CEOs.

"If you spend all day with him and his wife on the boat and see their interplay with other CEOs on the boat, that kind of thing, you get a gut feeling. . . ."

With Forbes, investigative yachting is no haphazard affair. That's why the guest list for the *Highlander* requires such careful planning. Every year Forbes targets about 150 CEOs who are ripe for an investigative cruise. And then during the fall, in a veritable investigative blitz, invitations go out to 25 CEOs at a time, for six weekend cruises with the Forbes family up the Hudson.

Then, after the CEOs and their wives have departed in their limos, the Forbes family gathers to share the journalistic fruits of the investigative cruise.

"After a *Highlander* day, Steve, Kip, and I—and my wife's got a good instinct—we discuss what did we think of so-and-so. . . ."

Sometimes, Forbes says, as often happens with journalists and sources, friendships develop between Forbes and the CEOs after they brave the river together. Sometimes such friendships advance the ongoing investigative enterprise, because they give Forbes and his reporters greater entrée to a company. And often, says Forbes, "the price of entrée is friendship."

These friendships—one hesitates to call them investigative friendships—"can sometimes creates stresses," he says, "when we, as we often have to be, are critical of companies run by people we know well."

In fact, Forbes is quite frank in his critical estimate of many CEOs. I don't know what these CEOs and their wives do wrong on the yacht, but they often don't leave a favorable impression.

"I'm surprised at the number of times," Forbes says, "the head honcho of a corporation can come across as not particularly impressive. Not just in personality but in perspective . . . things that bring into play other facets of his mind."

In fact, from what Forbes says, many of these CEO minds don't seem to *have* other facets: "Quite a few are not impressive either for their grasp outside their bailiwick, or —there are a surprising number that come across as not being heavyweights."

Okay, forget these narrow, dim-bulb CEOs for a moment—tell us about some you like, some who passed the scrutiny of an investigative cruise.

"Well, Roger Smith of GM," he says. "When I first read about him I thought, 'Oh my God, General Motors can't afford another accountant, another pencil sharpener. . . .' But, as you got to know him, you realized that he was a guy who really is *digging* redirecting General Motors. . . . I got that feeling from the man in two social gatherings— here, and then they spent the weekend with us ballooning in France. This little guy—when you realized this, you knew GM was not in the hole."

Who else?

"Jack Welsh at General Electric. He's another charger. He's not somebody with a striped-tie, bankerish type of essence. Here's a guy that's a fighter and aggressive. The same thing with John Opel at IBM. I mean, here's a guy who's redirected, reshaped, impressively expanded IBM."

Forbes likes these chargers, these aggressive guys who are digging the excitement of their CEO-ness. That's what he looks for: turned on, charged-up CEOs. Like Malcolm Forbes.

"To me a very revealing characteristic for evaluating somebody with big responsibilities is, do they convey a sense of excitement about what they are doing? Are they turned on by it? Do they convey a sense that they're just digging what they're doing? If they are, it's a great tip-off."

The word "digging" is a key one in the Forbesian pantheon of values. Not digging in the dreary Woodward and Bernstein sense, but *digging* in the neobeatnik, ecstatic, Kerouacian, blissed-out-on-the-beauty-of-Being sense of the word. I heard it again later on in his description of the joy of motorcycling, which the sixty-six-year-old Forbes still does with a kind of weekend gang in New Jersey: "Your *awarenesses* are all different. . . . You see more. . . . You're using a whole bunch of different senses, which is very relaxing because it's a different frame. . . ."

The time has come to shift the frame of this lunch, from the drawing room to the wine cellar.

The wine cellar is the inner sanctum of investigative lunching at *Forbes*. Most routine CEO lunches take place in the larger, less intimate setting of the main dining room and are attended by Forbes's editors, sons, and writers. The wine cellar is reserved for the really intensive investigative lunches, the ones in which the CEO is sweated by Forbes in a head-to-head session of investigative digging.

Actually there's very little literal sweating here in the wine cellar. For the sake of the wines the place is kept quite chilly. Forbes says 62 degrees, but it feels colder to me.

It's a bit austere and monkish, this cloistered little six-by-eight chamber. All four walls are lined from floor to ceiling with racks of aging bottles in repose. And hung from the ceiling are dozens of silver wine cups with dangerous-looking silver antlers projecting from the rims. Forbes's steward serves us a 1962 Château de Cros white in conventional wineglasses.

"White wines are easy," Forbes says dismissively. "Most countries make a good white wine. It's reds that are difficult. I've never had a red California that's comparable to a good, not necessarily the best, but a *good* Bordeaux. I'm not a connoisseur; I'm a consumer, but if you consume enough you form some opinions. We have a pretty good gamut here, practically every year from about 1890."

But the point of the wine cellar, of course, is not digging the wine, it's digging the CEOs.

"What we do," Forbes says, "is bring some CEO here who likes wines and is into wines. Sometimes we'll give him a bottle of the year of his birth. The only promise we extract from him is that if he opens it and it's vinegar, he won't tell us."

Apparently Forbes himself has had almost invariably bad vinegar experiences with the oldest, most expensive bottles in his collection.

"Whenever I've opened one it's always a disappointment," he says. That's why the CEOs are instructed to keep their mouths shut if their gift bottle turns out to be vinegar, too. "It would wipe out the value of the cellar," Forbes says. "We can't afford to know."

Still, he says, the birth year bottles of wine "make a great token of esteem" to the lucky CEOs who get them.

"What we do when we have a CEO here is give him one of these," he says, taking down a silver wine cup with antlers for me to see. "The stag's head is the Forbes clan crest," he explains. "We take these silver cups and we put two of them at his place, the big one for the red wine and the smaller one for the white. Then a year after he's been here, we engrave the date on them. We keep the big cup here in the wine cellar like a bagged trophy; then the year after the luncheon, we send him the small cup and say, 'This is the year you were here and we had an interesting session,' or what have you. The idea is we tell them that if their cup is in the wine cellar, anytime they're in the neighborhood they're entitled to come down here, take their cup out, and open any bottle of wine they want."

Sounds like fun, doesn't it? You'd think the CEOs would really go for an offer like that. A little CEO-only clubhouse. Their own silver cup, drop in anytime, maybe run into a bunch of other CEOs checking out the wine cellar. One of the perks of having arrived at the top of the corporate pyramid.

But according to Forbes "so far no one has felt the need" to take advantage of this generous offer.

I can see two explanations for this shyness on the part of these usually charged-up CEOs. They might suspect the free-wine offer is a subtle ploy of investigative lunching, a tricky way of uncovering which CEOs have too much of a weakness for a free bottle, suggesting perhaps a shaky hand on the corporate tiller.

Or on the other hand, it could be that *all* those gift bottles of birth year wines turned out to be vinegar. In which case few CEOs would be charged up enough to want to endure a second offering from the Forbes cellar, even from their own silver-antlered cup. Still, I envied Forbes his investigative wine-cellar setup. As a lesser practitioner of the investigative luncher's art, I knew I would have *many* more insights if *Manhattan, inc.* would supply me with an investigative wine cellar of my own.

In any case, the 1982 white wine he served me was quite pleasant, and perhaps under its spell, I tried to steer the conversation in a more philosophical direction. When I say, "I tried to steer the conversation" with Forbes, it understates the difficulty of such a task. The man is a forceful talker, he has strong opinions on everything and one opinion frequently leads to another, and trying to steer the conversation with him is like trying to deflect the 276-ton *Highlander* under full steam, with an oar.

But I thought it was important to try to get philosophical, because it was the other Malcolm Forbes I was most interested in. Not the hard-nosed capitalist tool, the charged-up super self-promoter, the maniacally acquisitive collector, the Malcolm Forbes whose image he himself dismissed as "that rich guy with the balloons."

No. I was looking for the other Malcolm Forbes. The one whose philosophical bent emerges cumulatively in his "Fact and Comment" column. The introspective Malcolm Forbes, the thoughtful reader, the curious, alert intellect. The one who scorns the lives of quiet desperation led by the narrow, dim-bulb CEOs.

People close to him testify to the existence, the importance of this introspective aspect. One associate who accompanied him on his recent Egyptian venture—the one in which he traveled in a balloon the shape of a sphinx—reports that Forbes experienced a kind of peak moment of introspection during his visit to the ruined pyramid of Tutankhamen.

There, it's said, Forbes gazed upon the long-buried ruins only recently disclosed to view after millennia beneath the sands, and was inspired to question the permanence of human endeavor, the nature of his own legacy for the future. It came in a year when Forbes turned sixty-five and when—though still charged up and vigorous—he suffered two brushes with death in motorcycle and balloon accidents. Did he have such a moment of introspection at Tut's place?

"It's a nice story," he says. "But it isn't true. I did say to my sons when I was standing there that 'you guys are lucky—when I die you won't have to dig a hole like this for me.' That's a fact. I found it fascinating but not any cause for reflection or genuflection."

But then he does begin to get a bit philosophical about Tut's tomb. "If anything, it illustrates the futility of any form of human efforts at immortality," he says. "Socrates and some of the philosophers—you can begin to identify with them. When you're young, you have utter confidence and certainty, and the rest of your life you spend realizing more and more that there's less and less. You understand? There's no certainty. But everyone discovers that for themselves."

"The impression I get from reading your 'Fact and Comment' column is that you're a contemplative person, concerned with things of the spirit, and—"

"That's what it's all about basically," he says.

"And yet look at yuppies, your readers. Don't you think these people are too busy, too concerned with success and getting ahead to think of—"

"No, I don't think so at all," Forbes says forcefully. "I think that's unfair to yuppies. What's deplorable about somebody that's turned on about starting a business or building one or climbing up the ladder? What the hell's wrong with that? It's somebody's freedom to do their own thing! And if you're going to do your own thing, don't you want to do it successfully?"

Lunch has been served (mushrooms on toast, poached salmon, chocolate mousse). I'm drinking coffee, and Forbes, sitting across from me, is smoking a huge black Macanudo cigar.

"There is a period," he says, "between a good wine and good cigar when introspection and perception are probably sharpened. I have often found that I write a lot of my two-line sayings then."

Taking advantage of this window of introspection, I ask Forbes about his relentless pursuit of objects of art, Fabergé eggs, collections of this and that. Does he see any analogy between the magnitude of these obsessions and those of William Randolph Hearst or Charles Foster Kane, who ended up with warehouses full of treasures locked away from view?

"I was often baffled as a youngster," Forbes says, "when I'd read about a person who'd be going broke and he'd have a warehouseful of things. I thought to myself, 'How could anybody have a warehouseful of things?' "

But now he's beginning, he says, to understand warehouse-scale collecting.

"I have never bought a warehouseful, but if I didn't have a lot of houses I'd need a warehouse because . . . I can't resist something that turns me on. I can better perceive why Mr. Hearst's dream of San Simeon—I can understand how he could end up with a lot of stuff he never used. I have nothing, very little, warehoused. We have paintings in what I call temporary storage."

What turns Forbes on about collecting, he says, is the thrill of the quest. And the competitiveness of it. He's charged up about his imminent assault on his eleventh Fabergé egg, soon to be auctioned at Sotheby's, the one that would put Forbes ahead of the Kremlin. The Capitalist Tool and the Communist Superpower each have ten of the jeweled eggs.

"Next Tuesday," says Forbes, "we will, up to a point, go after the eleventh Fabergé egg. It's an egg I turned down years ago because it wasn't aesthetically very pretty. But now the idea of having one more than the Kremlin is a turn-on."

Forbes expects the egg to cost him more than a million *if* he can outbid the Kremlin.

"We don't know; Russia might bid on it. After all, they don't like being outdone in the cold war, and they want to keep ahead of us in missiles. Maybe they want to keep ahead of us in eggs."

But if anything's a bigger turn-on for Forbes than beating the Kremlin, it's beating up on his rival Capitalist Tool *Business Week*.

More momentous than the superpower egg race is the

drive by *Forbes*—now number two in ad pages for all national magazines—to overtake *Business Week*, which is number one.

He loves to take shots at *Business Week*. Like the full-page ad he took out in the *Times* when *Business Week* hired away a *Forbes* editor.

The ad claimed that *Business Week* editor Steve Shepard had told the *Forbes* defector, "We want to be more like *Forbes*." I'd heard Forbes personally wrote the aggressive ad. Did he?

"I've never denied that and I don't deny it," he says proudly.

But didn't the *Business Week* editor deny he had used those embarrassing words?

"Wouldn't you deny it, if you were the editor of *Business Week*? Of course he denied it, but I can assure you that, from what I consider an absolutely totally good source, he said it. . . . At least I think he said it. There's no reason to doubt it."

"When do you expect to overtake *Business Week* in total ad pages?"

"Five years ago they were twenty-four hundred pages ahead of us. Last year they were about twelve hundred pages ahead. For the first four months of this year they're only two hundred pages ahead. And they come out twice as often."

Why is *Forbes* gaining?

"Because we are read with more intensity by people who . . . It's a guy with money reading our magazine. It's a successful person or a guy who's a yuppie and wants to be. He wants to know what the boss knows. He wants to *be* a boss."

"He wants to be you," I suggest.

"I don't know about that, but it's more fun reading *Forbes*."

It was about this point that the fun ended and the trouble started. Maybe it had been brewing already, a function of the fact that we were rival investigative lunchers. Or it could have been a question of temperament. Forbes is so relentlessly optimistic and sunny-minded it seemed to bring out that part of me that sees things through a glass darkly. In any case, what led up to the Offending Question and my being instantly ushered out was Forbes recounting his travels through Russia and China.

It seems he had a grand time motorcycling through the Soviet Union. The Russians loved his big American bikes. "They're a turn-on to them," he says, "because they're confined to small cc because of the huge price of gas."

And of course he loved ballooning through China.

"Creeping capitalism has knocked off China already, and it's eroding Russia. Communism as an ideology is absolutely dead," he proclaims.

And so the future looks rosy to Forbes. Rosier than it does to me: That very morning the *Times* had the first of its series on administration "contingency" plans to invade Nicaragua. In my dark view many would-be yuppies are going to die in the jungles of Central America. Which prompted me to ask what turned out to be the Offending Question:

"You're a capitalist; you've been to Russia and China. Nixon's been there. Conservatives go there. Why then does Ronald Reagan need to destroy the Sandinistas in Central America?"

Suddenly Forbes stood up.

He gave me a quick, hard stare. Suddenly he was John D. Rockefeller seeing Lenin in the mural.

Was there a Sandinista in the wine cellar?

Actually, I don't think Forbes thought I was a Sandinista. I think he realized he was face to face with something worse than a communist. A pessimist.

"Time to go," Forbes told me, "You've got more than enough."

THE FAST TYCOONS

———— • ————

A High-Concept Lunch with Don Simpson and Jerry Bruckheimer

> "What have you done? A treatment?"
>
> "No, a shooting script. At first I was held back by personal worries, but once I got started it was very simple. You just get behind the camera and dream."
>
> •
>
> "Authors get a tough break out here," Pat said sympathetically. "They never ought to come."
>
> "Who'd make up the stories—these feebs?"
>
> "Well anyhow, not authors," said Pat. "They don't want authors. They want writers—like me."
>
> —From *The Pat Hobby Stories*
> F. SCOTT FITZGERALD

Someday when you've got a couple of hours to spare, I'd like to explain to you why the long-neglected *Pat Hobby Stories* are the best things Fitzgerald wrote after *Gatsby*. Better than almost everything he wrote *before Gatsby*, too. And certainly better than anything he, or anyone else, has written about writers and Hollywood before or since. Forget *The Last Tycoon*. It's so choked with its own romantic effusions about visionary studio executives, he couldn't even finish it. Because he knew the other side of Hollywood. *The Pat Hobby Stories* are the view from below, a sharp astringent low-comic epic, a veritable *Dunciad* of hacks and feebs.

Fitzgerald wrote these stories for *Esquire* in the last few months before he died, while he was living in Encino on the lam from loan companies, tormented by debt and self-doubt, surviving by cranking out screenplays for Universal.

In the shambling figure of Pat Hobby, hack screenplay writer who—like Fitzgerald—has been on the decline since a brief blaze of glory in the Silent Era of the twenties, Fitzgerald did more than create a degraded image of himself and his own work. He captured for all time the exquisite self-loathing side of all writers, particularly those seduced and abandoned by the Hollywood muse. And despite the bitter comedy of their tone, he captured, through the lens of loss, the glamour and attraction of it all, the sheer seductive power of the medium to writers. Of what it's like, in doing a screenplay, to "get behind the camera and dream."

All of which brings us to our lunch today. The *Dreamstreet* lunch. Tell me how you like this as a High Concept: Let's do a lunch between a couple of hotshot Hollywood producers and a talented New York novelist. A "development lunch." The kind of thing that will embody all those complicated Fitzgeraldian ambivalences about writers and Hollywood. Let's see, what do you say we get Don Simpson and Jerry Bruckheimer to play the hotshot producing team? They're perfect for the part. They're *very* hot now; they're the ones who made *Flashdance*, the hottest picture of 1983, and *Beverly Hills Cop*, the monster hit of 1984. A lot of people are calling them *the* hottest independent production team around.

And they're available. They're in town for the opening of *Beverly Hills Cop*, they've got this multipicture deal with Paramount, where Simpson was head of production, and all the ex-Paramount execs at every other studio are trying to lure them away. Everything's moving fast for them. Let's call them the Fast Tycoons.

And let's get Richard Price to play the talented novelist. Another natural. He's best known for *The Wanderers*, but *Ladies' Man* and *The Breaks*, his last two books, are so wonderful, you could call him the Fitzgerald of the Jewish lower-middle class, only he's funnier than the doleful Scott ever was. In addition to being gifted, he's got several screenplay deals going, including one with Scorsese called *Night and the City*. And, of course, he's got a script "in development" with Simpson and Bruckheimer, too, a project that's close to his heart, and one that's got the lovely tentative title of *Dreamstreet*. Will the Hollywood hotshots make his dream? Or will they break his heart?

And hey, while we're at it, how about getting me to play the role of observer? I can bring the proper Pat Hobbyish perspective of envy and bitterness to the whole thing, having written a screenplay for Warner Brothers that was hot for about five minutes before being consigned to the terminal limbo of "turnaround."

Okay, now let's do this lunch at the Russian Tea Room —where else? It's where Hollywood does lunch in New York. Hell, we could even try to do it in the now notorious "Tootsie booth," as they call it here, after that fab scene with Dusty and Sydney. But no. That's overkill. No clichés here. "We're not cliché schlock Hollywood producers," Don Simpson has assured me. "We're something different."

Well, how do you like the concept so far? It's really got everything, don't you think? It's got Art and Commerce. The dream and the deal. Hollywood and New York. Caviar and blintzes.

And now let's choose just the right moment for it. How about the day after the night *Beverly Hills Cop* opens to record-breaking business, the day after *Variety* comes out with a piece praising the movie-marketing wizardry of the Simpson-Bruckheimer team, filled with all sorts of impressive-sounding distribution-strategy terms like "slide factor," "false-flag tactics," and "blind-bid prints." Don't you think all "the elements" are here?

And so here we are at the Tea Room; we've got a corner booth, but it's way in the back by the kitchen—look, these guys are hot, but they're not Dusty and Sydney yet. The whole place is buzzing and table-hopping, it's the whole borscht-sipping, *shashlik*-noshing agent-and-producer side of "the industry" at lunch. In fact, before we get a chance to give our designated cossack our drink orders, a Russian Tea Room regular table-hops over to congratulate them on last night's opening-night party for *Beverly Hills Cop*.

"Did you hear about the opening-night figures?" Simpson asks her. "Biggest opening in the history of motion pictures on a Wednesday—two point two million dollars, six hundred forty thousand people saw the movie."

"Really? That's fabulous."

"We're doing *Raiders of the Lost Ark* Saturday-night business on a Wednesday-night opening! It's unheard of."

"They're going to do a whole series of sequels now," says Richard Price. "*Westwood Cop, Brentwood Cop, Tijuana* . . ."

"We *are* planning a sequel already," Simpson says. "We're taking him to London. Eddie Murphy's going to London."

"*Piccadilly Cop*," suggest Price, "*Chelsea Cop* . . ."

I ask Price about the genesis of this *Dreamstreet* project he has "in development" with the Simpson and Bruckheimer team.

"I just started doing screenplays about two years ago," Price says. "And my agent says there's a guy Don Simpson and a guy Jerry Bruckheimer and they want to talk to you about a project, and Don basically said to me—" Price pauses and intones the following with proper High Concept portentousness: "East Coast. High School. 1984."

"I couldn't get more broad-stroke than that," Simpson recalls. "For four or five years I had it in our idea notebook, and when Jerry and I formed a company, one of the first things I wanted to get off the ground is this, and Richard is the guy we wanted to write it. We never went after another writer. *The Wanderers* is, I swear to God, maybe next to *Moby Dick*, my favorite book of all time. When I finished *The Wanderers*, I felt like part of life was over. I mean I was sad. I was like *depressed*. It pissed me off that he didn't write nine *Wanderers*."

In other words, Simpson seems to be saying, if I read him right here, *he liked the book.*

Price talks about the difficulty of moving from the vague High Concept parameters of East Coast. High School. 1984 to something he could get his teeth into.

"Doing a movie about a high school is just a minefield of clichés," he observes. "All Don said to me is 'East Coast. High School. 1984. What do you think?' And the first meeting we just sat there for two hours. They say there are only seven great stories in the world and the only one I could think of was fallen idols."

"Sam Goldwyn said there's only *one* story—a delayed fuck," observes the cynical Pat Hobby figure at the table.

Simpson, too, was aware of the "minefield of clichés" that East Coast. High School. 1984 needed to negotiate.

"Richard and I and then Jerry and I kicked around what the thematic notion was for a long time because it was never intended to be *Blackboard Jungle* nor was it intended to be *Valley Girls*, and it wasn't going to be *Teachers*."

What was it intended to be?

"It was intended to be a *look*," says Simpson. "That's

why I wanted Richard to do it, because I knew he had the eyes and the ears to go out and do the research which is critical to this, and make it real."

Meanwhile, Simpson is going about making it real on the studio production level.

"Now we get into the higher level of the business aspects," Simpson says. "When the Paramount management shifts began to occur, regime changes, Ned Tanen [Paramount's current head of production] called Jerry and I in and asked us to have lunch with him. He said. 'Look guys. We know what your next movie is going to be—*Beverly Hills Cop*, which everybody is high on.' And then he says, 'You've got two projects in development that I think are fabulous.' One is called *Top Guns*, which is going to be our next movie. They're committed to it. It's going to be in the theaters next Christmas; we're going to hire a director in the next probably two weeks. It's about the crème de la crème of naval fighter jocks. They go to a school called the Top Gun School."

This sounds an awful lot like *An Officer and a Gentleman Goes to Graduate School*, which is not surprising since Simpson oversaw the production of *An Officer and a Gentleman* when he was at Paramount.

"Top Gun School really exists," Simpson says. "In Fighter Town U.S.A., they call it. The town really exists. That was project one. Put that aside because that's not for this lunch. And he [Tanen] said, 'You've also got this project with this kid Richard Price.' He knew the one. He says, '*Dreamstreet*. Tell me what it's about.' "

I get Price to fill me in on what it's about, and he gives me a history of how it developed in his mind from East Coast. High School. 1984.

"I would get a lot of guest spots teaching writing in high schools because a lot of the kids had read *The Wanderers*. So I would end up teaching at like Our Lady of the Tax

Shelters out in Brooklyn. Then I taught in this school, Christopher Columbus High School in the Bronx, where the three key graduates there were Son of Sam, Christine Jorgensen, and Anne Bancroft."

"Come on," I say.

"That's what he told me, too," Simpson says.

"That was my local high school. And I started thinking about these kids, like white working-class kids, second generation up from the Bronx. The fathers are like mailmen, firemen, and these kids are into the Travolta look. These kids aren't *West Side Story* kids, but they aren't suburban kids either. The equivalent of Valley people, only the Valley people would hang out at some ritzy mall; these kids would hang out by Nathan's on Sunrise Highway. I always felt that when people write about Long Island they write about Fitzgerald's West Egg, but they don't think about places like Freeport."

I *knew* Fitzgerald would enter into this in one way or another. Price continues retracing the way he developed the concept.

"You ask these kids what they want to be. They want to be like *Mark Gastineau.* One kid said, 'I'd like to be a subcontractor.' I'd be asking the kids, 'Well, what do you want to be?' Three quarters of them would say, 'The Army . . . maybe the Navy.' It's like that Army ad—'*Be all you can be.*' That's all they thought they could be. They watch Apex Tech ads. There's like a despair level, but it's tied into economics. There's a cynicism that did not exist when I was in school. So I started thinking, what happens if you get a teacher who doesn't give a flying fuck about these kids, it's a job, and he gets seduced into taking up these kids' attitudes? And I went from there."

"It all sounds pretty bleak," says the bitter Pat Hobbyish observer, knowing that Hollywood doesn't make downbeat movies these days, certainly not bleak enough to suit his mood.

"No, no, it's not," says Price. "No, these kids come out on top and everybody—see the story is about an education. And every kid gets a little piece of what he didn't know he wanted but he realizes through the course of the story he wanted. Now if you want bleak, see *Teachers*. That got into despair with relish. This is the opposite. And I'm very aware of the despair thing—these kids I'm talking to, I don't want to betray their confidence and say, 'Thanks, kids,' and then do a *Zero for Conduct*. . . ."

"At present it's called *Dreamstreet*, not that we'll stick with it," says Simpson. "But the notion is that the kids today don't think Dream Street exists anymore and it's just because they don't know which way to turn to get on the street, but—"

"But it's about relearning optimism," says Price.

"That's the one, relearning optimism," says Simpson.

"This is what the meeting is like," says Price. "I say something and everybody goes, 'That's it!' "

At this point there's an interruption. A skinny kid—well, he's not actually a kid, as it turns out, but he *looks* like a Bronx Science kid—comes up to the table dressed in sort of denim-and-polyester Bronx-Science-goes-Beverly-Hills garb. It's Marty Brest, the wunderkind director of *Beverly Hills Cop*. What happens next is a kind of confused babble of voices on my tape, and I can't quite figure out who said what, but the transcript looks like this:

"Hey, Marty!"

"How you *doin'*, daddy-o?"

"Hey, meshugge, meshugge."

"Did you read where *I'm* doing *Dreamstreet*?"

"It's great, I love it."

"You've been developing it for years."

"Marty, do that thing with your glasses."

"Amazing, he must feel good."

"So I don' want to disturb your—"

"This is the Richard Price show at the moment."

"Da da da da da da."

With that fanfare, the frenetic Brest returns to his table and Simpson explicates.

"Paramount has asked us to start looking for directors for this *Dreamstreet* project, and we're all laughing because this is so incestuous. Richard here is writing a project for Marty at an enemy studio, and we want Marty to direct *Dreamstreet* because we all get along and we're all simpatico in our sensibilities."

"It's so inbred," says Price, "everybody should have hemophilia by now. What I realize about this industry is that you can never really say 'fuck you' to anybody because what goes round comes round."

"In any case," says Simpson, "Marty has this joke about us willing reality to our own—we create our own reality, and we've been hocking him for two months to do *Dreamstreet*. And then yesterday, *The Village Voice* comes out with this story, and he's quoted as saying, 'Well, my next project is going to be *Dreamstreet* written by Richard Price.' He was misquoted. The truth is he hasn't committed to it. It was subconscious. It was bubbling up some place."

Back to *Dreamstreet*, the concept.

"I don't want to do the cliché," Price says. "I really wanted to lay down a unique environment. It is like the East Coast version not of Valley Girls but of working-class people. So that's what I proposed as an environment. Then I just started writing. One of the characters I wanted to have was a teacher, like a Jimmy Breslin type who got knocked off the paper because he made up some stuff, and he's got to teach because he's got these two daughters in Bennington majoring in Marxist dance theory and banging black jazz musicians. So now he's got to teach and it's beneath him and he's pissed off. And to have this guy lock assholes with a real smartass kid whose brother owns a carpet clearance warehouse on the Miracle Mile. The kid wants to write. It's basically a father-son story because that's my turf, and I picked something very comfortable to me in terms of what I've done in literature because I felt like it was still a relatively new form for me and I didn't want to have to worry about writing about eighteenth-century China."

Once this was decided, Price says, producer Simpson took an active, almost collaborative role in shaping the first draft.

"I'd run down these scenes to him and Don would run down his take on these scenes. I read scenes to him over the telephone, but these phone calls would be four-hour phone calls with bad connections."

"Yeah, true," says Simpson. "Richard, by the time we were into the second draft, had literally read the entire screenplay to me in different voices at least twice. And he and I had this conversation about—I don't know, I picked up a quote some place, I said, 'Richard, writing a novel is the equivalent of the accumulation of detail. Writing a screenplay is the selection of the one detail that supplies the whole.' "

Perhaps this is the point to supply some details about the Simpson-Bruckheimer collaboration. I ask them how they got started working together.

"I hired Jerry to do *American Gigolo* and he pulled off—"

"To do it, meaning to produce it?"

"Produce it. The budget originally was eleven million dollars. John Travolta was committed to the project, then for personal reasons he had to withdraw. The studio canceled the movie. Paul Schrader, who wrote it and directed it, who was the *auteur* of the film, went nuts. He said, 'What are we gonna do? What are we gonna do?' And then he said, 'I know what we're gonna do. We're gonna get Richard Gere.' The studio, truth be known, didn't want to make it with Richard Gere and we were begging Richard Gere to do it and Paul went out and got Richard to say yes, and I'm going, what am I gonna do now? I go to my bosses Barry Diller and Michael Eisner, and they said, 'We don't want to make it with Gere.' [Eisner disputes this version of the story.] I said, 'We've got to make the movie.' They said, 'Great, you tell your friend Bruckheimer and your friend Schrader if they'll make it for five [million], we'll do it.' Knowing that it was impossible. I called Jerry at home. I had to trust him. He's my friend. I said, 'Can you do this for five? You've got to cut sixty percent of the budget.' Jerry said, 'I can do it and I'll get Paul to agree.' I told Paramount and they were boxed; they said okay, go ahead. And Jerry made the picture for four-eight. And that's what started us. He substantiated his ability as producer, and I got lucky and saved my job or I'd have gotten fired."

"How do you guys define your different responsibilities as a team now?" I ask Bruckheimer.

"We're interloping and we're interlocking all the time," he begins. "Don's initial strength comes from being a screenwriter and then he went into producing. He's considered to be Mr. Inside. He knows the inside of a studio backwards and forwards. He knows how you push buttons. Much better than I do. Since we've been together for almost three years now, we kind of go back and forth, but I guess I'm Mr. Outside: I'm out there thinking about the *look* we want—"

"Jerry's taught me everything about production," Don says. "I knew very little about it because as a studio executive you don't make movies. You make deals."

"That's why you hated it," says Bruckheimer. "There was never any completion."

"That's why I *loathed* it."

"You never get to come."

"It *is* coitus interruptus, yes. It's always beginning something you never complete. Coitus interruptus. And doing what we do now, you not only get to begin something, you get to see it through the burgeoning stages of the set, and then you get this day in the Russian Tea Room where your picture opens bigger than any—that's a good time. And that's what we're in it for. And all those middle stages. I knew the beginning of the process, but I never knew the middle. Over three years Jerry's taught me the middle. Jerry was an award-winning photographer when he was nine years old. He's got the best eye of any producer in the movie business. He can walk on a set and tell you what the f-stop is. Tell you where the camera should be. And his pictures have a particular look because of him. Jerry can do this with what we call the seven pillars of what we do. The writer and director, the cinematographer, the production designer, the film editor, and the music composer. I got six there. I missed one. And casting, yeah. These people are the pillars of every movie we make, and we make very, very, very careful moves to juxtapose them properly. And that's something he taught me—people. He knows what cinematographer for what picture . . ."

One thing Simpson didn't teach Bruckheimer was his own irrepressible volubility. Mr. Outside, Bruckheimer, is the silent type. I try to draw him out a little.

"How would you define this look he's talking about?" I ask Bruckheimer.

"I think if you look at the pictures that I've been involved in like *Gigolo*, *Cat People*, and *Flashdance*, it's—"

"Sensuous?"

"No, it's *contemporary*. They're all very contemporary. They're on the leading edge of design, fashion. We don't try to create trends, but we have, we did. *American Gigolo*—people started wearing ties again after that movie. We were the first ones to really bring on Giorgio Armani in this country, it helped change the way people dress. And *Flashdance*, another zinger. Don and I have a talent for finding talent. We hired a young designer who gave you the cutoff sweatshirt."

"Leg warmers, too," I contribute fondly.

"Leg warmers. All that stuff started to happen. There's a whole thing with dance studios and aerobics and all this kind of stuff that that picture helped generate. It was already building, but we helped make break dancing, too, with that picture. We saw these break dancers in the Roxy and the way they do these strange dances on the floor, and we said we've got to use this in *Flashdance*. And since then you've had six break-dancing movies."

"Let me ask you a question about lunches, since my column is theoretically a lunch column. Do you find a difference between L.A. lunches and New York lunches?"

"In L.A.," says Simpson, "you get lotte. You get *l-o-t-t-e* —that's the fashionable fish."

"Oh, there's a simple difference," says Bruckheimer. "We don't go to L.A. lunches."

"Why?"

"Jerry and I are not packaging producers," says Simpson, with a slight sniff of disdain for that breed. "The only reason we go to lunch in L.A. would be to sit down with agents to seduce them and woo them so they'll give us scripts so you can get elements for your movies. So ipso facto we don't do that. We go to *movies* at lunch. We may eat, we may not, but going to lunch is boring. In New York, lunch seems more appropriate. It's a lunch kind of place. This city is a lot slower paced for us. This is not a movie business town. I don't know, this is a cultural town."

"And where do you stay, which hotel?"

"I'm at the Regency. Jerry's very smart," says Simpson, answering for his partner. "He saw *Flashdance* was going to be a hit and he bought a loft."

"The thing about the Regency," says Price, "I feel like my whole screenwriting career is tied up with those red doors, knocking on doors. I'm always seeing some producer and director in the Regency. I just remember walking down the corridor and at the end of the corridor is money. It feels like—*Behind the Red Door.*

"But," Price says, "I always wanted to do this, do movies. I figured I'd establish myself as a novelist, so it's not like I'm going in there feeling bitter about being a pinch hitter or something. I know I'm a novelist. When you do a novel, that's your kid. This is like the men's club. I get away from my kid to see the guys at the club. It's a very different thing, and I don't put them on the same level. But I am having a tremendous amount of fun doing it, now that I feel like I cracked it, cracked the formula of it. I'd say this is the most fun year and a half of my life, which is to say nobody fucked me real bad yet. But I'm ready. I go in there with a chastity belt."

"Did anybody fuck you guys badly this year?" I ask.

"No way," says Bruckheimer.

"When was the last time?"

"Back in Anchorage, 1947," says Simpson, who grew up in Alaska. "No, it's been too long to remember. Since Jerry and I have been in the business together, nobody. When I was a studio executive it happened. Daily. Are you kidding? Oh yeah. When you're rejecting two hundred people a day, they're all going to take out their three fifty-sevens and shoot at you, and believe me they do. It's impossible to be well liked and be a successful studio executive. The two just do not go together."

Bruckheimer tells the story of how he got Simpson to quit his studio post as head of production for Paramount.

"I always knew he hated being an executive. He hated what he was doing. So this was when we were ready to do *Flashdance*. I walked into Don's office. It was like ten-thirty in the morning and I'd just see his energy was drained. I looked at him. I said, 'You're not happy. Why are you sitting here? I'm having a great time. We're down in a trailer; girls are coming in, beautiful dancers.' This guy is sitting here, people are yelling at him, and I said, 'Why don't you just come on and make a movie and have a good time?' He says, 'Oh man, I wish I could.' Then a day later he called me up and said. 'Guess what? I quit. Let's make this picture together.' "

"I walked into Mike Eisner's office," says Simpson, "and he looked in my eyes and said, 'You're going to do it, aren't you?' And I said, 'Here's my hat. It's done.' He looked at me and said, 'Okay, what do you want to do?' and I said, 'I want to produce *Flashdance* with Jerry Bruckheimer.' He said, 'You got it. You'll get to keep your entire contract as president.' And I get to keep my car, my house, all the perks, and that was it. It was that simple."

"Don was in a great position," says Bruckheimer, "because he has intimate relations with all the people like Mike Eisner, Jeff Katzenberg, Frank Mancuso. These are all close friends of his that worked together, they've gone to the wars together, and now they've split up and they're all in top positions at all these studios, very, very smart executives running different companies."

"We have a contract at Paramount that runs for another year and a half. We're happy and we intend to honor it," says Simpson devoutly. "But it would be a lie to say the other studios haven't been calling and asking what we're going to do when our contract's up and asking to talk to us. . . ."

I get Simpson back on the subject of Price's development deal for *Dreamstreet*.

"Actually, the point of this meeting," says Simpson, "there's certain things that Richard isn't even aware of yet. Because when I pitched the idea to Ned Tanen, I pitched him the '*Be all you can be*' stuff. I keep loving that. He could hook into that. And Richard's ability to write. And he says, 'I'm committing to *Dreamstreet* and I haven't read the script, I love it so much.' And I said, 'You should read the script.' But Ned's a real savvy guy and he was laughing. He said, 'I'm committing to the movie.' And then he read the script and he called about two days later. And he was ecstatic.

He said, 'Look, I'm assuming Mr. Price is going to come in and do another draft,' which is one of the things we're going to talk to Richard about in the next three weeks. But what Ned did after reading the script was commit to the movie. He says, 'Now that I've read it, this is a movie Paramount wants to make.' So we're really here to tell Richard Price that he's going to get the movie *Dreamstreet* made."

"Not only do I get all this good news," says Price, "but I get a free lunch."

What Does John Diebold Actually Do?

---◈---

The Eternal Mystery of the Automation Guru

I probably shouldn't begin this by telling you about the problem I had with John Diebold's "automated" washroom door, should I? After all, Diebold has an international reputation as an automation guru, and to begin by describing my embarrassing encounter with the automated washroom door might give rise to the impression that I thought it was some kind of *metaphor*. And that wouldn't be fair, because my whole preoccupation with the perplexing washroom door really reflects badly on me. Just demonstrates I've still got an attitude problem when it comes to automation and "the information revolution," deep-thinking management consultants, futurist gurus, and other such ornaments of our civilization.

No. I'm glad we gave this some thought. Let's save the

automated washroom-door thing for later. Wait till it comes up in context. See it as part of the larger picture.

Yes, let's begin with the Big Picture. Because the Diebold story transcends the petty pros and cons of the management guru trade.

The Diebold Question rises to the level of one of those Historico-Mystico Unsolved Mysteries that awaken in us a vast sense of wonder about the deep secrets of being.

Those giant stone heads on Easter Island, for instance. I *still* want to know what advanced civilization put them there. And Secretary of War Stanton—what *about* those links to John Wilkes Booth? How exactly *did* Dickens intend to end the unfinished *Mystery of Edwin Drood*? The rise of Inca civilization: evidence of Ancient Astronauts? Napoleon poisoned? Judge Crater alive? You know the kind of thing I mean.

And so it was, with the awe and trepidation that such questions inspire in me, that I approached one of those equally baffling riddles haunting and perplexing the inhabitants of contemporary Manhattan: *What does John Diebold actually do?*

For years I've been intrigued by this man Diebold. A woman, a casual acquaintance, once revealed she worked for The Diebold Group. She described the high-powered, expensive aura of Diebold, the man and the institution.

"What does he do?" I asked.

"It's kind of vague," she said. "He was the guy who invented the word 'automation,' and now he, well, he's a consultant, but . . ."

She trailed off. And never got more specific. At first I thought she was being deliberately evasive, but in retrospect, I realize that the question "What does John Diebold actually do?" was a mystery to her, too.

Then there was that feature in *New York* magazine a few years ago about that evening in John Diebold's drawing room. The room that originally graced a castle on the coast of Sussex in Queen Elizabeth's reign. A du Pont bought it, had it shipped here, and reassembled it in the East End Avenue apartment now owned by Diebold. The evening described in the article sounded like a very top-drawer event. Concerned tycoons, serious-minded socialites—Diebold dazzled them all by putting on a production of an Elizabethan court masque. Pretty impressive; it certainly made Diebold *seem* like an important fellow, but somehow I never got a picture from the article of what the guy actually did.

Now it's not as if we're starting off without any evidence. Like the Incas, Diebold has left us some clues. Recently, while patiently sifting through a jumbled midden of management-guru, Theory Z, Future Schlock–type books, I came across a curious volume called *Making the Future Work*, by John Diebold, "international Authority on Management and Technology." The discovery gave me hope that Diebold might do a lunch with me and allow me to ask him directly What He Does. You don't often get this kind of opportunity. The great stone heads of Easter Island don't give interviews, and Secretary of War Stanton never returns my calls. Diebold did.

Before our lunch, I studied the baffling book for further clues.

The jacket identifies Diebold as "the influential chairman of The Diebold Group, Inc., management advisers to the Fortune 500, governments, and leading public agencies. . . . For more than 30 years John Diebold has been acknowledged one of the world's foremost authorities in the field of computers and automation . . . has been featured on a cover story in *Time* . . . has been decorated by the governments of Jordan, Italy, West Germany, and France."

We also know that whatever he does, he's made a lot of important friends doing it. We learn this in the first couple of chapters of *Making the Future Work* in which Diebold frequently annotates various treasures of management-guru deep-think by adding that he received some bit of enlightenment "while trout fishing at my country home with my friend John McCloy."

In the brief space of two pages, he mentions "my friends Cyrus Vance and Daniel Yankelovich," "my friend Henry Rowen, former president of the Rand Corporation," and the doubly friendly "my friend Fred Friendly."

In a couple of instances he even identifies dead people as "my late friend Herman Kahn" and "my now deceased friend Mark Garlinghouse, general counsel of AT&T."

In fact, he can't stop thinking about his friends. "I am fond of quoting Charlie Brown," Diebold says at one point, and then advises us parenthetically, "not my friend the AT&T chairman but the 'Peanuts' Philosopher."

But, sad to say, if this book is any evidence, Diebold is, at best, the "Peanuts" Philosopher of management gurus.

In the same paragraph in which he quotes Charlie Brown—in case you forgot, that's the "Peanuts" Philosopher, *not* his friend the AT&T chairman—he also unearths a tired chestnut from another comic-strip philosopher: "I think that any further dodging of the real dilemmas of our society will bring us into the arms of that other comic-strip curmudgeon, 'Albert,' in 'Pogo,' who observed, 'We has met the enemy and it is US!' "

And then in a staggering concatenation of platitudes he tells us: "While I hesitate to overdramatize this situation, the alternative to making our vital institutions work is something we must avoid at all costs—moving toward an increasingly authoritarian government of either right or left. . . . Our late twentieth-century propensity to focus on symptoms rather than causes results in technofix—applying increasingly expensive Band-Aids to our condition. . . . We need to make the institutions of our society capable of dealing with life in the advanced industrial world in which we live."

It goes on like that. It's not writing; it's word processing.

Not since Joyce's endless-cliché chapter in *Ulysses* has Western literature seen a more sustained stream of platitudes. Interspersed with clip-job-like "case studies" of such already endlessly overdiscussed issues as regulatory gridlock, overlitigiousness, The New Biotechnologies: Threat or Menace?, and so on, Diebold gives us long excerpts from such sages as Ted Sorensen and the now deceased Herman Kahn, and such characteristically Dieboldian pronouncements as "The long-term horizon can be very distant," and "Why are libraries, in spite of some record-keeping advances, still functioning as they did centuries ago—as storehouses for paper books and paper references?" (Well, for one thing, burning all those outmoded books might violate those pesky EPA regulations.)

I could go on. There are certain passages in this book that might replace conventional means of torture in getting reluctant prisoners to talk. What hardened terrorist could withstand a sentence that gets under way with "I can't help but believe that some organized and ongoing assessment of alternative futures and the demands of these on our society would be useful so that in the daily prioritization that occurs . . ."

What's fascinating about this is what it seems to say about the collective intelligence of the Fortune 500 companies: *They pay this guy to do their deep thinking for them.* No, that couldn't be. They pay him, but not for this. This is just for the masses. The real stuff, and the kind that earned him the "guru of automation" reputation, the kind the Fortune 500 companies rely on, the really deep Dieboldian concepts can't be captured in mere processed words. It's not what he says, it's what he *does*. Whatever that is.

And so reading The Book only deepened my sense of awe at that eternal Diebold Question. And strengthened my resolve, in the course of my lunch with him, to ask Diebold directly what he does, to pin down something at least for future investigators to build upon.

Which brings us to the elusive "social strategy" puzzle. A little mystery within the larger Diebold mystery, a mystery that mystified even Diebold himself. The first thing I tried to pin down.

I first came across the term "social strategy" in its Dieboldian context in a slick, four-page folder on an end table in the anteroom of his Park Avenue office suite. The folder was *The Diebold Group, Inc. Administrative Newsletter.* It's filled with the busy doings of the many divisions of the Diebold empire.

Here we learn DIEBOLD TO KEYNOTE WORLD CONFERENCE ON ERGONOMICS. "Ergonomics," Diebold is quoted as declaring, "will play an increasingly important role in the development of user-friendly hardware and software, in the configuration of the automated workplace. . . ."

Meanwhile, we learn that the Diebold Multi-sponsor Continuing Programs have just completed the Sixty-third Diebold Plenary Meeting. (Theme: "What will the new world of intelligent technologies, so different from their simple machine forebears, look like?") And the Sixty-fourth Diebold Plenary on Kiawah Island looked to be a searching one ("The unquestionable elements of technological growth and expansion must be probed . . . from three different perspectives, that of the underlying infrastructure . . .").

But the really exciting development in this newsletter is nothing less than an entirely new coinage: "social strategy." Diebold Bossard Organizational Dynamics, Inc., identifies itself as "a professional consulting practice" that can put you in the "social strategy" picture. Because the words "social strategy" have undergone Dieboldization, they don't mean what you might think. "Simply defined," according to the newsletter, "social strategy" is "that set of *assumptions* which an organization appears to hold *about people* [italics theirs]." "Social strategy is revealed as the system of human values that people perceive as they observe or experience the activities of an organization. . . . Rapidly accumulating evidence suggests that, in these complicated times, social strategy may be the prime determinant of relative operational results achieved by competing organizations."

It that clear? Not what "social strategy" means—that's not clear at all—what's clear is that whatever it is, if you want your corporation to get to the top, you better have it. After all, it may be the *prime determinant* of success.

So this "social strategy"—whatever it is—must be cutting-edge stuff. The kind of thing you didn't learn about in *Theory Z*, the kind of thing you won't find in *In Search of Excellence*. The kind of thing that's brought to you exclusively by Diebold Bossard Organizational Dynamics.

Still, I thought maybe I could get Diebold to disclose just a *little bit* more about this powerful new management concept, "social strategy." And so shortly after I began talking to him—before we headed off to lunch—I asked Diebold, "Can you get a little bit more specific about what this 'social strategy' that your newsletter refers to is?"

Diebold is a tall, pleasant, fiftyish fellow who reminds you of no one so much as David Hartman. He's got that same furrowed brow, that same "concerned"-looking expression the *Good Morning America* host gets when he's really empathizing with, say, Suzanne Somers's career dilemmas.

When I ask Diebold to tell me about "social strategy," he gives me a quizzical stare. Almost as if he hadn't heard the term before this instant.

"Social strategy," I repeat.

He furrows his brow, as if searching the memory bank. "Then we have to get into whoever was doing that here. I'm not—it's not my term. Um, um . . ."

Trying to be helpful, I hand him the newsletter and point out the headline DIEBOLD BOSSARD FOCUSES ON SOCIAL STRATEGY—which, remember, is the "prime determinant" of organizational success "in these complicated times."

Diebold takes out his reading glasses, puts them on, and focuses on the mystifying "social strategy" paragraph. Reads the prose with a puzzled look.

"Oh," he says finally, although a bit tentatively. "This is in the context of organizing work for, um, if you tried to, um, have a, um, most effective, um, productivity in the, um, the work. . . ."

He pauses and remarks, a bit unnecessarily, "It's not an area that I've been working in, so, um . . ."

Here I seize the opportunity to ask the eternal Diebold Question: "What *are* the areas that you specifically do handle these days?"

"Um?"

"Well, you said this is an area you're *not* working in, so . . ."

"No, um, I mean, the use of the term," he begins, the "term" referred to being "social strategy," which he continues struggling to define. "The activity is the concern of how to, um, improve productivity by using some techniques a French firm we're associated with have developed. In terms of the improving both factory and office productivity, and I think the use of the term 'social strategy,' I've never heard it used, so that's why, um . . ."

Okay, Diebold's not right in charge of the inventing-new-words-to-consult-about division of The Diebold Group anymore. He's beyond that. He's looking at the Big Picture, now. The future.

Ergonomics, for instance. I mention that he's set to keynote the coming World Conference on Ergonomics, which the newsletter says "will take place in Los Angeles, Chicago, New York, Amsterdam, Düsseldorf, Helsinki, and London."

What is ergonomics again?

"That was my reaction when I was asked to keynote,"

he says. "It's not my term, but it's the interface between the human being and the machine. . . ."

Well, these terms were all terrifically illuminating and useful, but they didn't give much of a clue to what Diebold does day to day. I ask him what he did *that* morning.

And in fact he did conduct some business that morning. He did have a 9:30 meeting.

"It was a meeting on a, well, a venture that we're forming in a new area."

"Can you be a little more specific?" I ask. "You don't have to mention the name of the company."

"It's a company that will be in the communications field," he says. "Communications in the voice and machine mode. People use 'communications' for publishing. I don't mean that. Hardwire communications, in that sense."

That's as specific as he gets on that subject. He explains that his schedule is "particularly skewed right now" because he is serving as foreman of a grand jury in the afternoons.

"But tonight I have a dinner at my home here in New York for the head of policy planning for the German Foreign Ministry. This will simply be a stag dinner for a group of people to talk about foreign policy. Also technology, because they're very interested in the impact on their country. I tend to find that I use stag dinners. I tend to do that very frequently to try to have the opportunity to have a long discussion with a person who's a major player in that area."

Diebold has some mildly interesting thoughts about the cultural values of European society that tend to inhibit entrepreneurial growth. About the importance of making failure easy.

"It's very difficult in that society because in the European area, the premium on not failing is very high and in America you can fail and start over. It's one of our national strengths. In Europe the consequences of failure are much greater and the result is that you find far fewer young people who will go out on their own and try to start new businesses."

"I believe you've written," I say, "that the mildness of U.S. bankruptcy laws is one of our strengths."

"The bankruptcy laws are very important because people are able to start over again. In Germany, the guy who is legally the CEO of the German company has something like twenty-seven years of personal liability if his venture goes bankrupt. You don't find very many ventures being started."

Somehow I wondered if those Manville Corporation asbestos workers would have the same enthusiasm for the enlightened bankruptcy laws Diebold proposes.

It was getting to be time to proceed to Lutèce. As we were gathering our things up, I decided to ask Diebold about his attitude on the new generation of management gurus, rival entrepreneurs in corporate deep-think.

"I noticed in your book," I say, "you made a couple of disparaging remarks about people following 'trendy Japanese management theories.' "

"I wrote one of the first things ever about looking at the Japanese in the seventies," says Diebold. "It was a guest editorial in *Business Week*—simply saying that one ought to look at the Japanese, there's a lot one can learn from the Japanese." One ought to look at the Japanese, Diebold now says, but not too *hard*. "In the last few years, you've had a lot of people trying to wholesale say we should, but you just can't wholesale copy this sort of stuff, and I think a lot of them are silly. But as I say, I think I was one of the very first people to actually come out in praise of it and say you ought to look at the Japanese. . . ."

"What about *Theory Z*, do you think that's one of the copycat books?"

"I don't like any of them—I think life is much more subtle and much more complex. I don't like easy solutions to complicated problems."

Easy solutions to complicated problems. Which brings us

to the automated-washroom-door problem. A complicated solution to an easy problem. Diebold popped into the washroom, which was located at the far end of his office, near his desk. When he emerged, he said he needed to consult his assistant about something, and told me as he left the room, "Use the washroom if you'd like."

I approached the place that Diebold had just emerged from, but couldn't find a door leading to the washroom. There was just some sleek wood paneling. I could have sworn I saw Diebold emerge from a door in this wall. But where *was* the opening? I started feeling with my fingers along the interstices of the paneling. There it was. An aperture. This must be the edge of the door. But it didn't seem to offer any easy way of getting it open. It didn't seem to offer *any* way. I can't say how long I stood there clawing to get the door open. It seemed like hours.

And then I heard Diebold returning. I certainly didn't want to have him catch me clawing at this wall like a fool. Could this be some kind of trick? Some clever Dieboldian demonstration of the limit of human problem-solving ability? Did he pull this on clients to throw them off balance, make them feel they needed a guru in "these complicated times" with invisible washroom doors?

I heard Diebold a few feet away from reentering. I straightened up so it wouldn't look like I'd been flustered by the door problem. So I'd look like I'd just been standing here next to his desk.

No. That looked bad, too. He'd think I was snooping, trying to get a peek at the Dieboldian vision of the future taking shape there. Proprietary stuff that. Industrial espionage. Theft of the future. No. I had to crack the washroom door and get inside. I attacked the aperture in the paneling with the frantic desperation of *Escape from Alcatraz*. And suddenly my fingers found something. I don't know what or how, but a little metal thing suddenly popped out at waist level. I pulled it and got the door open just in time. Safely inside I tried to get a glimpse of the maddeningly elusive washroom-door mechanism. And then I saw it. There was some kind of button hidden away in the crack between the door and the door frame. As I reconstruct it, you have to push the button to make the metal handlelike thing pop out, at which point you are able to use the handle to open the door.

Now, you can look at this push-button washroom-door-handle arrangement in two ways. You could look at it as 1939 World's Fair Automatic Home of the Future stuff—an antique futurist vision of a life lived in sleek streamlined surfaces with no distractingly utilitarian protrusions like handles.

Or you could look at it as a really dumb device. It's not really automation, but it does use a push button to complicate a simple process. I suspect some designer got carried away with the automation theme of the enterprise and made sure everything that could be push-buttoned would be push-buttoned. Still you'd think the man who is hired by the Fortune 500 to integrate automation into their infrastructures, or whatever, would be able to tell an inappropriate use of technology when he saw one. Couldn't he have told his designer: "Hey, put a handle on my washroom door, will you?"

I think the useless, ridiculous push button is a metaphor for all that's wrong with the computer and automation obsession: the idea that things are automatically improved by putting a button or a screen between people and experience. If you ask me, the entire automation and information "revolution" and all the gurus that flack for it have contributed about as much to the advancement of the human experience as the button on John Diebold's washroom door.

The oddest thing is that from then on I found myself getting to like Diebold. Partly because I began to suspect

Diebold himself didn't take the management guru thing too seriously.

We were in Diebold's car on the way over to Lutèce when he told me something that made me see him in a kindlier light. As Diebold's driver, Mustafa Sala, skillfully piloted us through the noon rush, I asked Diebold to tell me how he got so interested in Chinese culture.

He said it had begun after reading the great scholar Joseph Needham's epic work *Science and Civilization in China*.

"I got hooked on that," Diebold tells me, "and then I got to know Joseph, and he asked me if I'd be chairman of his trust, which I am. I've gotten, between Joseph and this group, all the key Chinese flow-through both in my home and here. We've never tried to do business in China; this has been an entirely intellectual thing. I try to keep windows open on a lot of worlds. I'm very interested in foreign policy and have considerable interest in Europe, which is probably why our business is there rather than the reverse, the interest in it. There was a period when I was on a first-name basis with every European head of government. That's no longer the case," he adds a bit wistfully.

Suddenly touched by his genuine enthusiasm for Needham, I got a new illumination about who Diebold really is.

Do you know how they select the top lamas in Tibet? When the old one dies, they go out into the countryside and try to find a child who was born at the *exact instant* the lama passed on. That way there is some assurance that the soul of the lama leaped from the moribund body to be reincarnated in the new baby.

That all makes perfect sense, of course, but look at it from the point of view of the chosen child as he's growing up. *He* knows he's just another peasant kid, no different from his brothers and sisters. But from practically the moment he can speak, *everyone in Tibet hangs on his every word as if he were a God-Sage*. He knows he's just an ordinary guy, but hell, it's nice work if you can get it, why argue with them? Why not play along with it?

I have a feeling that something like that happened with Diebold's transformation into God-Sage of the Age of Automation. He coined the word "automation" at just the right instant, just when the age was being born. Found himself acclaimed the dalai lama of modern management gurus. He didn't have an abundance of blinding insights after that, but he didn't have to. Once people acclaim you a God-Sage, everything you say seems like a blinding insight to those in search of that kind of enlightenment. And so Diebold decided to play along with it. It was a good gig. He's a thoughtful, sensitive guy, the kind of person whose favorite pleasure probably was spending long hours immersed in Joseph Needham's fascinating multivolume work on the history of technology in China. But what the hell, with the management-guru business going, he'd have plenty of time to do that. Time to meet Joseph Needham. Time for trout fishing with John McCloy. Meanwhile, just keep spinning off Diebold Groups, Diebold Institutes, Diebold Public Policy Studies Programs, and the like.

And who can blame him? It's a nice life. When Diebold's not hosting deep-think dinners for techno-baffled Europeans in his private dining room or in his transplanted Elizabethan digs, he can be found having lunch almost daily at Lutèce.

Moments after we're seated in Diebold's corner table downstairs, chef André Soltner comes over to greet Diebold warmly and tip him off to something special he's whipped up today.

"I made a *mille-feuille*, almost like a napoleon with a mousse of smoked salmon for a filling, maybe as an appetizer. On the *plat du jour* maybe you would like we have a breast of Muscovy duck which we sauté. Make a sauce with the fresh black currants."

We agree to give them a try.

"And," Soltner adds, "I'll send you a little soup just to taste for your tongue."

"You know my weakness," Diebold says, laughing.

"I once almost owned an interest in this place," Diebold tells me. "The first chef who owned it, chef André Surmain, was crying to me one day about how he was going to have to go out of business. He only had fourteen tables. This was a genuine rose garden here." Diebold, the apostle of progress, says he misses the days before the rose garden was uprooted to make room for additional tables. "I went home from lunch sitting at this table where I've always sat," Diebold says, "and I wrote a letter which I had the wisdom not to send, offering to buy an interest to keep the restaurant going, because I felt they tried to do everything right and they really did. . . ."

Well, this is all very nice, and the food is still just right. The *mille-feuille* is especially intense and creamy, but, intoxicated as I am by the smoked-salmon mousse and the bottle of Sancerre Diebold has ordered, I know I'm here on a mission. I'm here to find at least some answer to the ever-elusive "What does John Diebold actually do?" question. Even if he only consults and thinks about thinking now, there must have been some concrete achievement beyond coining "automation" behind his management guru empire.

"Most people know you coined the word 'automation,' " I begin, "and that since then you've been consulting for a lot of major corporations. Are there specific corporations —can I say that Exxon, say, is reorganized this way because they consulted with John Diebold, or IBM decided to change its approach to this or that because of John Diebold?"

"I'd rather not, in the sense that if we do our—" He pauses. "There's an old Chinese maxim that the best leader is he who, after the battle has been won, the people say,

'We did this by ourselves,' and I think that's the way; if you do your job right, it shouldn't be that you say I reorganized XYZ. The problem is most of the things we do you can't talk about in specifics. Sometimes you can. Sometimes in the public sector you can because they're public. What can I say to be helpful to you?"

"I suppose I'm looking for examples of how Diebold and The Diebold Group changed American management, changed the American corporation," I say. "Are there things that you can point to that are modes of innovations, automation, whatever, that are your influence? How is American business different today because of what you've done?"

"I suppose one way to look at it," Diebold says, "is simply we have been working with a lot of very good companies for a long time and presumably would not be if they were not making some practical use of it. Another way to look at it is that I think a lot of ways of looking at problems, concepts, and ideas are things that we've done a great deal to not only produce but to work on the dissemination of the concepts and of ways of thinking about them. I mean I hope my own contribution is that in terms of changing perceptions of things."

Well, that all seems pretty clear in a sense. And the Muscovy duck arrives and it's very good, but there's something missing from Diebold's plate.

"It's beautiful," says Diebold as the waiter sets down our plates, "but I didn't get any berries."

"You didn't," I observe. It's true. My lovely lean slices of duck are dotted with gleaming dark currants.

"I think I got your berries," I say.

"Discrimination," says Diebold to the waiter, pointing at my currants.

"Oh," he says, "I forgot the berries." He hurries off to get some berries.

He wanted berries; I wanted answers.

But by this time, I was getting desperate; it was a mind-bending challenge to my ingenuity as a reporter. I found myself twisting every stray subject I could into another go-round at the Big Question. We were, for instance, talking for a moment about the device on my tape recorder that allows it to pick up voices out of noise.

"It's very important," Diebold remarks, "because the background noise here is horrible."

"Speaking of noise," I say, "wasn't that the essence of your theoretical discussion of automation, right, the distinction between the *bit* of information and the *noise* surrounding it?"

"Either you've done your homework," says Diebold, "or you've done a lot of reading."

"Both I guess," I concur modestly, the good pupil. "Help me out, though, with finding the *bit* of information that's what John Diebold *does* as opposed to—I've read lots about The Diebold Group, but I guess I'm trying to get a sense of—you know what I mean, what—"

"What am I good at? I'm good at ideas. I guess fundamentally I'm a man of ideas and often—I'm finding the same problem with this book, which I never in a million years expected—is getting people to focus on ideas. They're so used to thinking in terms of the crises that they cannot focus on the fact that those are symptoms. They just don't want to do it. They walk away. I learned today the book has won a—I hope I get it right—a George Washington Medal of the Freedom Foundation."

"This one, *Making the Future Work*?"

"Yeah. But it's a terrible problem to get—years later people say, '*Yeah, obvious*.' It's like that Japanese thing I cited this morning."

He's referring to what he regards as his prophetic editorial in *Business Week*, which suggested we "take a look at what the Japanese are doing." He wishes he'd gotten more attention and credit for what he regards as *his* discovery of Oriental management wisdom. "I never had a letter. I never had anyone ever mention it. At the time, I thought this was a good thing, a new look at Japan. Eight or nine years later it's very fashionable. That's the story of my life."

Lunch is drawing to a close and I return to the Big Picture again. To Diebold's final chapter in his book, "A Guiding Vision."

"You talk about, in your book, the need for a guiding vision. You talk in Chinese terms of the various visions, Legalism, Confucianism, Taoism, and then you say I'm sorry, I'm not going to give you a guiding vision. Now this is very disappointing."

"Some people find that," Diebold concedes. "It seems to me that to recognize the need for that doesn't mean to me that you've got to be able to say, 'Ah, I've got it right here,' and you check out number three. As I say in the book, when I started I had no anticipation of suggesting anything. When I finished, I decided that, well, Jesus, it's not such a minor thing to maybe let us in the interim period before someone arrives with something that can then be agreed upon, that direction for society, let's focus on the need for getting the process right. I don't think that's minor."

"It seems to me from reading between the lines of your discussing of the various Chinese visions, that of those four, Confucianism would be closest to your—"

"Please don't try to say I'm a Confucian."

"Come on, this can't be really controversial. This is not going to get you in trouble to say that of the four Chinese visions, Confucianism is—"

"Okay, okay, okay, but I mean I don't want to see a drawing of me as a Confucianist."

Okay. Just to make sure, I'm adding a little note to this piece for the art director: *No drawings of John Diebold as a Chinese sage.* We don't want anyone to mistake him for Confucius.

GRILL TALK

———— ❧ ————

Helen Gurley Brown and Liz Smith at the Four Seasons

Could we talk about Balzac for a moment here? The morning of the day I was scheduled to meet Liz Smith and Helen Gurley Brown for lunch, I had just finished reading the astonishing *Le Père Goriot* for the first time. And "got" for the first time the Balzacian visionary apprehension of social existence.

Got it, and saw what a perfect lens it is through which to examine the physics of power and magnetism that light up the circuits of Manhattan.

He writes, Balzac, of Parisian society at a time when Paris was the capital of the civilized world, a place constantly quivering with a frenzied consciousness of power, status, and money. He doesn't see it as a moralist, exactly. Balzac is more like a physicist: He sees the human comedy as a dance of highly charged particles crisscrossed by vectors of ambition and desire. He sees individual personalities, like particles, colliding with and attracting each other, their paths twisted by the powerful magnetic fields of money and love.

And just as a physicist uses a cloud chamber to capture and record a frozen instant of the drama of particles and forces, so Balzac uses such "cloud chambers" as dinner parties, masked balls, boarding-house breakfasts, and bordello evenings to project the configurations of forces and personalities on a common scrim.

All of which is to say that you could think of the Grill Room of The Four Seasons at lunchtime as one of the key cloud chambers of contemporary Manhattan society. And you could think of Liz Smith and Helen Gurley Brown as physicists of ambition and desire.

You could also think of them as two powerful women in the quintessentially male-power Grill Room. The place where the power lunch was *born*, for God's sake. Born on whatever momentous occasion it was that Michael Korda, who has practically *condo-ed* the power table here, decreed that ordering Perrier and small portions—those dainty *paillards* they serve here—means you have the lean and hungry confidence of a Power Guy.

On the other hand, you could forget the power equations and just think of Liz and Helen as two women who have known each other for twenty years, ever since Helen took over *Cosmopolitan* while Liz was working there as an entertainment writer.

Or—and this is your *final* option—you can just hope that when the three of us sit down, I'll keep my Balzacian vision to myself and let the two of them talk. Which is almost exactly what happened.

Liz: I saw you here the other day with Grace Mirabella, Helen.

RON: Is this a regular place for you?

HELEN: No. A, I don't go to lunch; B, nobody ever believes you; C, the minute you say you never go to lunch, you run into your twelve not-dearest friends or dearest enemies, just the people that you say you never go to lunch to, and there you are having lunch. It's not exactly handy, because I'm at Broadway and Fifty-seventh, and this is Fifty-second and the other side of town, and since I like to take buses, it takes . . . I started out at eleven-thirty this morning.

RON: You still take the bus?

HELEN: I took the number twenty-eight, and I got off at Lexington and whatever. Here I am. I *adore* The Four Seasons. It's pure heaven.

LIZ: Let me tell you a great story about Helen and buses. One time I went up to have dinner with her. This was when I was a freelance writer. I said, "I just grabbed a cab and came up here." She said, "You took a cab?" Then she started telling me how she couldn't stand ever to take a cab and she always took the bus, and I said, "For heaven's sake, they even gave Mrs. Vreeland her limousine. You make millions for The Hearst Corporation. You've got to start treating yourself better." So finally she let a lot of time pass and she said, "I've started taking a cab one way now." I couldn't talk her into a round trip. She still takes the bus. Now the best part was she said, "If I don't take the bus at least once a day, I don't know what's going on with my girls." You see, those *Cosmopolitan* girls ride the bus.

RON: So what is going on with the girls today?

HELEN: Well, I get on the bus; I put on my makeup; I study my notes; I read the paper. It's really—I'm really taking the bus because I'm cheap, and I don't talk to anybody on the bus. Who know's what's going on?

[*Liz's Bloody Mary arrives, along with my beer and*

Helen's Perrier. Liz orders the steak with fried onions, Helen gets the salmon and—well, do you care what I ordered? I ask Liz to survey the room and tell me what kind of crowd it is today.]

Liz: Well, I was thinking that we should go someplace where a lot of people come over and say hello. Generally that does happen here, but today there really isn't anybody here that I know. I mean, the last time I was in here, I knew everybody, because all the agents come here. This is the publishing lunch place, and it's always full. You always see Michael Korda and Leo Lerman and— that day I was in here, I saw Leo Lerman, Tina Brown, Helen, and two or three editors and publishers. You always see them. You know, Morty Janklow comes here, Swifty Lazar. I have this theory that people come here because they can't be overheard. This room—not the other one, but this room—is a great deal-making place.

Ron: Is it the architecture, the setup of the tables, that makes it?

Liz: Yeah, that's my theory. The tables are so well separated that you can sit back to back and still not hear what people behind you are saying. And you know Jackie Onassis is in here all the time. This is her big deal-making place.

Helen: Liz, I think that article about Truman Capote and his ex-friend [Lee Radziwill] is the best thing you've ever written.

Liz: I'm glad you like it. That's why I was having lunch with Tina Brown. She said, "Why didn't you sell that to *Vanity Fair*?" and I said—you know the *Daily News* was just launching this new section called "Sunday People." It was a nice kickoff for the section. But I could have made a lot of money selling it.

Helen: *Vanity Fair* spends money. I did something sort of rotten last week. I never make speeches, and I didn't this time, but I went to a magazine convention, a publishers' conference. I said I couldn't make a speech, but I would answer questions. They were very snotty questions, like "At your age, how can you edit a magazine for such young women?" and "Is it true that you're cheap?" We discussed that already. But I said yes, and then I mentioned what I paid for book excerpts. They said that you can't be cheap with writers because they won't write for you. But book excerpts—I said that *Vanity Fair*, speaking of them, had paid fifty thousand dollars for a Norman Mailer excerpt, and I just let the clouds roll by, and a month later I paid five thousand dollars for the same material, because I figured, how many people read *Cosmo* who also read *Vanity Fair*? And I mentioned some more magazines by name, saying they had paid eighty thousand dollars for Jane Fonda, and I let the clouds roll by, and I paid five hundred dollars each for a couple of exercises from her new book. And it was sort of rotten to mention names because it made them sound so extravagant.

LIZ: I think it's great. I think as we grow older we should be more specific.

HELEN: You're always specific.

LIZ: No, I'm very weaselly, but—

HELEN: How you stay out of trouble as well as you do, I can't imagine.

LIZ: I don't know, but I do. I was thinking how I feel hated today. Sometimes when everything goes wrong, four thousand people call and complain. I had this item last week that Gavin Macleod and his wife had gone back together. You know he divorced her, and then she was brokenhearted. Her name was Patty. But they had gone back together and so forth, and they had both gotten religion. Well, today the *Star* says that they've gone back together. It's just taken my story and rewritten it. But

then the *Enquirer* and the *Globe* both say that he's going
to marry this evangelist, so—

HELEN: Makes you wonder.

LIZ: But you see, I got the item from somebody who
knows them so well that it would never occur to me to
try to reach them and ask them. They weren't going to
make a comment anyway. So now I've got to try to reach
them and say, "Hey, were they right? Am I wrong?"

HELEN: Did you get religion or didn't you?

[*Liz tells another fascinating story involving religion.
She told it to us with the tape recorder on, but I think I
should probably tell it as a "blind item." Let's call it the
tale of the Princess and the Conservative Intellectual. Liz
says she heard it from a very well-known, recently deceased author.*]

LIZ: He told this horrible story about [the Princess]
putting the make on [the Conservative Intellectual]. How
she decided that [the CI] was the person she wanted, so
she called him up or ran into him somewhere or something, and she said to him, "I want to discuss my religion
with you. I feel that I'm a lapsed Catholic," and so forth
and so on.

HELEN: What a neat idea. I've never thought of that.
But then I'm a lapsed Presbyterian.

LIZ: Haven't you heard this? So he comes to her apartment to discuss how she can get back into the fold. And
he has this long conversation, this deep conversation about
religion and so forth and so on, and she comes on to him
like crazy, and he just acted like it wasn't happening and
continued talking about religion, and then he left.

HELEN: What a lovely story.

LIZ: How's my boyfriend [*referring to Helen's husband,
movie producer David Brown*]?

HELEN: He's making a movie in Europe. It's *Target* with
Gene Hackman and Matt Dillon. It's a mystery-thriller.

CBS is putting up the money, Warner is distributing, and so far it's going very well. Do you want to know about my life?

LIZ: I do. I want to know.

HELEN: My life, of course, is talking to David twice a day and getting his mail to him and sending him the things that he's forgotten. I sent all of his Dunhill suits to Paris because he needed them before I was arriving. They got there, and they stayed in customs for about a week. And then we had to pay a thousand bucks to get them out of customs, and I said, "Send them home." And on the way home they got lost, and we never saw them again until very recently. So that's David. We've taken care of David. Tomorrow night I'm going to give a fund-raiser for the National Abortion Rights Action League. I'm not very big in charities, but this cause is so special.

LIZ: Why didn't you call me?

HELEN: Well, they're just asking men. They're asking about seventy-five rich men.

LIZ: Oh, that's great.

HELEN: Isn't that cute? It's a nice new kind of fund-raiser.

LIZ: When I used to work for Helen—

RON: Was Helen your first boss in New York?

HELEN: I wasn't her boss, and she didn't work for me. She was a contributing editor at *Cosmopolitan.*

LIZ: She was the hardest boss I ever had.

HELEN: She wrote the movie reviews for fifteen years, and they were wonderful. She wasn't thrilled that she wasn't able to write anything rotten. But now you've come around to that way of thinking, Liz, because you don't hurt people in your column.

LIZ: Once in a while I do let somebody have it.

HELEN: Very rarely. You are well known for looking on—

LIZ: The bright side?

RON: What was Liz like when she first came to work for you?

HELEN: She was already there, so in a sense I was working for her. She had written these sensational articles about the Burtons and people that couldn't be gotten to, like Mike Nichols and Julie Andrews, who were gigantic stars at the time, so when I came in she was the big hoo-ha already, and I don't know—

LIZ: Helen just kept me on is what happened. *Cosmopolitan*, when I first started working for it, was sort of a general interest magazine like the old *Saturday Evening Post*, and of course it had six readers. And Helen and David had given them this wonderful idea.

HELEN: She was working with Rex Reed, whom she discovered, whose mentor she was, and she had gotten him the job reviewing movies at *Cosmo*. Then she sponsored Benton and Newman, who went on to—

LIZ: They were just my friends.

HELEN: They were doing a little column called "Cosmo Tells All." I think what happened to all of them is wonderful.

LIZ: The nice thing was, we became good friends. We just remained good friends.

HELEN: We're twenty years old now, do you know that?

LIZ: Our friendship is twenty years old. This is fantastic, fantastic. Can you believe it?

HELEN: You don't really drop people, do you?

LIZ: I don't have time to see anybody, though. I have to go out so much for business that I don't do too much just for my own pleasure. Once in a while I have lunch with Barbara Walters, because you know how dishy she is.

HELEN: Have you seen her recently?

LIZ: I went to her house to dinner about three weeks ago and met her new boyfriend, who is very cute. He owns Lorimar Productions. He owns the damn thing.

HELEN: It's rather serious.

LIZ: I don't think she's been seeing him that long. I mean, the point is they've just started seeing each other. And she looked beautiful that night. She gave a nice dinner for the Goldbergs. You know them, Wendy and Leonard. He used to be Aaron Spelling's partner. Now they're mortal enemies, I guess, and they're not partners anymore.

HELEN: Do you have a feeling this is *My Dinner with André*—you and me?

LIZ: Well, Ron is observing us, you see.

HELEN: Would you like to say a little something, Ron?

LIZ: Throw yourself right in here, Ron.

RON: Okay, I have a question about southern women. Is it any coincidence that the two of you, both powerful women in New York, are from Texas and Arkansas?

LIZ: Do you feel like a powerful woman in New York, Helen?

HELEN: No. And I certainly don't feel like a little girl from Little Rock. But I guess I feel more like a little girl from Little Rock than a powerful woman from New York. I'm buying time here because I want to think about the southern background. Ron, I don't think it has anything to do with anything. I think we have other things in common—strong mothers—and we had some trouble in our growing-up years.

LIZ: We had sibling troubles—

HELEN: Had sibling troubles, which maybe still exist to this very moment. And we had making it in New York as a common bond.

LIZ: Both of us were very much motivated by the movies.

HELEN: A crush on the movies developed very early, and we both went to the movies—not together, because she was in Gonzales, and I was in Little Rock.

LIZ: I think we were motivated by the movies to wish for a more glamorous existence.

RON: I wonder, Liz, if there's a new kind of Hollywood star in your column—studio heads, people like Barry Diller.

LIZ: I think it's only confined to people in the business. I don't think the reader cares. But I do it if I can get the story, because it gives me a lot of credibility within the business, and it's important to show you know what's going on. And I try to explain it in such a way that if readers do want to read about it, maybe they'll be interested. I think I said in that story about Barry Diller that the public might feel they knew him better because he had been going out with Diane Von Furstenberg.

HELEN: You know, somebody you have handled nicely and fairly is Pia Zadora, who really is quite an engaging young woman, and she just—

LIZ: Well, I like Pia Zadora.

HELEN: I like her, too, and she's been so maligned.

LIZ: And I think Pia Zadora could really do something, but I think that her husband ought to get out of her scene, and until he does, she won't ever, I think, be anything except a joke. But he wants to be part of her act, and it turns the press against her. I told her that, and I told him that. I was very frank with them.

RON: What did you say?

LIZ: When they first asked me to have a meeting with them, I said, "Why don't you get out of her number?" He can't. He's this older guy who's so proud that he's got this beauty, this sexy young wife, that he—it's the most important thing in the world. And she's got this Polish mother who's saying to her all the time, "Do what he wants to do. Agree with him. Don't argue." Da, da, dum.

RON: Let me ask you both a question about men in New York.

LIZ: Well, ask Helen. She's the expert on men.

RON: I'll ask you both. We know women have changed their roles a lot. They have more power. Have men changed in any significant way? Powerful men in New York?

LIZ: Fabulous question.

HELEN: I'm thinking of three powerful men, whose names I won't mention, but they're married to women who are beautiful, traditional women. And all three women have lobbied for, campaigned for, struck for some kind of career. And it wasn't easy because one of the women is in her early forties, and two are in their early fifties. Two out of the three have finally made it happen, and their husbands don't quite know what hit them, because they're so wealthy and they're so powerful—my God—that people keel over when they come into a room. And they say, "Why would she need this? What is the problem? Why am I not enough? She has those beautiful children." It's a traditional, clichéd story. So, based on those three men, I would say they may not like what's happening, but they definitely are going along with it.

LIZ: I notice at an awful lot of things I go to socially that the husbands are all somebodies, and the wives are like ciphers. They never speak, and it makes you wonder if there aren't a lot more like them.

HELEN: I see those women, Lizzie, but I also see women of the kind I'm talking about, who want something of their own. I'm going to name just one for an example. Roone Arledge's wife. He is Mr. Mogul at ABC, and she wanted some kind of career. I don't think that's why they have separated. If your husband is Roone Arledge, you really don't need to do it for yourself, but she felt that she did. And the DeLoreans. Before he fell under such trouble, she was trying her damnedest to get an acting career going.

LIZ: She wanted to do something, and I think that was proved the minute he won the case and she left him. She had been trying to leave him for a long time, I think. She never objected to what he had done or anything, she just wanted to realize herself.

HELEN: The real corridors of power are in the U.S. government and local governments—New York State, New York City, California. We haven't hit there yet. We will sometime. There is this business of biology. Women have the children, and men have not yet taken on much of the nurturing. There are no such things as paternity leaves for men, so somehow the woman gets stuck taking care of the baby—hello, Marvin; Marvin Josephson—we have a long way to go. For instance, the Reagan administration—let's forget about whether we think it's good or bad or whatever. But the whole attitude of the Reagan administration and the whole structure of it—the social structure of the kitchen cabinet and all that stuff—seems to me to be embracing the past in such an extraordinary way. All of those women are women who look good and sharp all the time, and give good parties.

LIZ: And then they have this throwback to religion, which is the most frightening thing I have ever observed in American life, because it's so disastrous, so absurd, to let those fundamentalists become an actual power block.

HELEN: Do you know what my theory about that is? I think there are maybe millions of people out there, fundamentalists and members of other organized religions, who just never got over the idea that women have learned to enjoy themselves sexually without guilt, and they are totally preoccupied on the subliminal level with the idea that women go to bed and don't have to suffer. They don't have to have any guilt, and they don't have to have babies. Up until now. So these people are saying, "Okay kid, you've had your fun, you f——d everybody"—don't use that word in print—"now you're going to have to pay. If for any reason a little squiggle of protoplasm gets through and you conceive, that's it. The door clamps shut, and you're going to have the baby whether you like it or not."

RON: Let me ask the two of you this: You see all these executive women now in middle management, in law firms and on Wall Street. Do you think that in their struggle to get to the top they're repeating the same mistakes that men make? Aren't they falling into the same values— just thinking about getting ahead?

HELEN: I don't think that's a mistake, just to want to get ahead. I think that's terrific. You can also fit in your social life, your love life, and your life with your children. You just have to be well organized. You give up long social lunches or a couple of golf games. But no, I don't think women are making the same mistakes. If women don't work hard and aren't totally work oriented in the marketplace, they won't get anywhere, and—

LIZ: A lot of them can't get anywhere anyway, no matter how good they are.

HELEN: It's been pointed out by lots of people other than me that we are a bit nurturing in the marketplace. We want to be nice to people and kind to men and charming and sexy, and we may not come on really as strong as we should because we don't want anybody not to like us. We've got to be loved.

LIZ: We really deeply believe, all of us, in this thing that women should be sweeter, more tender, more compliant. And I think women believe that more than anybody, don't you, Helen?

HELEN: Yes. I keep trying to get them to separate the two ideas. In their personal lives they can be sweet and compliant and adorable, and even passive if they want to. But in their business lives they've got to put all that aside. These are two separate spheres.

LIZ: There are a few women maybe who don't care, but I think we're all really, really very much—

HELEN: Man oriented.

LIZ: Women still see men as authority figures, even when they don't want to. And also, I just think that they want to be pleasing.

RON: Don't you think this is also true of men—that they do all they do, build their buildings and whatever, to impress women?

HELEN: I think men are totally enthralled by women, but in a different way. Women are totally—

LIZ: I think men are still mystified by women.

HELEN: They still are.

LIZ: And I think they remain mystified. I think they think we're all great mysteries, and it's up to them to figure us out.

HELEN: And they go around asking silly things, like "What do women want?" What women want is the same thing that men want. We want—

LIZ: Respect and luxury and everything else.

HELEN: Love and sex and a place to live and warmth and food and clothing—all the creature stuff. But we also want the power, the glory, the money, the recognition, the achievement, the success. So when a man asks me that dumb question, I just say, "Think what *you* want." I've got a dental appointment, and I'm going to have to leave both of you here. Would you turn this thing off for one second? I want to ask Lizzie something.

DISORGANIZED CRIME

———— ● ————

James La Rossa Defends the Late Alleged Godfather

Did you ever come across the story of the bloody run-in between Meyer Lansky and Joseph P. Kennedy? It surfaced a couple of times in print, and although it may be apocryphal, it certainly reflects something real.

The way the story goes, back in the twenties there was a jurisdictional dispute of some sort between the underworld bootlegging operation run out of Boston by Joe Kennedy and the one run out of the Lower East Side by Meyer Lansky and Charles Luciana. When negotiations fell through, it is said that Meyer Lansky—widely regarded as "the Jewish Godfather"—caused a convoy of Kennedy-owned trucks to be ambushed on the road, in the course of which a high percentage of the Kennedy drivers and guards were shot dead.

Shift now to Washington in the late fifties when Joe Kennedy's sons Jack and Bobby are relentlessly hounding and grilling the heirs and associates of the same Lansky-Luciana gang that allegedly blew Joe's drivers away.

If the story is true, does that mean the Kennedy brothers' "crusade against organized crime" in the fifties and sixties should be looked at as little more than a family gang vendetta pursued by other means? That would be going too far. But the story does suggest that Italian Americans do have a legitimate grievance at the way their gangs are viewed as somehow more sinister than other ethnic-group gangs. A narrow focus on Sicilian gangs disregards the "achievements" of earlier-arriving ethnic groups. For a hundred years before the Sicilians reached Ellis Island, for instance, America was run by two notoriously vicious and murderous WASP gangs—the southern plantation owners and the northern factory owners. And until very recently, descendants of the leading families of those WASP gangs ran a kind of mafia of their own that was involved in murder, heroin, and corruption. It was known as the Central Intelligence Agency or, in the colorful slang of that ethnic group, "the Company." The crimes of the Italian Mafia are not necessarily more evil than the crimes of the WASP gangs. Just more illegal.

Still the recent slayings at Sparks Steak House demonstrate what a spell the old Godfather myths have over us. The execution of an alleged Godfather on a midtown sidewalk—like a ritual slaying out of *The Golden Bough*—still has a primal fascination about it. And so an opportunity to talk with James La Rossa, the noted trial attorney for the late alleged Godfather—and the last non–family member to see Paul Castellano alive—was hard to refuse.

It was the alleged Godfather's last sitdown. No, it's not fair to call it a sitdown. But it was the last time alleged Godfather Paul Castellano *sat down* before the reputed Gambino family head got back into his limo for the ride that took him to his fatal rendezvous with mob-linked executioners on the sidewalk in front of Sparks Steak House.

The site of this final conference: a Madison Avenue address twenty blocks south of Sparks—the law offices of James La Rossa.

The time: 3:40 P.M., Monday, December 16, 1985. Castellano's trial on murder conspiracy and theft charges was not in session that afternoon, and La Rossa had not expected to see his client until Tuesday.

"It was a surprise visit," La Rossa is telling me over lunch at Nicola Paone three weeks after the day his client was blown away.

"He walked into our office and brought gifts for my secretary," La Rossa recalls. "That was the purpose of his coming here."

But Castellano ended up sitting down with La Rossa and talking business.

"We spent an hour talking about the case so far and what I believed was going to occur the next afternoon when we were going to resume. And within an hour he was dead."

"Tell me more about that last conversation," I ask La Rossa.

"In effect what I was saying to him was 'The trial is over for you—the rest of the witnesses are not going to implicate you.' That opinion was based on the discovery material. So we were talking about going to the jury. We were talking about summations. We were talking about a break that was coming up over the Christmas holidays. We both talked about how much we needed it."

Was Castellano planning to go away?

"He was anticipating going to Florida. His family owns an apartment in Pompano Beach."

They were tired, but they were both feeling good about the trial, La Rossa says. He was confident he was going to win it, and Paul Castellano was confident, too.

"He was very pleased. He wanted very much to hear this verdict. He thought he won. I thought he won. The other defense lawyers thought he won. I think the jury thought he won. If you read the Sunday *Times* article the week before he died, they said in effect the government's case fell apart. There was a feeling in the courthouse."

The reason for that feeling? La Rossa had just completed cross-examination of the key prosecution witness against Castellano—the only eyewitness to link the alleged God-father to the case.

The way La Rossa tells it, his cross-examination left that witness for dead.

"They had one witness, really, who put Castellano in the case," says La Rossa. "His name was Montiglio, and by the time I completed cross on Montiglio, he had admitted to committing perjury on six different occasions. He admitted to being addicted to cocaine during this period of time. He had never implicated Castellano until October 1985, when the jury had been selected. Notwithstanding that he had been interviewed on sixty-eight different occasions by [FBI] agents, assistant U.S. attorneys, and grand jury appearances where he'd implicated dozens of other people and never once implicated Castellano. I think the jury disbelieved him, and I think it was evident in court."

"How was it evident?"

"There was a point in the cross-examination of Montiglio where seven or eight of the jurors actually turned their backs on him," says La Rossa.

"What do you mean? They turned around in their jurors' chairs?"

"In their jurors' chairs," La Rossa says.

"To look at the wall?"

"To look away from him. They were shaking their heads in disbelief," La Rossa says.

Who was this guy Montiglio?

"He was a nephew of probably the number two defendant in the case, Anthony Gaggi. Montiglio had met Castellano on numerous occasions at his home; he was the only one that had face-to-face experience with him. He was the only one who could really tie up the case for them."

"What was the purpose of his testimony? To say that profits from the stolen-car ring were—"

"Yes, had gone up to Castellano. He had testified in 1983 and 1984 that he had no personal knowledge of whether any money had gone up to Castellano. And then on October 4, 1985, which was one week into the jury selection, he suddenly recalled an instance where he delivered a package of money to Castellano. But he was such a poor witness I don't think there's any way the jury would have found Castellano guilty."

Still, there has been speculation in other quarters that another kind of jury was observing the courtroom duel between La Rossa and Montiglio. And coming to another kind of verdict on Paul Castellano.

There was, for instance, the cryptic but fascinating Jimmy Breslin column that appeared two days after the Sparks restaurant slayings. Breslin has in the past demonstrated an uncanny ability to come up with inside dope in mob-related cases—his reporting on the Lufthansa heist and its bloody aftermath, for instance. And this column was the first to link the activities of a certain rather exclusive "hunting and fishing club" in Queens to the Castellano hit—a linkage Breslin seems to have made almost before the cops did. But Breslin makes another startling linkage in that column: He links a verdict on La Rossa's cross-examination of Montiglio to a verdict on the life of Paul Castellano.

Breslin's column, it must be said, was written in the guise of a story about the semimythical "Un Occhio," an alleged underworld elder statesman to whose thoughts Breslin claims privileged access. Still, the utterances of Un Occhio have proved remarkably prescient in the past, and because of Breslin's Queens Boulevard sources, his account must be given some respect.

According to this account, certain powers-that-be in the mob requested a progress report on the Castellano trial. An observer reported back that "the nephew put the money into Paul Castellano's hands, but the attorney made him out to be a liar on the stand." Still the bottom line was not good: The jury might well go ahead and convict anyway. On the basis of this report on the courtroom showdown, Breslin's column indicates, a decision was made that Castellano's leadership abilities would be fatally impaired by a conviction and a further decision was made to fatally impair Castellano's life.

Undocumented speculation, yes. "Gibberish" is La Rossa's word for such theorizing. But it is a fact that Castellano's execution came just five days after the completion of that epic cross-examination. It gives the subject of that particular courtroom confrontation an added fascination: It might well have been a matter of life and death.

"Just how did you damage the witness, this Montiglio?" I ask La Rossa after we order drinks (club soda for La Rossa).

"He admitted to the planning of robberies all over California. He admitted to use of drugs. He vehemently denied that he ever sold drugs, but after an hour of cross-examination on the subject, he admitted that he was present when the drugs were handed to someone else. He had a gun on him when the drugs were handed to someone else. He picked up the money at various times when the drugs were delivered to someone. He continued to break the law and lie about it even after he was put in the witness protection program."

"Why would the feds go with such a—?"

"I think they just wanted Castellano so badly, and I think they were three quarters of the way into it when they realized what kind of trouble they were going to have. And there was no way to back out of it. I think they made a mistake and I think they would have lost the case. The jury was so turned off by the witnesses that even mentioned Castellano's name that it was incredible. I mean, we had this witness the papers called the gay hit man, he—"

"You had the gay hit man in this case?"

"Yes," says La Rossa, smiling at the memory. "Vito Arena."

I'd forgotten about the gay hit man, or thought somehow he was a witness in the Pizza Connection case or one of the other mob trials going on downtown.

You remember the gay hit man from the tabloid headlines, don't you? He was the prosecution witness who admitted to three grisly rubouts, which will not be described here.

La Rossa attacked the gay hit man's testimony by eliciting from him a litany of the special privileges he'd demanded from the prosecution in return for testifying. These privileges included the installation of his convict boyfriend in a protective-custody cell adjoining his and housing the boyfriend there a month after he should have been released on parole. He also got the hit man to concede on the stand that he'd demanded the prosecution provide cosmetic dentistry for his boyfriend's teeth and Bruce Springsteen tapes for them to listen to or he'd "call La Rossa."

But the great moment in La Rossa's cross-examination of the gay hit man—and I think it's fair to say one of the great moments in the history of cross-examination—was this bizarre exchange:

LA ROSSA: Now let me take you back just about five weeks ago. . . . Did you tell Mr. Mack [the prosecutor] that you wanted a mini-operation to have the fat sucked out of your face, cheeks, chin, and neck? Did you say that?

ARENA: Yes.

LA ROSSA: Did you say you need a nice profile because you look like a cyclops?

ARENA: I felt that my appearance was awful. . . .

LA ROSSA: And did you further tell Mr. Mack, 'La Rossa is going to dress up all the defendants and I am going to look like a bad guy'? Did you say that?

ARENA: If you look at the baby faces on them and you look at me . . .

The fat suction request is more than an amusing sidelight to the trial. Like the threat to "call La Rossa," the concern with how La Rossa would make him look is a tribute to the rep he has as a courtroom tactician. La Rossa estimates he has a 70 percent acquittal rate in jury trials.

How will the Montiglio cross-examination affect La Rossa's rep? Would he, as he insists, have gotten the alleged Godfather an acquittal on the basis of it? We'll go into that a little more deeply in a bit. But first I wanted to hear a little more from La Rossa about how he got to know the late Paul Castellano.

"When did you first represent him?"

"I defended him in the Eastern District in 1976. It was a case where he was accused with seven other people of lending money at usurious rates. It was a one-loan situation where the issue was whether or not he had charged twenty-five or thirty percent interest annually. At the time our usury law was twenty-four percent. The judge was quick to note it wasn't much different. And the judge dismissed the case."

"Why, for the triviality of the percent or—?"

"He said the government did not have sufficient evidence to give to the jury."

"Why did Castellano come to you as a lawyer? Had you defended other alleged org—"

"By 1976 I represented a lot of people who were fairly well known. I had represented judges accused of bribery, of corruption. I represented city commissioners. I represented what the government perceived to be organized-crime figures. I have represented nursing-home operators. I have represented Perry Duryea, a gubernatorial candidate at that time. I represented Congressman Bert Podell. I was probably the major defense counsel through the Nadjari [anticorruption] days. I didn't know him, so where I fit, in that respect, with Mr. Castellano, I don't know. Obviously, he came back to me recently because of the initial defense."

"You hadn't represented him between the '76 case and the two recent indictments?"

"I'd represented him in the sense that he'd been subpoenaed a number of times before grand juries and had never been charged with a crime. He started to come to me again about the beginning of 1983 because he perceived unusual surveillance. Based on that surveillance and the kind of subpoenas he knew from other lawyers were being served, we assumed he was a target."

"And what kind of guy was your client?"

"He's a different kind of personality," La Rossa says. "A very sophisticated guy for someone from that world. Well taught personally. Well read. He read *The Wall Street Journal*, to give you an idea. He was more interested in business than almost anything else. He loved to talk about business. He could give a symposium on what he thinks about Lee Iacocca, for instance, and so on and so on."

"Really? What did he think of Lee Iacocca?"

"He thought he was marvelous. He thought he brought the American republic back. You know, that type of thing."

"What kind of business would he talk about when he talked business?" I ask La Rossa.

"He'd talk about the meat industry. His family had been in the meat business for years. He talked about which businesses he thought were on an upswing, what he thought about locations for property, that kind of thing."

"A student of the economy?"

I think La Rossa picked up a hint of skepticism in my voice.

"I don't want to take this beyond the point it should be," he says. "I'm not going to suggest to you it sounded like the Wharton School of business. But you would have believed him to be a business manager."

"What about the leaks the *Daily News* and the *Post* have been getting from law enforcement people about the tapes that were made from bugging Castellano's house? They say Paul Castellano died because of what was on those tapes. Badmouthing all the other guys, talked too much, that sort of thing. What's your reaction to that?"

"I'm under a gag order about the tapes, but I think it's gibberish. Everybody seems to know the answers the day after. As for me, La Rossa, I can't conceive of that being the reason. I have heard comments that he was—well, there was one leak. Goldstock [director of the state's Organized Crime Task Force] said they were afraid he was going to become an informer. Gibberish."

"Did the feds make an attempt to turn him into an informer?"

"If they did, I never heard about it. And I'm sure I would have. It's all gibberish."

I thought this might be an appropriate point to step back from the details of the Castellano case and get La Rossa's views on organized crime in general. Early in his career he'd served in Bobby Kennedy's Justice Department as an assistant U.S. attorney in New York's Eastern District (Brooklyn, Queens, and Long Island).

"What was your view of Bobby Kennedy's crusade against organized crime?"

"I think it was probably the first time that Justice had ever really focused on it. Obviously, Hoover didn't share his enthusiasm at that point. I don't know how I can answer your question honestly. We really weren't focused on it like they are today."

"What I'm trying to get at," I explain, "is this: Did you think that this crusade was misguided, that they were going after a chimera? Or was the organized-crime thing that Bobby Kennedy and the Justice Department were trying to expose, was that real?"

"I don't think I'm equipped to answer that, really," says La Rossa. "Other than what I read in the newspapers and what I saw on television, I wasn't in that position within the U.S. attorney's office where I was sharing information with Mr. Kennedy."

"Well, what's your belief now?"

"Well, my belief is that there's obviously organized crime in the United States. It comes in multifacets. I believe that there's a group of Italian Americans who are involved in criminal activities, and you can call them whatever you want. I believe that there are Cubans in south Florida who are involved in criminal activities. And I think we've glamorized the concept of Italian organized crime by calling it the Cosa Nostra or Mafia or whatever you want to call it. Is there a group of Italian Americans who participate in organized crime? The answer to that is obviously yes. Do I believe that it's what everybody thinks it is? The answer to that is no."

It was here that La Rossa introduced an intriguing new term for the phenomenon he doesn't like to call Mafia, Cosa Nostra, or organized crime: *disorganized* crime.

"If, in fact, Italian Americans banded together in the kind of criminal activities that certain prosecutors would like us to believe, they would be a lot better organized. If I had to describe American criminal activity, I would call it *dis-*

organized to begin with. Some of it's downright sloppy. But I don't see it as organized as everybody would like to think. I think there are gangs of people. The West Coast is having trouble with motorcycle gangs. And they're having trouble with right-wing organizations that are killing people. They're gangs—that's organized criminal activities."

It was time to order lunch. La Rossa asks for the salmon, which the courtly waiter has described as "fresh, fresh, fresh, Mr. La Rossa." I ask for the veal chop. La Rossa seems to be a valued regular patron here at Paone's, a place known for catering to powerful "permanent government" types from the world of politics and business.

La Rossa looks tanned today; he says he's just come back from one week's vacation with his family.

"Where were you?"

"We were in Florida. We have a house in Fort Lauderdale. We spent a week down there."

"Were you able to get this stuff off your mind?"

"I think so. For a week. It's been a long hideous period. Very troubling, you know. When you sit next to somebody for eight weeks, obviously you develop some caring for him, and he was a caring person to begin with. He was very thankful for everything you did for him. He was very considerate. I got a phone call from Murray Kempton apparently ten minutes after it happened, before it came across the wire with an identification. Kempton told me, he said, 'Is it possible it's your client?' I said, 'I don't think so. I think he should be home at this point.' I was wrong. It was unpleasant, to say the least."

I turned to the question of Castellano as alleged Godfather. "I read the 'commission' indictment [the federal indictment that charged ten alleged leaders of organized crime with being "the commission" that runs the Mafia], and while it goes to great length to show everyone conspiring to extort money from cement contractors, nowhere in the indictment, it seems, is Castellano singled out as chairman of the commission. Am I right?"

"That's correct."

"Now on what basis is all this talk that he is or was *the* Godfather?"

"Because the prosecutor decided to get up and say it. There's nothing in any evidence. . . ."

"Nothing in the tapes?"

"Absolutely nothing. The incredible part of it is that if they decided to make one of the others the chairman of the commission, they could have done it just by vocally saying it. It's as simple as that. That's exactly what I'm driving at in terms of solving the murder the next day. Everyone gets up and has an absolute reason why it occurred, and I think it's as ridiculous as naming somebody the chairman without any proof."

"What was his reaction to being thus named chairman?"

"That it wasn't true. In effect, 'Why are they charging me with something that I'm not? Why are they doing it?' He proclaimed his innocence completely throughout."

"Now, you've been quoted calling the commission indictment 'a fairy tale that dates back to 1900.' Just how were they going to prove the history that far back?"

"I assume one of the agents was going to take the stand and give the historical background. I think it was pleaded in that fashion to get publicity. . . . I called it a poor Puzo novel. And that's the way it was written. Especially when you're preceding any defendant's birth date at that point."

"Then they had the commission established in 1931?"

"Yeah, it went on 1940, 1943. They tried to take Joe Bonanno's deposition, you might recall. They were attempting to use his book as a treatise on the history of— take Bonanno's book and go to the indictment. There's a chapter called 'The Commission' in his book, and the indictment and the book are word for word, including, interestingly enough, the nickname that Bonanno's associate gives to someone—'Earthquake.' "

"Albert Anastasia?"

"Albert Anastasia. He said in the book, 'I nicknamed Albert Anastasia "Earthquake." I never mentioned that to anyone, but in my mind I called him "Earthquake." To myself.' And then in the indictment it has 'Albert Anastasia a.k.a. Earthquake.' So obviously that had to come from Joe Bonanno's thoughts."

"You attacked the use of all those nicknames in the indictments—like Big Paul and—"

"We got a ruling that the government was going to be forced to produce proof that they were used, and up to the point that he was killed, there had been no proof of 'Paulie,' 'Big Paul,' or any of that business. The only witness that knew him called him Mr. Castellano, and when asked on cross whether that was how he referred to him in the past, he answered yes."

"How did you address him?"

"Mr. Castellano? I called him Paul."

"How would you describe—had you become friends over the years or . . . ?"

"Well, the answer to that is yes. I liked him. He was a very interesting man."

"Tell me a little more about who he was."

"Like I said, he was a very considerate man. He was very pleasant. He was interesting to be around. I never heard of any other life from him—he wasn't that kind of a man. Just a pleasant, nice man. You might describe him almost at the time he was killed as somebody's grandfather. And not much more than that."

I ask La Rossa for his assessment of U.S. Attorney Rudy Giuliani, who's been spearheading the attack on organized crime that hit his friend Castellano so hard.

"He's very bright," La Rossa begins. "Very energetic. And very ambitious. I can't tell you whether he's going to run for public office or not. You've heard all the declamations. But I think being a prosecutor is a frightening thing. Frightening in the sense that when I was one I was always so terribly concerned that I'd make a mistake and somehow the wrong person would go to jail. When you start getting personal ambitions involved in decision making, I think it becomes frightening."

"Do you think Giuliani has gone ahead with cases that are not solid because of personal ambition?"

"I think the acquittals speak for themselves. Don King is a perfect example. I wonder if Don King was an unknown who had no notoriety, whether he would have been indicted under the same circumstances. I seriously question it. And I think that's what's happening. I think cases are being made of noteworthy people for the sake of noteworthiness. The other concept I disagree with is this throwing as many people into a case as you can, what they call mega-trials. The Federal Bar Council asked Giuliani to address the group on the prosecution's view and for me to take the defense view. There's a reason they put all these defendants in the same case. You hope it's going to work the same way as the ferryboat does to the garbage when you sweep everything into the pier. I don't think it's right."

There's another thing La Rossa doesn't like about the current organized-crime crusade: the attack on alleged "mob lawyers."

"I resent the Kaufman Commission [the President's Commission on Organized Crime, headed by Judge Irving R. Kaufman] referring to lawyers as mob lawyers."

"Did they use that term?"

"Yes, they did. When Judge Kaufman was pressed, he said, 'I'm not talking about all the lawyers.' But he doesn't define what he is talking about. When I was a prosecutor,

I was an attorney representing the government. Now I'm an attorney representing the defendant. Not any particular kind of attorney but any cases that are tempting to me in terms of interest, something I enjoy doing for a period of time. And to label the bar in any fashion whatsoever I think is horrendous."

I ask La Rossa if he recalls Roy Cohn's comment to me about mob lawyers. I've brought along a clipping of it and read it to La Rossa to refresh his memory.

"Cohn was talking about the difference between lawyers who represent organized-crime figures and lawyers he called mob lawyers. He said: 'I have enough of a varied practice that I can't get tagged as a mob lawyer. I don't like mob lawyers. I can't stand them. Know why? They have only one thing to sell. Loyalty. There's only one problem: They lose practically every case.' What's your reaction to that?" I ask La Rossa.

"I think that's gibberish, absolutely. I was surprised that Roy said it. What's a mob lawyer? Is the mob lawyer the first-class practitioner who the organized-crime figure retains when he's indicted? Or is he the guy that does the little real-estate deals for him or helps him do certain things that are maybe not legal or illegal. There are lawyers who are dishonest. There's no question about that. But are you talking about the lawyer who walks into the courtroom and tries an Abscam case on Monday, an organized-crime case on Tuesday, represents a doctor on an income tax violation, flies to Chicago and represents a senior partner in a law firm on a bribery case, represents a judge for bribery in North Carolina? He's a mob lawyer because on that one occasion he represents somebody who the government decided is an organized-crime figure?"

"I think Cohn was trying to distinguish a person like that from a quote 'mob lawyer' who—"

"I don't like his quote," says La Rossa. "I don't like people being tarnished by wide brushes, okay? Go back to my friend Roy Cohn's McCarthy days—there were some fine artists and musicians that had to move out of the United States because they were blacklisted. I don't share his enthusiasm for pointing at people. He's done that all his life. He's done it all his life."

Has the government made an attempt to smear people defending organized-crime figures?

"Sure, the Kaufman Commission did. And there were a rash of subpoenas issued to lawyers involved in—"

"RICO [antiracketeering] cases?"

"Exactly. But they backed off. The rules now, as I understand them, are that the United States attorneys cannot subpoena an attorney's records who's defending a person in a criminal case, unless he gets the approval from the attorney general. We had a three-month period with twenty or thirty subpoenas. I mean obviously that was a threatening gesture. To me it was."

"You didn't get one?"

"I didn't get one, no."

"Do you feel under pressure because you're handling these high-profile cases in this area?"

"I've been doing it too long to worry about that. But I think it affects young lawyers. I hear them talking about it. But at this point I can't do anything else. I'd never make a plumber or carpenter. I have no place to go. Plus I love what I'm doing and I'm fairly good at it."

Our fish and veal arrive.

"The food is always good here," says La Rossa.

"What about Castellano?" I ask La Rossa. "Was he known as a person who liked food? Because it was on the day he was shot that *New York* magazine came out saying Sparks has the best steak in town. Do you think that was the reason he was going there?"

"No," says La Rossa. "I know he'd been to Sparks before. I'd eaten in Sparks with him myself."

"Did it ever cross your mind that you might have continued your conference with him and gone on there and have been in the middle of this?"

"Had I accompanied him to the restaurant? I guess my time wasn't up. Fortunately. It has crossed my mind and my family's, obviously. It's caused us some distress."

"Does this sort of thing come with the territory?"

"It's never happened to me before in my twenty-eight years. Never lost a client in that fashion. I hope it doesn't come with the territory."

"Did you go to the funeral?"

"Yes, I did."

"What was it like?"

"It was quiet. The family. Very small group. It was a sorrowful funeral. His family obviously was shocked by the fact, and it's much like death in any family. There was that reaction."

"Did you know Bilotti, the man killed with him?"

"Yes."

"And how would you describe him? Was he his driver?"

"He was a constant companion. He drove the car for him. He went to lunch with him. They seemed to have a father-son relationship. I can't tell you what he was or what he wasn't, but he was somebody that was with him at all times."

"What was your reaction to the *Times* story that the murder was really designed to get rid of Bilotti because he had been the chosen successor?"

"That's typical of all the other theories that have been thrown around. I have no knowledge of it. And I think it's ridiculous to manufacture a story like that at this point."

"Who do you think is manufacturing these stories?"

"To some degree, law enforcement people. I've seen conflicting theories advanced by Goldstock, by the Justice Department employees, by the FBI. Everybody is getting up and advancing their pet theories. But they're not advancing it as theory, they're advancing it as fact."

But what about the theory La Rossa is advancing: that Castellano would have beaten the rap in the racketeering case because La Rossa had beaten the witness Montiglio on the stand?

After lunch I take La Rossa up on his offer to provide me with a transcript of the courtroom battle. Outside Paone's, La Rossa signals for his car and driver and I wave off the cab I've hailed. On the ride over to his office, La Rossa speaks proudly of his four children: two daughters in college, a son who's a stockbroker, and another son who graduated from Sarah Lawrence and wants to be a writer.

In fact, if this kid was smart, he'd get hold of the 250-page transcript of the Montiglio cross his father handed me. The tale that emerges from this transcript makes a great contemporary underworld novel—call it *The Godson*. The saga of Dominick Anthony Montiglio and how he came to be a witness against the alleged Godfather takes us into a world Puzo never imagined; there are resonances here of late-Chandler L.A. evil and a contempo glint of *Miami Vice* coke sleaze. It's a kind of morality tale, too, in its own way, a tale of how a figure from the anarchic whacked-out world of contemporary disorganized crime came to point a fateful finger at one of the last tycoons from the Age of the Godfathers.

When we first meet Dominick Montiglio in the transcript, he's living the L.A. high life. He's the bodyguard for a guy he describes as "the largest coke dealer in Beverly Hills." The nephew of a reputed organized-crime figure back east, Montiglio's really carved a niche for himself out west. He's hanging out at the Daisy on Rodeo Drive. He's carving a new identity for himself, too, it seems, spending time with musicians (guess why) and outcall-service girls like this one called Chelsey who works at a place called "Coco Cabana West—An Experience to Remember." He's begun calling himself a songwriter. Meanwhile, he's carving something else: a hole in his septum "big enough that you would see the light shine through it" because he's doing a quarter ounce of coke or more a week and cooling out with 'ludes and Jack Daniel's. But it's okay: He needs something to calm him down on those nights when he has the nightmares about being back in Nam.

He supplements his salary from the Beverly Hills coke king with side ventures with friends, some of whom are Colombians and Cubans. Like when this girl known as Wicked Wanda learns of a house in San Diego where a horde of coke is waiting for funding. Well, Montiglio ends up driving with Wicked Wanda and a guy named Angelo to this house so they can speak to people there, which is apparently done—with a gun—while Montiglio waits outside. He waits outside a lot while friends rip off heavyweight coke people with guns.

This California lifestyle was going pretty smoothly for Montiglio, except for the septum problem, until he came back east and got involved with a woman named Danielle. His downfall. It seems that Montiglio was involved with some French Canadians who were moving mega-quantities of Quaaludes down from Montreal. A girl named Danielle was involved. Well, one thing led to another and Danielle became Montiglio's girlfriend, which was nice until Montiglio was arrested in a Hickory Pit restaurant on a charge of trying to extort twenty thousand dollars from a man named Winnick, in collaboration with Danielle and her friends from the friendly North. There was some indication that Montiglio had represented himself to this Winnick guy as a convicted murderer who'd just done time in Dannemora. Montiglio maintained that he was trying to collect on a loan he'd made to Winnick to start a "belt-buckle business."

Detectives investigating were skeptical of this and apparently presented Montiglio with a difficult choice: If he started talking to them about his reputed mob-leader uncle, for instance, they would drop the extortion charges against his girlfriend, Danielle.

It was a choice between love and family, or perhaps love and death. Montiglio chose Danielle, and in the spring of 1983 he began talking—about the past, about the murder and racketeering activities of a car theft crew said to be run by his uncle, allegedly under the patronage of Paul Castellano.

Specifically, Montiglio described a meeting at a place called the Gemini Lounge where he's given wads of cash in rubber bands—car-theft-crew profits—which he personally delivers to Paul Castellano at a Brooklyn luncheonette.

And it is this story that—if the jury believed it—could have put Paul Castellano away.

In his cross-examination, La Rossa gets Montiglio to admit to repeated perjuries in his grand jury testimony. He gets him to admit to crimes—like the Wicked Wanda caper—he concealed from prosecutors until La Rossa revealed them in court. He gets Montiglio to admit to crimes he committed in his new "clean" identity in a southern city under the witness protection program.

Then he zeroes in on the Gemini Lounge story—the one that puts the racketeering profits in Paul Castellano's hands. La Rossa reveals that Montiglio's recollection of the money transfer came after two years of repeated sworn denials that he'd seen any such thing. The belated production of this smoking-gun-type testimony is not just a detail he's overlooked; it contradicts his previous testimony on that specific point. Had I been a juror, had there been no explanation offered for this contradiction, I would have had difficulty voting to convict after La Rossa's cross.

However, since I'm not a juror and wasn't in the courtroom, I thought I'd put La Rossa's claim that he'd have gotten Big Paul a walk to *my* idea of an ultimate jury: Jimmy Breslin and Murray Kempton, who both had covered the trial. It gave me an excuse to call two of my favorite writers and probably two of the best judges of human nature in these situations.

What about it: Would the jury have let Big Paul off on the basis of La Rossa's cross? Breslin said no, emphatically. Sure, he said, La Rossa made the witness "look like a fucking lunatic," but he pointed out that "Jimmy the Weasel Fratianno admitted to thirty-two murders but still got juries to convict on his testimony."

Kempton said no, judiciously. He thought La Rossa had been at the top of his form in the cross, but he somehow suspected that because of the sheer number of charges, the jury would have convicted Castellano of something.

But don't try to tell that to James La Rossa. For him the judgment on Paul Castellano came too harshly and too soon.

THE FRANTIC SCREAMING VOICE OF THE RICH AND FAMOUS

———— ❧ ————

The Blossoming of Nouveau Journalist Robin Leach

Could you do me a favor? It's important—I wouldn't ask you otherwise. Before you get comfortable, before you read any further, could you just run out to a bookstore and pick up a copy of the paperback edition of the new Wallace Shawn play *Aunt Dan and Lemon*?

Don't worry. I'm not going to ask you to read the whole play, at least not now. But I would like you to read the eighteen-page "appendix" Shawn calls "On the Context of the Play." Trust me on this: It's the single most provocative piece of writing I've come across this year. It's easily the best essay on New York in the eighties and the rich and famous consciousness of our time. And frankly I'm just not sure I can communicate with anyone who hasn't read it yet.

Because it is in this essay that Shawn gives a beautiful

name to the most emblematic personality-change process of the eighties: *blossoming*. What *est* was to the seventies, blossoming is to the eighties.

Now please don't go confusing blossoming with "fluffing out." Fluffing out is something entirely different. "Fluffing out" (according to a *New York Times* report on executive woman culture) is the term used by hard-nosed career-conscious women to describe less single-minded women who have allowed themselves to drift behind the career curve, a character flaw fatally signaled by the telltale choice of fluffier "pussycat" bows over simple silk-band executive bow ties.

Blossoming is not for pussycats. Blossoming is for tigers of both sexes. Blossoming is—well, this is how Shawn describes blossoming:

"As I write these words, in New York City in 1985, more and more people who grew up around me are making this decision; they are throwing away their moral chains and learning to enjoy their true situation: Yes, they are admitting loudly and bravely, we live in beautiful homes, we're surrounded by beautiful gardens. . . . And if there are people out there who don't seem to like us . . . well, then, part of our good fortune is that we can afford to pay guards to man our gates and keep those people away. . . . The amazing thing I've noticed about those friends of mine who've made that choice is that as soon as they've made it, they begin to blossom, to flower. . . . They develop the charm and grace which shine out from all people who are truly comfortable with themselves. . . . These are people who are free to love life exuberantly."

Blossoming is seductively beautiful to behold, Shawn writes, but he finds something more than a bit sinister about all these people blooming all around him—something that suggests to me the sinister, soul-stealing blossoming of the pod plants in *Invasion of the Body Snatchers*.

As his friends blossom around him, Shawn confesses a longing to succumb, to blossom himself—"a fantastic need to tear that [childhood moral] training out of my heart once and for all so that I can finally begin to enjoy the life that is spread out before me like a feast. And every time a friend makes that happy choice and sets himself free, I find that I inwardly exult and rejoice, because it means there will be one less person to disapprove of me if I choose to do the same."

Welcome, then, to the blossoming world of the rich and famous.

The Cross-promotional Hotel Deals
of the Rich and Famous

When I asked Robin Leach to choose his absolute, ultimate favorite lunch spot for an interview, his reply, through his publicist, was: Nicole's at the Omni Park Central.

Nicole's at the Omni Park Central?

Yes, that's his very favorite place, she assured me.

Did I miss something? Why is it I can't recall Nicole's at the Omni Park Central being mentioned in the copious chronicles of the rich and famous in the same breath as Mortimer's and Le Cirque? Had Nicole's blossomed overnight? Or could it be that Nicole's at the Omni Park Central was one of those fabulous secret *hideaways* of the rich and famous? One of those incredibly unassuming places they seek out to escape the glare of publicity (with the possible exception of Robin Leach and his camera crew, who are allowed in to document their "passion for privacy").

Well, Nicole's at the Omni Park Central turns out to be a pleasant enough place. Although it's tucked into the Seventh Avenue and Fifty-sixth Street corner of the Omni Park Central, it's not exactly a hideaway kind of place, and there don't seem to be any rich and famous customers in evidence.

Still, there is a sign announcing WE HAVE BEAUJOLAIS NOUVEAU!

Could that nouveau touch be why Robin Leach chose this place? *Lifestyles of the Rich and Famous* might be said to have given birth to the successor to the New Journalism: the Nouveau Journalism.

But, no, actually there's a more complicated reason why we're at Nicole's at the Omni Park Central, Leach tells me.

"See, in January we're doing a show, not really a *Lifestyles* but a two-hour special I'm involved in called *SuperModel of the World*. And Phillip Georgeas, who used to be the manager of the Berkshire Hotel, which is right near our office, is now the manager of the Omni Park Central, and he's agreed to put up the models from around the world who are going to be in the pageant, and so he's told me to make use of this place for everything. I'm a great believer in loyalty and—"

"Now *SuperModel of the World*. Just what is—?"

"Eileen and Jerry Ford have done this *Face of the '80s* thing for the past three years through Telerep, which is my producer and syndicator, and in a sense what we're doing with *SuperModel of the World* is—if 'rich and famous' has become a generic expression—we're going to rich-and-famous-up the *Face of the '80s*."

The Network Ripoffs of the Rich and Famous

Think about that: *We're going to rich-and-famous-up the* Face of the '80s.

In fact, he's already done it. Robin Leach has succeeded in rich-and-famousing-up the face of the decade. Certainly the face of the eighties as seen through the eyes of the Nouveau Journalism's shameless imitators in the Infotainment World.

The Sunday night before my lunch with Leach, I watched

60 Minutes and *Lifetyles of the Rich and Famous* in succession and the comparison was not flattering to *60 Minutes*, whose centerpiece segment that night was a seemingly endless Harry Reasoner report from the Palace Hotel in St. Moritz.

This consisted mainly of extended footage of Harry Reasoner sitting in expensive old rooms telling us how old and expensive they were, how many rich and famous old people stayed in them. He couldn't seem to get over how old and famous and rich everything was. It was very sad and it lacked the nouveau vigor of a Robin Leach segment.

I asked Leach what his reaction to this craven and inept copying was.

"I'm not arrogant," Leach begins, "but I am *overjoyed* that some of the techniques that we use on *Lifestyles of the Rich and Famous* have been adopted by *20/20*, *60 Minutes*, and particularly the Barbara Walters specials."

He believes he blazed a path, a clearing in the national consciousness that permitted Rich and Famous Journalism to blossom.

"We took the rich out of the closet. It was now respectable to talk about wealth. And having us be the pioneer in making it respectable, it appears that a lot of other shows on television had to devote a segment within their programs to the rich and famous but without calling it such."

Still, Leach's pride as a craftsman is offended by the failure of his network imitators to *understand* the editing concepts of the Nouveau Journalism.

"I have the greatest respect for Don Hewitt and the *60 Minutes* gang," Leach avers. "But I honestly think we did a better job with our Donald Trump piece than they did, because we had the inside of the house in Connecticut and they just had him in his suit and tie *outside* the house. We actually had the tour inside."

He's critical of *60 Minutes*' ponderous TV technique, too.

"I don't know the shooting ratio that *60 Minutes* uses on its pieces, but there is a rule in *our* office that I like to see the visual of what we do change every three seconds. My idea of a dream piece is never to see a shot of people talking, and if you can, do a five-minute piece where you never see the face of the person talking in a close-up, except maybe once. So in terms of the Palace in St. Moritz I can only assume that we would have shot far more than they did, and we probably would have done it with a celebrity, like we did with Loretta Swit in Portofino. You'll find, Ron, as you get to know me through this lunch," he confides, "that I am very, very serious and very, very diligent about what really is bubble gum and bubble bath and froth."

But before we got any deeper into the serious techniques of the Nouveau Journalism, I wanted Robin Leach to clear up a mystery that had the whole town talking that month. Just what treasures were concealed in . . .

The Lost Briefcase of the Rich and Famous

The mystery announced itself overnight when big bold REWARD! posters suddenly appeared—practically blossomed —all over midtown. Robin Leach's briefcase was missing. Reward. No questions asked.

But of course questions *were* asked. Questions were asked by those for whom watching *Lifestyles* was a secretive, shameful vice, by those for whom it was a camp cult classic. And the questions were, of course: What fabulous secrets of the rich and famous, what absolute ultimate inside dope on their intimate doings in those hideaways of theirs, could have occasioned the feverish high-profile search for the lost briefcase?

What *was* the story of the missing briefcase? I asked Leach after we'd placed our drink orders (a Bloody Mary "very spicy with not much vodka" for Leach, a beer for me).

"It's more than a briefcase, really," Leach explains of the purloined satchel. "It's halfway between a briefcase and a small suitcase—it was the whole contents of my desk, which I'd taken to Connecticut for the weekend. Monday morning I took a taxi to work and stopped at a newsstand to pick up the *News* and the *Post*—I never read the *Times*—and regrettably, as we found out afterward, the cab driver had recognized me, and when I got out of the cab she just took off with it, with the briefcase inside."

"She probably thought she was getting the priceless secrets of the rich and famous," I suggest.

"I have no idea. But she would have got the private phone numbers of everybody in the world and a lot of plans and story ideas."

What a haul: the private phone numbers of everybody in the (rich and famous) world. Instant access to the ears of the rich and famous speeding away in the back of a cab. Into the hands of who knew what kind of terrorist or opportunistic insurance salesman. No wonder the all-out campaign to get back the briefcase of the rich and famous.

"I hired a private detective," says Leach. "It took us eight days and—*whoa*, excuse me, love—"

This latter is to the waitress passing by.

"They have the new Beaujolais," he tells me. "*Whoa*—we've got to try the new—sweetheart, instead of the Bloody Mary could I have a glass of the new Beaujolais? Would you like to try it?" he asks me.

"I'll stick with my Heineken."

"Well, then," he says cheerily, "I shall make up for both of us."

Leach returns to the quest for the lost briefcase of the rich and famous. "The private detective managed to find the cab and the cab driver, and he met her on Eighth Avenue and Forty-fourth Street. As she told the story afterward, within ten seconds of taking off with it she didn't want to carry on with what she'd done—she was from Ecuador and she must have panicked about getting arrested. But instead of coming back, she took it home and put it in her bathroom and never opened it."

Listening to this tale left me with an image of that lost briefcase standing there unopened in the bathroom of the frightened Third World immigrant—an obscure object of desire plucked from the inner sanctum of the First World, seductive but too threatening to touch. Clearly the woman was just not ready to blossom.

Our waitress arrived with a glass of the Beaujolais Nouveau.

"Good health, Ron," says Leach pleasantly. "This is my first glass of this."

He sips. Appraises.

"It's nice," he says. "Certainly better than last year's. . . ."

The Pornographic Exploitation of the Rich and Famous

I was walking down Broadway in the Forties a week or so before my lunch with Leach and I passed a porno theater marquee promoting, with lavish displays of bare flesh, a movie called *The Decadent Lifestyles of the Rich and Famous*. The subtitle promised to take you "Inside Beverly Hills." Or maybe that was the title, and *The Decadent Lifestyles of the Rich and Famous* was the subtitle. But you get the idea.

I asked Leach if he'd seen the film. It came as a surprise to him. He was visibly disturbed.

"Oh, we have to stop that," he says quickly, taking out a notepad to jot down a reminder. "Thank you very much. Is there really?"

"Yes," I assure him.

"No," he groans. "It hasn't been advertised in any of the

papers because we'd have caught it. It's for the lawyers."

"It's amusing though, isn't it?" I ask.

He doesn't look amused. He's even less amused at my next question.

"Don't you feel that in some ways *Lifestyles* is a little bit like porn for the wealth-obsessed, the way—"

"Oh no," he says, shocked at the notion. "Now, Ron, let's be friends. How can you ask that question?"

"You don't think so?"

"No, come on. How could you describe anything that we do as even edging toward that? Where's the tease?"

"Well, isn't it a sort of voyeurism, getting to see forbidden—"

"Well, you can't say it's forbidden. You can say private, yes. It's not forbidden. And we are *so* mom and apple pie on the show. I mean, yes, we had the Playmate of the Year because she just picked up a hundred thousand and there's a little bit of bare shoulder—"

I try to explain to Leach that I'm not accusing him of literal sexual pornography but the pornography of wealth.

"When people say they watch *Lifestyles*," I explain, "they almost always say, 'I have a shameful confession to make: I never miss *Lifestyles*.' But they say it as if they were confessing to watching an X-rated movie."

Leach groans. I continue to try to explain the porn comparison.

"See, they confess it like it's a forbidden pleasure because there's that strain in the American character that disapproves of lust for possessions, lust for material goods— there's always that tension between the Puritan side and the expansive side, right? So when people say they like your show, they tend to say it like they're confessing a forbidden lust."

Leach is still not buying this argument.

"That doesn't make it pornographic by any stretch of the word."

"Not in the sense of sexual or perverse but in the sense of dealing with forbidden lust, see—"

"What's the definition of pornography?" he asks me.

"Arousing, provoking lust. How about that?"

"Arousing, provoking lust. If we do that, I'm the happiest man on earth. Do you really think we do that? No."

"Lust for beautiful homes. Lust for expensive—"

"There is no avarice," Leach says. "There is no avarice. We are the Gray Line bus tour and we don't cheat you, because when you take the Gray Line bus tour you see the stone wall, you don't go over the top of it. We take you through the front door. There's nothing more than that. We've taken the rich out of the closet. It's no longer wrong to be rich. When Ronald Reagan came back into the White House, there was a certain amount of glamorous life clinging about again. Remember that came about more or less in the same time as shows like *Dynasty* and *Dallas* were creeping on to television. . . . That's why I always describe *Lifestyles* by saying, if the script writers of *Dynasty* and *Dallas* merged those two shows, they couldn't come up with the wealth that we have on our show every week, because real-life wealth completely overshadows what Hollywood could create. So we made rich people respectable, but our viewers do not watch this with lust, which might be your definition of pornographic. There is no lust in watching this."

The Secret University of the Rich and Famous

Leach is continuing to refute my porn analysis of *Lifestyles*.

"We get odd letters from people who say, 'When you were covering Cher's house, there was a shot of a coffee table.' Or, 'Could you please send us the name of the company that manufactures the wallpaper in Donald Trump's apartment." Now I don't think that's lust. And that's certainly not avarice. That's somebody that wants to go out and buy the same kind of wallpaper. I'll tell you a story, a story that does my heart good because there's a little bit of the moralist in me."

This tale of the morally improving value of *Lifestyles of the Rich and Famous* begins in a liquor store near Leach's little house in L.A. (he says he rents it for $550 a month). Leach goes there, he says, because he gets a good price on Cristal champagne—his only conspicuously rich and famous personal taste.

"One day when I was at the checkout with my wine for a Saturday night dinner, the manager came over to me and said, 'Mr. Leach, I just want to thank you because you've changed the Saturday nights in my house, and I can't tell you how grateful I am.' He said that he had two teenage boys, and until the time *Lifestyles* went on the air, 'I despaired of those boys.' He said, 'They never did their homework, they were out on the streets Saturday night. And I knew sooner or later they were gonna wind up in trouble.'"

But instead, says Leach, they wound up in front of the TV set absorbing the secrets of the rich and famous.

"He told me, 'Those two boys of mine started watching *Lifestyles* and now they don't go out. They sit there with two notepads. Those two kids of mine have decided they've got somehow to get to Brown University.' And I said, 'Why Brown University?' And he said, 'Because they found out that's the major common denominator of all the rich people. So they figure if they work hard at school now and they got to Brown University, they would get an education that would enable them to live like this.' "

Despite this heartwarming evidence of his salutary effect on the youth of America, Leach disclaims any sweeping mission of social improvement.

"If we've provided the little bit of impetus for somebody to better themselves, then socially we've done something.

But we're not in it for that. Our mission in a given hour is to entertain. To make people feel good. . . . I mean it never rains on *Lifestyles*. We—"

"It never rains?"

"We'll show snow," he says. "But we prefer sun because it makes people feel better. But it never rains. The roses are always in full bloom. . . ."

The Rich and Famous Parties of the Rich and Famous

But don't get the idea that the poor and aspiring are the only ones who watch *Lifestyles of the Rich and Famous*.

The rich and famous watch it too! They love to see each other blossom.

"I was on a flight back from shooting Khashoggi's fiftieth birthday party this summer"—an event he describes as "the single most momentous party in European history"—"and a passenger from London told me he'd enjoyed a show he'd seen in New York. He told me that David Rockefeller watches it every Sunday night with a gaggle of friends."

"David Rockefeller has *Lifestyles of the Rich and Famous* parties?"

"Yes," claims Leach. "He gives little cocktail parties and then everybody toots into the television room to watch the show. Then they all go to dinner."

The Sad Mercedes Dealer in the Totally Nouveau Nation of the Rich and Famous

When I asked Leach about his most satisfying Nouveau Journalism coups, he cited his hour-long special on the high-flying life of Adnan Khashoggi, once reputedly the world's richest man. And he was particularly pleased with *Lifestyles'* videotaped raid on the kingdom of Brunei, home of the current world's richest man, the sultan of Brunei. Oil discoveries in this tiny Malaysian principality have given the sultan a reputed income of $155 million per day. And the trickle-down from that has made most of the other two hundred thousand inhabitants pretty wealthy (per capita income of a million dollars or so per year).

For some reason the sultan refused *Lifestyles* an interview. Perhaps he was holding out for Portofino with Loretta Swit—who knows? But Leach was undaunted. He just hopped ashore with a camera crew and did a profile of Brunei itself, a tiny nation that is totally rich and totally, unashamedly nouveau.

"What I found amusing," Leach tells me, "is that Brunei is a country that just ten or eleven years ago, before they discovered oil, exported bat droppings as fertilizer to Australia."

"Bat droppings?"

"Suddenly they found oil and gas. So the sultan's new in those terms. It's nouveau riche."

How nouveau? So nouveau it almost sounds like a parody of nouveau-ness.

"This is an extraordinary place to go," Leach tells me, "because you can't imagine—I mean to me the fun part was interviewing the Mercedes-Benz dealer, who was the unhappiest man in the place."

"Why was he unhappy?"

"Well, you see, everybody there buys Mercedes and there's no place to drive them. There's only one road in the whole country, which is mainly a clearing in the jungle. So they buy them not to drive but as status symbols to put in their front gardens. They stack them on top of each other. Like lawn ornaments. You know, they have four of them, they need five. They have five, they need six."

Sounds like the perfect country for Robin Leach, doesn't it? Or does it just sound like Beverly Hills?

"But how could the Mercedes dealer be unhappy?"

"Because," Leach says, "he's on a strict allocation from the factory in Germany and he can't get any more cars."

The Highbrow Literature of the Rich and Famous

I asked Leach to give me an assessment of his rivals and imitators in Nouveau Journalism.

"I think *People* magazine does a very good job, but I think it's too highbrow for the audience it's after," he says.

"*People* too highbrow?"

"The quality of the writing is above the audience, a little too artsy-craftsy. *US* magazine, on the other hand now, has the graphics, the punch, the color, the look that really appeals to that audience. Still, however, any way you cut it they're both glossy versions of what the *Star* is. The *Star* to me is more honest. But these are the growth vehicles of the publishing industry, let's be honest."

The Germ in the Mind of the Rich and Famous

The product of a lower-middle-class family in the non-U section of Harrow, Leach got his start in the Nouveau Journalism covering garden shows.

Of his horticultural coverage Leach says, "I know you'll find the analogy in here somewhere, and it's not quite true. But I would focus on the biggest squash. I would focus on the biggest cauliflower because I really believed that that's what people wanted to read about."

He went on to write gossip for Fleet Street tabloids and then came to America and soon got himself the prized post of gossip columnist for Murdoch's *Star*. His place in history as an auteur of info-tainment culture, however, was assured by his participation in the creation of *Entertainment Tonight* and his four years as *ET*'s show-biz-gossip correspondent.

I'd read somewhere that Leach had left *ET* over "philosophical differences" with then executive producer and fellow info-tainment *auteur* George Merlis (The Man Who Created *Good Morning America* As We Now Know It). You could think of Leach and Merlis as the Leibnitz and Newton of their genre, inventors of the calculus of info-tainment. In the same way that profound philosophical differences over the nature of nothingness (the concept of "the infinitesimal differential") divided the inventors of the calculus, so too is the difference between Leach and Merlis an unbridgeable gulf.

"I disagreed with the whole direction of *ET* under Merlis," Leach tells me. "They wanted to cover the business side of show business. My belief is that the viewer does not want to understand the box office take for the week and how it affects the corporate boardroom of the motion picture studio."

And what does the viewer want?

"The viewer wants to see the stars partying with champagne."

The schisms behind the scenes at *ET* still rankle Leach. "Do you know there was a memorandum sent around by one of the executive producers that stopped party coverage?"

"Really? *ET* stopped party coverage?"

"For a short period of time. Then that was followed by a short period of time when they said, 'You don't eat the shrimp when you go to cover a party. . . .'"

The shrimp ban was only a symptom of a deeper philosophical difference. Like the failure of *ET* to understand the importance of furniture shots.

"My real difference occurred—the reason that *Lifestyles* began as a germ in my mind was that it used to greatly aggravate me that we would be able to go off and do wonderful interviews in people's houses and we would never see the chair they were sitting on."

This absence of furniture shots may not seem like a fundamental philosophical inadequacy to you, but to Leach it's a vitally important issue. He wanted to do fewer close-up head shots of movie stars talking about their "commitment to the work." He wanted more of their fabulous lifestyles and expensive furniture.

"If you see a blond bombshell in a bubble bath," Leach sums up, "I think it's far more believable than her claim she wants to do Shakespeare down the road."

The Intimate Floorplay of the Rich and Famous

"What about the sex lives of the rich and famous?" I finally got around to asking. "Is sex better when you're rich and famous?"

"Is sex better when you're rich and famous?" Leach considered. I thought he'd probably have a lot to say on the subject, but unfortunately he seemed to interpret my question as another go at the pornography issue.

"We really don't get into sex on our show, contrary to what everybody might think, including you."

"Well, there are a lot of hot-tub shots."

"That's not sex," Leach says. "Sex is—be it in the bedroom, or on the living-room floor, or in the mink coat—the act of making love. That's what sex is all about. There's a lot of intimate floorplay—foreplay—on *Lifestyles* and Cristal champagne and romantic candlelight. I don't think because we show people in hot tubs or people in the bubble bath that's done for sexual reasons. That's done because that reflects their lifestyle. Movie stars *do* take bubble baths. Movie stars *do* study scripts in their bathtubs. Movie stars *do* like to ease their tensions by going into the Jacuzzi. Whether that's sexual I don't know."

Did you catch the Freudian slip Leach made in the middle of his defense of Jacuzzi Journalism? He said "floorplay" for "foreplay."

What's fascinating about this slip, what's so perfectly rich and famous about it, is the hierarchy of urges it seems to reveal. Usually in a Freudian slip a sexually charged word subverts an "innocent" everyday word, revealing the deep and turbulent tide of the unconscious beneath the surface of the stream of consciousness. But in Robin Leach's slip —"floorplay" for "foreplay"—furniture-related urges (floors, floor plans, home furnishings) appear to be far more primal than those of sex.

The Main Fear of the Rich and Famous

"One of the reasons that *Lifestyles* works," Leach is telling me, "why it isn't the show that people hate, is our writing. Our writing is—"

"Did you say why it *is* the show that people hate?" I ask, mishearing him.

"Why it isn't. My main fear was that it would be the show that everybody hated. What I had to do was kick it off at the very beginning to make it the show people *love* to hate, *then* the show that they loved. And the trick is—there are two tricks. First of all, in all of our pieces there is a *story*. A beginning, a middle, and an end. We look for heroic rags-to-riches sagas. We're subtly not selling but subtly carrying out the legend of the American dream and I feel very strongly about this in America. It was true in my case and it was true in a lot of people's cases. You do not have to be born with a silver spoon in your mouth to make it in this country. I come from a country where you have to be born on the right side of the tracks. . . . You don't in America. So within all the sugar of what *Lifestyles* is all about, there is a little pill in there and that little pill says: 'You must keep this. You must maintain what we have in this country. There is everything right about free enterprise. There is everything right about capitalism.' "

Sure, *if* you can get into Brown University.

The Ten Commandments (or Whatever) of the Rich and Famous

Leach has lost track, in the course of this passionate homage to his adopted homeland, of the other trick, the other one of the two tricks he said make *Lifestyles* the show you love to hate instead of the show you just purely hate.

"The reason the show works and the reason people don't get jealous and don't become envious or all the other commandments—thou shalt not avarice, thou shalt not covet, and thou shalt not whatever—is because there is a little tongue-in-cheek humor in the writing."

It is in this tongue-in-cheek tone, particularly the hyper-inflected servile ingratiating tone of *voice* that verges on self-mockery in its overawed statement that is Leach's greatest creation. I think he wants me to believe that it's intentionally *ironic* and therefore "subtle," a favorite self-descriptive word he likes to bestow on his work.

The Subtle Journalism of the Rich and Famous

Toward the end of our meal (Leach had the steak tartare, I had the cassoulet), Leach turned to me and asked me with heartfelt seriousness: "Do you sense as a journalist that there is a subtle journalism in *Lifestyles?*"

"Well," I began, judiciously weighing my words, not wishing to offend Leach, who is, with his low-key Fleet Street sense of humor, a likable guy. "Well, you do get access to worlds that are little seen, so in that respect it's *interesting* journalism. Interesting anthropologically, in a sense. I also sense there is a kind of tongue-in-cheek distancing in the voice and the writing—a kind of deliberate overstating for effect. Is that what you mean—?"

"Mmm," he says and proceeds to tell an anecdote that I

believe is meant to illustrate the subtle journalism to be found on *Lifestyles*.

"I remember getting excited when we were doing Princess von Thurn und Taxis and I said, 'By any chance does the butler deliver the helmet for your motorcycle on a silver tray?' She said yes, and I got it and I loved it. Do you know in Redondo Beach in California on Saturday nights it is de rigueur to watch *Lifestyles*, dressed in tuxedoes and fancy long gowns in your hot tub?"

"In the hot tub?"

"They wear the tux and long gowns in the hot tubs and they hire butlers to bring them little snacks. It's sort of like the *Rocky Horror Picture Show* cult."

And speaking of *Rocky*, don't you think someone should introduce these West Coast party animals to David Rockefeller?

The Frantic Screaming Voice of the Rich and Famous

But we were talking about Robin Leach's voice, I think.

"The reason for the frantic screaming voice," he tells me, "which has been described as halfway between the adenoids and the Atlantic, is because, just as the picture changes every three seconds, I want double the amount of copy in there to cover it. That was a conscientious decision to wall-to-wall it with copy—instead of the normal thirty words a minute I try to get sixty words a minute. That's how we decided to write it, to help drive the pictures. I mean there are two Robin Leaches. There's the man that's having lunch with you today and then there's the man who's selling washing machines on television Saturday nights."

At this point the waitress—a pleasant middle-aged woman—returns with my credit card receipt.

"Come back real soon," she says, lingering.

"We will," says Leach cheerfully.

"Thanks again," she says again, eyeing Leach.

"I don't talk like I sound on television," Leach is telling me, apropos the two Robin Leaches.

"You're a celebrity, aren't you?" the waitress asks Leach.

"No," he says modestly.

"You're an actor?"

"No."

"You *are*," she insists.

"Do you watch *Lifestyles of the Rich and Famous*?" he asks her.

"Yes," she says, scrutinizing him.

"You do? Well, that's me."

"Oh yeah," she says. "The voice. Oh, very sexy voice you have."

"It must be the English accent," says Leach.

"Yes," says the waitress. "*The Equalizer*. I like him, too."

ASKING JESSE JAMES
IF HE'S EVER SEEN A
TRAIN

🍎

The Gentlemen Players of
Sotheby's

The way I've heard it," I'm telling John Marion, chairman of Sotheby's, "the saying goes that Christie's is for gentlemen and Sotheby's is for players. Is that a fair characterization?"

"Isn't the saying supposedly that Christie's are gentlemen trying to be auctioneers and Sotheby's are auctioneers trying to be gentlemen?" asks Marion.

"No, it's *businessmen*," says David Nash, chief of Sotheby's fine arts department. "Sotheby's is for businessmen who want to be gentlemen."

"I think they've got that backwards though," says Marion, who now runs Sotheby's North American operations.

We're probing this mystery at a restaurant on Lexington Avenue called Gino that is the regular lunchtime haunt of

Marion and a host of art and auction-house types.

"Tom Armstrong of the Whitney goes to lunch here every day," Nash tells me. "You see a lot of people from the Metropolitan here every day."

At the table next to us the world's leading autograph collector and dealer is lunching with a rare-book collector. At the table behind us several dowagers are discussing family history.

"Of course Mrs. Roosevelt dumped Jimmy," one says. "She had a chance to marry a Whitney."

Get the picture?

Meanwhile we haven't quite clarified the Sotheby's/Christie's, gentlemen/businessmen equation.

Nash is not satisfied with the attribution to Christie's of a more gentlemanly identity.

"I know for a fact that we have more lords on our board than they do. We have a much higher lord quotient."

"Is that something new? An LQ?" Marion asks.

"Even rising to earl," Nash continues. "The earl of Westmorland. They don't have an earl, do they?"

"We have two earls," adds Marion.

"Two earls, four peers of the realm," Nash says. He enumerates the four peers of the realm.

"So are you saying the equation of Christie's with gentlemen and Sotheby's with players is unfair?" I ask.

"We definitely have a higher quotient of Old Etonians," Nash says.

"Old *Italians*?" I say, mishearing him. The noise level in Gino is very intense.

"No. Old *Etonians*."

"Old *attorneys*?" asks another party.

"No," says Nash patiently. "Old *Etonians*. People who went to Eton. And then there were the Old Etonians [who left]. There were two I believe."

"Two?" says Marion.

"There was ———. And there was The Other."

At the mention of The Other, there is a discreet silence from the Sotheby's contingent.

"There is something about these Etonians," says Nash. "Useless men who believe life was created for their entertainment. They're intensely interested in everything in an amateurish way. . . ."

Well, okay, Sotheby's is just as gentlemanly as Christie's, but the stakes in the contention between the world's two leading auction houses are more than sporting these days: The New York offices of the two international firms compete for close to a billion dollars in sales each year.

And you can find support for the view that in the past decade, of the two gentlemanly institutions, Sotheby's *has* been the player. Not always a winning player. But a high-stakes player. First there was a costly Bloomingdale's-like expansion and marketing push, designed to reach out beyond the confines of the traditional Antique Money clientele of the auction house. Then Sotheby's abandoned its cramped but dignified Madison Avenue location across from the Carlyle to light out for the territory of the Far East on York Avenue, where its vast and modern new headquarters raised eyebrows—but not, for a while, profits. This made the house vulnerable to a takeover bid from a couple of New Jersey entrepreneurs Sotheby's board characterized unmistakably as the Wrong People. Finally, last year there was the last-minute rescue by White Knight financier A. Alfred Taubman (whose wife, incidentally, once worked as an assistant at Christie's).

In the past year things seemed to have settled down at Sotheby's, which is preparing to celebrate its one hundredth anniversary in America. There is still controversy, of course. The state attorney general recently charged the firm with selling Hebrew manuscripts it didn't have proper title to. Sotheby's is contesting the claim. But through it all Chief Player John Marion has presided over record-shattering evenings in the auction room, including one this spring in which a collection including eleven little-known Impressionist works sold for a total of $39.2 million.

Marion is no gentleman. Not in the Old Etonian/Peer of the Realm sense. He's a master auctioneer, son of an auctioneer, and he grew up in New Jersey.

"It's not in my makeup to be a world-class scholar," he tells me. "You learn more by handling the objects. By seeing them over the years, what they mean to people and their heirs. I'm selling items now from estates of people who bought from my father. You like to see them come around again. You learn to appreciate the cycles in this business."

What he offers instead of scholarship to the clients at an auction—his chief asset, he says—is his voice.

"It's very hard to establish your personality in an intimate way with somebody who's thirty or forty feet away," he says. "That you do with various things—eye contact, mannerisms, especially your voice, making people feel comfortable. After all, you're talking about people spending an awful lot of money in a very pressurized atmosphere. Your voice is something you're born with. It's something you have or you don't have."

And Marion's voice is impressive. At first because it's so unassuming. No snooty Brit overtones, no hale-fellow English-huntsman warmth. Just very direct, very dignified, with a hint of the warm timbre that recalls certain Anglophile masters at Yale, but not unpleasantly.

The appetizers arrive. Both Nash and I receive beautiful plates of delicately aged prosciutto and ripe figs.

In his office before lunch Marion had proudly shown me a painting he was particularly pleased with. It was a work by a once-obscure American landscape painter named Metcalf. The vogue for this previously—and justly—underrated American school had pushed the painting's price from seven thousand to fifty thousand dollars in its last sale. It looked murky, clouded, very unreconditioned. "It's in *very* original condition," Marion told me.

That's just the kind of place Gino is. Very original condition. Its old-fashioned, red-sauced Italian home cooking makes it a dignified unretouched antique, if not an anachronism, in a neighborhood obsessed by the pale, virtually anorectic, nouvelle northern Italian cuisine in fashion now.

"Look at that wallpaper," Marion says.

It is a sight. Blood-red with fanciful zebras rampant and some random arrows from invisible bows.

"They had a flood here, and they were going to replace the wallpaper, but they couldn't find anything like it."

I can believe that. In fact, from the antique patina of what looks like food stains at table level, I can believe they haven't washed it.

But despite this, perhaps in fact because of it—because of its undesigned, bad-taste authenticity—Gino has become a hot restaurant lately. Dotted among the dowagers are Eurotrash types, their all-hemisphere tans the color of aged prosciutto, dining with Hollywood blondes as young and fresh as the figs.

The talk at our table turns to the big Sotheby's coup of the past season: the Dreyfuss collection sale. This was that consignment that went for a record one-evening total of $39.2 million. What made it such a coup was not just the dollar figures, but the fact that these paintings had never been on the market before. They had disappeared decades ago into the hands of a reclusive collector, and when they reappeared last year at the height of a renewed frenzy of multimillion-dollar prices for Impressionist works, most of them hadn't been seen for years, even by experts.

Except for Sotheby's Nash. His inside knowledge of the collection was a factor in getting Sotheby's the consignment to sell it. "The collection was formed by Mrs. Dreyfuss when she was married to Julius Wolf," Nash explains. "Later she married Sylvan Dreyfuss, who was an English watch-importer. And my father was in the watch business. And so when I came to America in 1963, I got a call from Mr. Dreyfuss saying did I want to see his wife's collection. It was at some little hotel—the Lombardy, that's it. After he died she became more and more reclusive. The paintings were put in storage, so I did have the advantage of having seen the collection as very few others had. I didn't discover it singlehandedly, but it was a very little-known collection."

Of course, with a collection like that it was not merely a case of finders keepers.

"We had to demonstrate to the executors of the estate that we had the better track record in this field," Nash says. "That we were willing to offer better terms, a better marketing program. That we had several advantages over our competitors—better exhibition service, larger number of catalog subscribers, those sorts of things."

Those sorts of things—marketing and the like—are becoming increasingly important as the art and auction world becomes subsumed into the world of commerce and investment. New money and new people are changing the clientele of Sotheby's, Marion says.

"People who have made their fortune in the stock market when their companies have gone public, computer whizzes, Wall Street people . . ."

"Twenty years ago," says Nash, "one knew everybody who was going to buy a one-hundred-thousand-dollar picture. All ten of them."

Gino comes around to supervise main-course orders, and Marion introduces me to the distinguished old gentleman. "My father started taking me here when he was an auctioneer," Marion says. "Gino came to my wedding." He recommends, and I order, the "Chicken Gino."

Nash talks about the dizzying effect of spiraling prices on new clientele.

"Just about this time last year, this doctor from Riverdale

came in with a painting by Schiele and asked me if we could get him fifty thousand dollars for it. I told him I thought we'd get him close to a million. He almost changed his mind, telling me, 'I was selling this to simplify my life; that kind of money will complicate it.' And I was kicking myself for blowing the sale, but eventually he did decide to sell and it brought two point two million."

Auctions that exceed expectations have become commonplace lately. But what was his most *disappointing* night with a gavel? I ask Marion.

"One time I was in Denver trying to sell a train. And we had worked so damn hard on this train. The *Silver Star* or something like that. A great big stainless-steel train. We hauled the whole thing up there and there wasn't a bid on the bloody thing."

"And there was that horrible yacht, too," reminds Nash.

"Yeah, the *Sequoia*."

"Nixon's presidential yacht?"

"Yeah. There we had three networks, all the lights, and I looked out there and I think there was one bid."

"I would say the most disappointing sale was the transponder," says Nash.

The transponder sale. What they were auctioning were time shares in the transponders to beam up to a communications satellite.

"In theory it was a wonderful idea," Marion recalls. "The final sales total was ninety million dollars on seven lots. The largest single auction sale in history. The first bid was fourteen and a half million, and as I went along I was wondering what happens when you get over ten million dollars in an auction—what kind of jumps do you make after that?"

Marion enjoys this aspect of the memory immensely. "It was a *true auction*," he says rhapsodically, conjuring up the beauty of the pure dynamics of auction forces at work.

"By 'true auction' I mean it started out very high when

demand was highest, went down to a point where it was too low, and then went up again as supply was dwindling."

So what was so disappointing? I ask.

"Unfortunately," says Marion, "we couldn't get the sale through because at the end of the day the FCC annulled it. They said we couldn't sell seven identical services for different prices. They didn't understand it," he says wistfully.

Marion launches into several more tales about large-scale unconventional auction innovations Sotheby's tried out during the years when the firm got its "player" image. I get the feeling he loved those days, that selling overpriced Impressionists and overvalued American landscape paintings gets a little boring no matter how high the price. The man was born to sell. Anything.

But Nash is not so comfortable during this part of the lunch.

"We're not a general auctioneer," he interjects a bit stuffily, pronouncing the words "general auctioneer" as if it's clear that's done by people "in trade," not by gentlemen.

Marion is unfazed and unstoppable in his enthusiasm. "We did sell the *Orient Express* in Monte Carlo," he reminds Nash. "That was very successful. Then we sold another train. . . ."

The talk turns to questions of value and price and the difference between the two. Hasn't some kind of hysteria taken over the bidding for Impressionists recently? I ask Marion.

"There is something psychological to it—once you've gone through the million-dollar barrier for a painting a number of times, it's much easier for people to think in those terms. And now that we've broken the ten-million-dollar barrier . . ."

"I think we broke three records last year," someone else in the Sotheby's party says. "The most expensive single work ever sold at auction was the twelfth-century illuminated manuscript *The Gospels of Henry the Lion*, for twelve million dollars. Then there was the Turner, the most expensive picture ever sold, for ten million dollars; then the single most successful evening, the thirty-nine million dollars for the Dreyfuss collection of Impressionists."

"You can liken what's happening with the Impressionists now," says Marion, "with what happened with old masters in the twenties. The real trick I think is to figure out what are going to be the old masters/Impressionists of the 1990s."

And just what might that be? I ask.

"You tell me," Marion says evasively.

I turn to Nash.

"I wouldn't tell you if I knew," he says, sounding a bit hostile.

Later I will get an answer to the "real trick" question from Marion, but only after I push him into a discussion of the question of whether a lot of art at auction these days is overvalued.

"Prices are going up," says one of the Sotheby's men, "because many collectors of contemporary art are competitive businessmen who are not used to losing in the office, and so when they get into the auction . . ."

"We saw a couple of years ago that kind of hysteria in the jewelry area," Marion says. "Where there were a lot of speculators involved and the price was going up by the hour, but you couldn't predict what anything was worth. When that happens it's not good. There was a shakeout."

He concedes that the vogue for American landscape painters of the nineteenth and early twentieth centuries is a question of what he delicately calls "relative value."

The "relative value" that pushes up the price of these often undistinguished works seems to be more a matter of what the ad agencies call "product positioning," if you listen to Marion's explanation for their popularity. Among the new yuppie breed of enthusiasts, he says, "People want to be involved, they want to collect. They look at the Impressionist market and it's pretty expensive territory. . . . In the American market there are many, many more opportunities."

It's kind of sad to have one's low opinion of "new collector" types of confirmed: They'll take a bad painting as long as it's a good investment.

But I guess it shouldn't be news that the art world has become an epiphenomenon of the stock market. Marion recalls the "electricity in the air" on the evening of the sale of the Havemeyer collection of Impressionists in 1982.

"You did have that feeling. Everyone was on the edge of their seats. . . ."

Why was it so special?

"Because it was a signal. The end of the recession."

Are there any artists whose market is declining in value these days? I ask.

"Well, the Balthus exhibition did very little to help his general popularity," Nash says. "Balthus paintings are still in the tight grip of what's almost a cult. I think the exhibition really proved him a disappointing artist. And I think the recent de Kooning show, instead of stimulating the market, depressed it. There were two big de Koonings offered for sale, both very famous. One, supposed to bring maybe a million dollars. There was no bid on that level. They took a chance on a second picture and got away with it for something like eight hundred fifty thousand dollars."

Why the disappointing results with the de Kooning? I ask Nash.

"I don't think it was a good exhibition. I think there was too much emphasis on later work, which is very, very repetitive. The work of a man who's run out of steam artistically."

Since we are playing the market game and he's the chief player, once again I try to get Marion to tell me what he

thinks the solution to the "real trick" in the art market is
—to figure out what will be the old masters of the 1990s.

"Okay. I'll say American paintings of the twenties and
after," he says.

And what does he see as the most foolishly overvalued
group of paintings?

"You're asking the wrong person," he says smiling. "That's
like asking Jesse James if he's ever seen a train."

TRUMP:
THE ULTIMATE DEAL

———— • ————

In Which We See the World Through the Eyes of Kaddafi's Pilot

Forty-eight hours before our scheduled lunch, Donald Trump called to cancel it. He'd had severe second thoughts, he said, about the advisability of revealing the extent of his involvement in the delicate—and explosive—subject I'd wanted to discuss with him.

"I'm dealing at a very high level on this," he said. With people in Washington. In the White House. There was too much at stake for him to risk the wrong kind of exposure on The Subject.

The Subject has itself been the subject of considerable delicate prelunch negotiations between Trump and the magazine. Trump was enthusiastic when he first heard I wanted to focus on The Subject.

That's great, he said: The Subject is far more important than any development deal he's ever done, than any deal of that sort he'll ever do. The life-or-death nature of The Subject transcends mere real estate. He's pursuing it as if it were the biggest deal of his life. The Ultimate Deal.

But now he's changed his mind about talking about it. "It's awesome what's at stake here," he said, "and some writer who's cynical could come along and try to make me look like an idiot and ruin my credibility." In addition his PR adviser told him he shouldn't talk about The Subject at all, he should only be plugging the success of the Trump Tower Atrium. Cancel the lunch.

After further negotiations, however, we arrived at a compromise. We could talk about the Trump Tower Atrium *and* The Subject. Or we could talk about talking about The Subject, which I believe is where things stood when I arrived at Trump's office.

Trump was on the phone with some midwestern senator when I walked into his office. He was promising to buy a table at some kind of fund-raiser he wouldn't be able to attend. While I waited I got a chance to gaze at the three-sided panoramic view of Manhattan through the tall windows of Trump's office. I got a chance to watch Trump upside down in the gold mirror tiles on the ceiling above his desk.

When Trump got off the phone we talked about The Subject and quickly negotiated the following deal: Trump would agree to talk about The Subject as long as I'd agree not to reveal in this article just what The Subject was.

Just kidding. See, that's just the kind of thing Trump is worried about. And that's why—as I write this—I've come to feel protective about Donald Trump. I want to protect him from my own most cynical instincts, the side of me that might be tempted to go for a cheap joke, an easy laugh at the expense of Trump's involvement with The Subject. Because when I first read a couple of references to Trump's interest in The Subject I have to admit I was skeptical, perhaps even cynical. But I've come to believe, from listening to him talk about it, that Trump is sincere about it.

This is a painful conclusion for me to come to in certain respects. Because The Subject is nuclear weapons proliferation and Trump's crusade to find a way to halt it before a wild-card nuke deals death to millions. And because I've become convinced that Trump's involvement is, well, serious, I have to abandon all the easy jokes and wisecracks I could have made if I thought it was some weird ego trip by an overambitious real estate promoter eager to thrust himself into the national arena.

Since I *don't* think that's true, I won't be able to make sarcastic remarks about nuclear war being bad for real estate values, about the danger of landlords acquiring neutron bombs as a way of dealing with stubborn tenants blocking condo conversions, about co-oping the missile silos and sending surprise eviction notices to the Soviets.

Actually, it was more than Trump's *sincerity* that convinced me to abandon such unworthy material. Something else convinced me. As soon as I heard of Trump's initial enthusiasm for talking about The Subject, I went out and got a copy of the *Bulletin of the Atomic Scientists* special issue reviewing the sorry state of the nuclear nonproliferation treaty. And then read, for the first time, *Deadly Gambits*, Strobe Talbott's inside story of the Reagan administration's pathetic and fraudulent nuclear weapons negotiations with the Soviets. The *Bulletin*'s report was distressing, but the Talbott book was worse, a sickening chronicle of bunglers and clowns engaged in Machiavellian bureaucratic maneuvering, the main purpose of which was to find the most effective means of deceiving the American people. Pretending to seek an arms control agreement while deliberately sabotaging any chance of a real deal in favor of foolishly conceived arms-race escalations such as the notorious "Dense Pack" mode of basing the MX. Remember the Dense Pack basing mode? That was Caspar Weinberger's brilliant solution to the alleged vulnerability of the MXs he wanted to build. The genius of Dense Pack was to group all the MXs into one big missile field on the untested theory that hundreds of Soviet warheads targeted on this concentration would crash together in midair *over* the target and blow themselves up by "fratricide," leaving the MXs totally untouched.

If Congress could listen to Weinberger propose spending billions of dollars for this mad-as-a-hatter scheme without having him medicated, I could certainly listen to Trump's plan to halt nuclear weapons spread, and take it seriously.

After all, these people—Weinberger's Dense Pack of "defense intellectuals"—not only did not want to make a deal, they wouldn't know how to make a deal if they did. And one thing Donald Trump knows how to do is make deals.

And so it occurred to me in the aftermath of reading *Deadly Gambits*: What could we possibly have to lose by placing *all* nuclear negotiating in the hands of Donald Trump? At least the guy knows how to negotiate. And after all, it's not without precedent for a smart businessman to come up with a brilliant deal in the nuclear weapons field: Many historians of the arms race argue that the United States and the Soviet Union missed an irretrievable opportunity to stop the arms race before it could begin back in 1946 when the Baruch Plan was rejected. Financier Bernard Baruch, you might recall, proposed that both superpowers place all atomic technology under the control of an international authority that would prohibit weapons development. Rejection of the Baruch Plan is regarded by many as one of the great Lost Opportunities in modern history.

Perhaps someday history will look back with similar regret at the Trump Plan for halting nuclear weapons spread—another Lost Opportunity. Or, if Trump gets his way with this, the way he does with other deals, it's not inconceivable that history will look back on the Trump Plan's *acceptance* as one of the few hopeful developments in the course of a miserable century. In any case, you read it here first.

"My uncle who just passed away was a great scientist," Trump is telling me as we make our way out of his office to the elevator. "He was a professor at MIT. Dr. John Trump. In fact, together with Dr. Van de Graaff they did the Van de Graaff generator. He was the earliest pioneer in radiation therapy for cancer. He spent his whole life fighting cancer and he ended up dying of it."

It was his uncle, Trump tells me, who got him started thinking about The Subject.

"He told me something a few years ago," Trump recalls. "He told me, 'You don't realize how simple nuclear technology is becoming.' That's scary. He said it used to be that only a few brains in the world understood it and now you have a situation where thousands and thousands of brains can easily understand it, and it's becoming easier, and someday it'll be like making a bomb in the basement of your house. And that's a very frightening statement coming from a man who's totally versed in it."

Downstairs on the sidewalk outside Trump Tower, Trump gazes at a crowd of chanting demonstrators across the street.

"Who are they?" he asks me.

"They're anti-Marcos. They say he's buying the Crown Building on the corner."

"Marcos doesn't own it," Trump says. "They think he does, but it's not him, it's somebody else."

Still, this sudden manifestation of Third World strife on his doorstep is a kind of confirmation of Trump's fears, which center on a Third World madman getting the bomb. Like Kaddafi.

Particularly Kaddafi.

Because Trump's got inside information on the character

of the Libyan dictator. From Kaddafi's pilot.

"I have a pilot who works for me who used to be Kaddafi's pilot," Trump is telling me as we head through the crowds on Fifth Avenue in the direction of "21." "He's a highly trained American pilot. And I asked him, 'What kind of guy is Kaddafi?' And he told me, 'Mr. Trump, you've never seen a man like this. This man would get onto his plane, and he'd slap his subordinates in the face. A total schizo.' "

The pilot quit Kaddafi, Trump says. "He was being paid a fortune—he's a great pilot—but he said, 'I couldn't stand it. He'd get into the plane, he'd scream, shout, slap people. He was crazy. You never knew. Hair-trigger.' "

Hair-trigger. Trump foresees a situation soon when such hair-trigger heads of state will have their hands on multiple nuclear triggers.

And it drives him crazy that nobody in the White House senses the danger.

"The fact is, it's already very late. It's one of the great problems of the world. Not *one* of them. It is *the*. And yet it amuses me that when people in Washington talk about the big issues they talk about tax reform. The hours and hours and money and worse that's spent on this ridiculous tax-reform issue. If one half of the same effort were devoted to this much more important issue, you might be able to solve it."

"What explanation do you find for the lack of action on nuclear arms spread?" I ask Trump as we approach the spear-topped iron gate of "21."

"I'll tell you why," Trump says. "People just don't believe the inevitable. You know, there's a feeling that it's always going to happen to the other guy. I read something the other day about a football player who played five years and he saw a lot of guys getting hurt and he never thought it could happen to him. All of a sudden his knee's gone and he's out forever. You know—he's gone. He never thought it could happen to him. Never thought."

Inside "21" everyone greets Trump effusively. And me, suspiciously: An officious functionary sidles up to me and tells me to straighten up the knot of my tie. I think of various irresponsible remarks to make on the order of "Hey, fella, when Kaddafi gets the bomb, you'll have more important things to worry about." But I resist the temptation. More is at stake here, I remind myself, than a cheap remark.

Upstairs at our corner banquette, Trump is greeting some sycophantic admirer, and this time a captain sidles up to me, points to his tie, and nods significantly at me. Evidently I haven't straightened my knot sufficiently yet. I see him standing there pointing at his ridiculous little tie, and just pity his lack of awareness of the nuclear proliferation crisis, which, if you ask me, will make all questions of tie-straightness irrelevant.

We order drinks, a Heineken for me, a prim Virgin Mary for Trump, and he continues on the blindness of U.S. policy makers.

"I believe they're sort of fools," Trump says. "They only think about Russia. Russian and U.S. weapons. But the summit is a joke. It's not about the real nuclear problem. You have countries like France that are openly and blatantly selling nuclear technology."

Trump is very down on the French.

"They've got an arrogant head of the country, who I think is a total fool, and he's trying to make up for his losses by selling this technology to anyone, and it's a disgrace. It's a disgrace."

So what's the solution? I ask him. How do you get the French to stop, how do you get French technology out of the hands of the Pakistanis at this point?

"I think you have to come down on them very hard economically or whatever way," Trump says. "I think the solution is largely economic. Because there are so many of these countries that are so fragile and we have a vast power that's never been used. They depend on us for food, for medical supplies. And I would never even suggest using it except on this issue. But this issue supersedes all other things."

He pauses.

"I guess the easy thing would be to say you go in and clean it out."

"Like the Israelis did with the Iraqi plant?"

"I don't necessarily want to advocate that publicly because it comes off radical. And you know, without a lot of discussion prior to saying that, it sounds very foolish and this is why I get very concerned about discussing it at all."

Suddenly there's an interruption. A guy leans over the partition that divides our banquette from his, and in a loud, braying voice calls out: *"Hey, Donald, I want a piece of that deal."*

The intrusive mover-and-shaker is apparently under the impression that Trump and I are negotiating a deal.

"Hi, Jack," Trump says. "You want a piece of the deal?"

"Sure, Jack," I was hoping Trump would say. *"We're figuring out how to go in and clean out the Pakistani bomb-making facility at Islamabad. Care to handle munitions procurement for us?"*

But instead Trump says blandly, "How are you? Good, Jack," and returns to the problem of getting the nuclear genie back in the bottle.

"It's really a bothersome thing," he says. "I don't want this story. In fact, I would have preferred not having any story, and when I heard it was going to be about this I said forget it entirely. What I would have liked was a story on how well the Atrium at Trump Tower is doing."

"Well," I said to Trump, "we can get into that. Would you like to start out by telling me how well the Atrium's doing?"

What followed was the single most surprising moment

of our conversation. The one that convinced me that Trump's interest in the nuke-spread issue was genuine.

He brushed aside my offer to listen to the Atrium success story. And never once returned to it. The master salesman passed up a chance to make a pitch. Instead he returned to The Subject.

He spoke about *Deadly Gambits* and the bureaucratic sabotage that has destroyed the possibility of a deal on arms control between the superpowers. And why our negotiators wouldn't know how to make a deal if they found one staring them in the face.

"I will tell you," Trump says. "There is a vast, vast amount of difference between somebody who has consistently made great deals—and I don't say me, by the way—of whatever nature, and there aren't that many of those people, by the way; you have maybe a roomful of them in the whole country. There's a vast difference between somebody who's been consistently successful and somebody who's been working for a relatively small amount of money in governmental service for many years, in many cases because the private sector, who have seen these people indirectly, didn't choose to hire these people, any of them, because it didn't find them to be particularly capable. But then, years and years later they get slightly promoted, promoted, promoted. The private sector has passed them by and all of a sudden *these* people are negotiating the lives of you and your children, your families, and I tell you there's a tremendous amount of difference."

He pauses in the midst of this impassioned analysis.

"You know, a while ago you asked me to talk about the success of Trump Tower Atrium—it really does pale. It's hard to get off this subject."

What about deal making as an art? I ask Trump. What separates those born with it from those who don't have it?

"It's a total skill and art. See—again, I don't want to say

I have it. I don't want to come off saying that. I'm just talking about some people. Some people have an innate skill. There's an ability to make deals. I mean I've gone into meetings when I've seen my people who are highly paid, very bright, they went to Harvard, they say the deal is dead. I'll go in and make the deal. Not only will I make the deal but I'll make it better than they could have. And on the other hand, I'll hear people telling me that such-and-such a deal is guaranteed. It's one hundred percent. It's going to happen. And I'll look at the people and I'll say, 'That deal will never happen. They will never make that deal. I'll guarantee it.' A certain other deal, they'll say, 'No way it can happen.' I'll say, 'They're dying for it, it'll happen.' That deal will happen. The other won't happen. I've seen sure things where it was blown because people didn't know what they were doing. I've seen sure misses that were made successful because of the ability to sense that a deal could be done."

Since we're on the subject of deals, I ask Trump to fill me in on his most recent deal-making efforts.

"I did the big deal with Hilton in Atlantic City a month ago," he begins. "That was a very big deal: I bought the largest gambling casino in the world. I just bought the St. Moritz Hotel. And of course there's Lincoln West."

"What are you going to be doing with that, will you be scrapping the original plan?"

"Yes," he says, "I don't want it. I turned it in. I'm going through a whole zone change. It's going to be an unbelievable project. Unbelievable. It's going to be spectacular. Throughout the world they'll be talking about this thing."

"Will it include the world's tallest building?"

"Well, between you and me, I'm looking at it and it's probably the only site you could have it on because it's so big. It's over one hundred acres. The West Side waterfront from Fifty-ninth to Seventy-second streets. I bought the site for one hundred million dollars, and right after that two blocks to the east it was five hundred million dollars for a site that's two and a half acres. And I have the whole waterfront for one hundred million. It's a great piece," he says, deeply satisfied as he contemplates the deal. "I think it's maybe gonna be the greatest purchase."

How great?

"This *will* be the biggest project in the history of the city. The West Side is booming. I bought—I mean I had a long-term right to it—I bought at a time the city wasn't thriving as it is. It'll be the most spectacular project ever if I get to do what I want to do."

But what about that deal Trump seemed to disparage, that two and a half acres a little bit east of his mammoth Lincoln West site, the Coliseum tract, the one that developer-publisher Mort Zuckerman and Salomon Brothers paid close to a half billion for? Wasn't this a deal Trump bid on himself? Does he regret not getting it?

Trump has strong feelings about the Coliseum deal Zuckerman made. But they are closer to ridicule than regret.

"No, I don't regret it. Never once. When I heard what they bid for it, I said, 'I didn't lose. I won.' You don't win when you're paying too much for something."

"They paid too much?"

"Even if it works incredibly well, which I don't think it will, at that price they couldn't make any money. If it worked out moderately well, they could stand to lose a great fortune. And if it worked out badly, forget it. It's just too much money."

"Could it sink them?"

"I don't know if it could sink them because I don't know what their financial condition is. I know this: I think it's a *catastrophe*. Hey, I bid two hundred million dollars less and somebody said, 'What would happen if you got it?' I said, 'I'd ask for a recount, because the price *I* bid was ridiculous.' "

"What do you think was going through *their* minds, or

what convinced them to pay half a billion?"

"Maybe nothing. Take my word. Everybody was in the two hundred million to three hundred million range except some were less than two hundred. They paid five hundred because they paid four-sixty plus they had to spend forty, fifty million on the subways, plus the carrying, plus to knock down the big building, and it's going to cost them ten for demolition. So they'll end up spending five hundred fifty million dollars before they get a shovel in the ground."

In addition to the financial catastrophe he sees for the Coliseum site, he also sees a potential physical catastrophe for the city's trouble-plagued convention center in the West Thirties. Trump owned the land for the site and offered to build the convention center for $250 million. The people who got the building contract are now three years late and $200 million over budget. But Trump has more than an I-told-you-so for the convention center deal: He has a warning. He doesn't think the sky's falling, but he's worried about the roof.

"That roof is so large nobody knows what is gonna happen. You don't have space-frame builders that can build a roof that large. And if you know anything about space frames . . . that roof will leak like a sieve, and who the hell knows what's gonna happen when they have five feet of snow on a glass roof?"

"Do you think it's dangerous?"

"I don't know. I mean I would hope not. But tell me what's going to happen if you have a five-foot snowfall and it's sitting on a glass roof. I know I would prefer being at another location. . . ."

Trump thinks the Golden Age of deals in Manhattan real estate may be coming to a close.

"There were some big buyers in the bad time back around '75," he says, "and I was one of those people."

For the latecomers he sees slim pickings.

"I mean, when a guy pays five hundred million dollars for the Coliseum," he says, returning to the deal his new rival in town just made. "That's not successful. That's paying top, top dollar. It's unfortunate as opposed to the advantage I had of buying things years ago when the prices were different. Today you can't buy a little grocery-store site someplace on the West Side for what I paid for the Tiffany location, which is the best location probably in the world."

The Golden Age of great deals is ending, and people are working with mere scraps and patches now, he says.

"They put together these half-baked sites in the middle of a block with a half a block here, a half a brownstone there, a fourteen-foot entryway from the other street because it's zoned industrial. I think they'll be killed."

And he doesn't see anybody making a killing in the office tower market either.

"I think office space in midtown won't be doing particularly well. Downtown is not doing well either. I'll tell you, Ron, the ones that are going to be hurt very badly are those that are working in marginal developments in marginal properties, and you see a lot of them. I think these people are going to be absolutely killed."

And what was the greatest deal Trump made in the Golden Age of dealing? He won't specify, but he does speak with special fondness of a certain Atlantic City deal that gives him what he calls "infinite return."

"That was the casino in Atlantic City I started to build, and then Holiday Inn came in. They put up about two hundred twenty million dollars to build a hotel I'd already started. I was under construction. I was on the third floor and they came to me and they wanted to put up money and guarantee everything, and I said to myself, 'Why should I own one hundred percent and have maybe two hundred fifty million of my own money in the deal when I can own fifty percent and have nothing in the deal, and in fact have a guarantee that if the place should ever lose money, *they* guarantee it?' So they guarantee it and they get no management fees, nothing. I own fifty percent of that casino for zero money in and substantial money out."

"That sounds like a pretty good deal."

"In the true sense that's what they call an infinite return. It's not a return on the investment. It's an infinite return because I got fifty percent of the casino for nothing. That'll make a lot of money."

And then there was the deal he almost made, the one that might have brought him not infinite return but infinite regret.

"I was going to go into the oil business two and a half years ago with a very big stake in a company which couldn't miss and just at the last moment I decided not to. And the company, it was a very, very, very, very large group of companies privately held by a lot of very—at the time—wealthy individuals. And I'll tell you, it filed for bankruptcy. That was in a way the best deal I ever made in that I *didn't* make it. That would have taken everything I had out of Atlantic City. It was one of those sure things that I decided not to go into that everybody had me convinced I should. It would have cost me hundreds of millions of dollars."

"What made you decide to back out at the last minute?"

"Well for one thing, there was something about digging holes in the ground that didn't really interest me. You know, I was talking to a guy who's in a very successful electrical-cable business and he passed Trump Tower and he said, 'Donald, the thing that's beautiful about your business is that you can *see* it. I spend hundreds of millions on cables and I throw it in the ground and no one gets to see it. There's no gratification. But look what you have—you're artistic, it's *your* building.' So with this oil—I was talking with the geologists and they were talking about different standards of probabilities that there'd be oil under the ground and I said, 'This is ridiculous. It's a total crapshoot.' So I didn't go in on it. If I'd made that deal we probably wouldn't be talking today, unless you were here to ask me, 'How did you blow it all, where did you go wrong?' "

But the thrills and perils of deal making no longer have the same excitement for Trump these days. Not compared with The Subject.

"Nothing matters as much to me now," Trump says.

He's been "spending so much time on this other thing," he says, meaning The Subject, that he's hardly had time to think of conventional deals. Because he's on the track of a much bigger kind of deal, his Ultimate Deal. The Trump Plan.

Of course, he doesn't call it the Trump Plan. And he denies that he wants to be the one to make the deal. But he's convinced there's a deal there to be made, that it's now or never, and that the people down in Washington are not doing anything to get the deal done.

Why don't they have the sense of urgency you feel? I ask Trump.

In part, it's the Kaddafi's Pilot Factor, he says.

"Those people think that because we have it and the Russians have it, nobody will ever use it because they're assuming everybody's not necessarily mad. They don't see Kaddafi walking into an airplane and slapping his subordinates and screaming like a madman on the airplane to the pilots. The man is a psycho.

"I mean, what if he's got the bomb and something happens like the time we shot down two of his planes. And he's enraged and he can't see straight and he's got twenty missiles pointed right at the United States. Washington. I mean, do you think there's a chance he won't press the button?"

"And then there's the briefcase bomb."

"Carry it in your briefcase, right. I'm not even talking about airplanes and missiles. You'll walk in with your damn tape recorder," he says, pointing to my innocent Sony, "and you'll say it's a tape recorder and nobody will be able to tell the difference. I mean, that's where it's going to be in twenty years."

But what makes him think he can do anything to forestall the wild-card nuke horror he envisions?

"I don't think I have to be the one. I'm not saying this to promote myself. But it has to be somebody of only a few people. Somebody who has the ability to make a deal. Because there's a deal there to be done absolutely. But not by the present players," he says, referring to current American negotiators and Reagan negotiators. "They have no smiles, no warmth; there's no sense of them as people. Who the hell *wants* to talk to them? They don't have the ability to go into a room and sell a deal. They're not *sellers* in the positive sense."

So what is the deal Trump thinks can be done? What is the Trump Plan?

It's a deal with the Soviets. We approach them on this basis: We both recognize the nonproliferation treaty's not working, that half a dozen countries are on the brink of getting a bomb. Which can only cause trouble for the two of us. The deterrence of mutual assured destruction that prevents the United States and the USSR from nuking each other won't work on the level of an India-Pakistan nuclear exchange. Or a madman dictator with a briefcase-bomb team. The only answer is for the Big Two to make a deal now to step in and prevent the next generation of nations about to go nuclear from doing so. By whatever means necessary.

"Most of those [prenuclear] countries are in one form or another dominated by the U.S. and the Soviet Union," Trump says. "Between those two nations you have the power to dominate any of those countries. So we should use our power of economic retaliation and they use their powers of retaliation and between the two of us we will prevent the problem from happening. It would have been better having done something five years ago," he says. "But I believe even a country such as Pakistan would have to do something now. Five years from now they'll laugh."

"You think Pakistan would just fold? We wouldn't have to offer them anything in return?"

"Maybe we should offer them something. I'm saying you start off as nicely as possible. You apply as much pressure as necessary until you achieve the goal. You start off telling them, 'Let's get rid of it.' If that doesn't work you then start cutting off aid. And more aid and then more. You do whatever is necessary so these people will have riots in the street, so they can't get water. So they can't get Band-Aids, so they can't get food. Because that's the only thing that's going to do it—the people, the riots."

"But what about the French?" I ask Trump. "They—"

"I'd come down on them so hard," he says. "Because I think they've been the worst example of—"

"But they already have the bomb. Do you think they'll give it up?"

"Well, I tell you if they didn't give it up—"

"Look, they blew up the Greenpeace ship—"

"They've got the bomb, but they don't have it now with the delivery capability they will have in five years. If they didn't give it up—and I don't mean *reduce* it, and I don't mean *stop*, because stopping doesn't mean anything. *I mean get it out.* If they didn't, I would bring sanctions against that country that would be so strong, so unbelievable . . ."

Okay, I didn't say the Trump Plan was a sophisticated diplomatic document. It's a little crude at this point. It's a *vision* of a deal. It doesn't have the imprimatur of the military geniuses who came up with Dense Pack. Think of it as a kind of Modest Proposal.

That's why I feel protective about Trump. It's not that

I think he's got the solution, but I like the visionary urgency he brings to the problem. I like the fact that he's using his Washington contacts, the access his money buys him, to bug the torpid Reaganauts to do *something* rational in the nuclear realm.

Trump drops enough names, off the record, to convince me he does have high-level contacts, that he may indeed be "dealing at a very high level on this."

I don't know how seriously they take him there, I get a sense that he's probably—to his credit—made a pest of himself, that the D.C. people probably regard Trump's calls on The Subject with the same enthusiasm as the guests at the wedding feast regarded the prospect of listening to the Ancient Mariner's tale. Remember the way Coleridge's glittering-eyed stranger began buttonholing the guests at the feast to tell them of the vision of horror he'd beheld out there in the watery wasteland, the hellish encounter with the albatross that haunted him still.

Trump is a bit like the Ancient Mariner here at "21." In the midst of the manic chatter of feasting deal makers, he's haunted by the vision of a madman in the desert wasteland, the vision of Kaddafi's pilot.

Hey, Donald! I want a part of that deal!

That kind of deal doesn't seem to gratify him the way it once did. He's looking for a deal of a different sort. The vision of Kaddafi's pilot has made Trump a stranger at the feast.

STILL HUNGRY AFTER ALL THESE YEARS

———◆———

The Frantic Screaming Fat Cells of Mayor Ed Koch

"I love garlic," Ed Koch is telling me. "I love garlic on everything from lettuce to crabs." There's even a story about the mayor and garlic on strawberries, but we'll get to that later.

Meanwhile, we've just arrived at the Bridge Café, the mayor's favorite lunch place. We've been shown to the mayor's table, the one they keep open for him every day by the window, and he's explaining to me how this place has adapted to the particulars of his garlic obsession.

"Whatever I'm served here is prepared with garlic, meunière-style," he says. "Sautéed meunière-style it does not have that garlic smell. So I can go about my business after lunch without feeling I'm going to offend someone."

The fastidiousness about offending may come as a surprise to those who are familiar with the mayor's peculiarly stinging way with words. This is, after all, the man who boasted, "I don't get ulcers. I give 'em." It might come as a surprise, for instance, to the leaders of the state's public employee unions, the entire state legislature, and the governor, all of whom were raked over the coals of the mayor's wrath and scorn during the hastily called prelunch press conference we have just come from.

The occasion for this attack was a pension bill passed by the legislature in the closing hours of its session, a bill the mayor claims will cost the city $1.7 billion and benefit only seven hundred union pensioners.

"A raid on the treasury in the dead of night" and "a billion dollars ripped out of the hide of the city of New York" were some of the choice phrases he had for the measure. "A billion and a half dollars for seven hundred people," he concluded scornfully. "How do I join that union?"

In the backseat of the limo on the short drive from City Hall to the Bridge Café I found the mayor looking at the notes I had taken on his remarks. He pointed to the last line. " 'How do I join that union,' " he said, quoting himself with some satisfaction. "I like that."

After that fire-breathing performance, it's garlic time at the Bridge Café. "I have lunch here three times a week minimum with Dan, sometimes five times a week," the mayor informs me. Dan is Dan Wolf, founding editor of *The Village Voice*, a longtime friend, unpaid adviser, and lunch companion. Koch dedicated his book *Mayor* to Dan Wolf, "the wisest man I know." Wolf (for whom, I should note, I once worked), was described by *The New York Times* as the one man who says no to Ed Koch. He's noted for his propensity for making acerbic comments on the mayor's tendency to grandiosity: Wolf is widely credited with describing the mayor's book as "the greatest love story since *Tristan and Iseult*—the one between Ed and himself." To his credit, this is a propensity the mayor seems to encourage, since he has installed Wolf in an office next to his, and has him sit in on crucial meetings, both lunch and nonlunch, to get his firsthand evaluation of people and situations.

We order drinks. Wolf, press secretary Bill Rauch, and I order beers. The mayor orders coffee. And describes his regular lunch procedure:

"Sometimes I'll invite two or three other people, a deputy mayor or some top staff people, commissioners, to join us. I'll just call them up that morning, ask them to make lunch. And I tell them, 'Don't feel if you have other plans that I'm gonna be upset." And if they say they have something to do and want a rain check, I say, 'Good.' And then I never call them again."

He pauses. "Not true. Just kidding," he says laughing.

The waitress appears to announce the specials. The mayor orders soft-shell crabs prepared in his garlic meunière fashion. No appetizers. I decide it is important to appraise scientifically the mayor's idea of garlic intensity. I order the crabs, too.

"Lunch forms a wonderful break in the day," Koch continues. "There are maybe three places I go to on a regular basis. The Bridge, Roeblings at the Seaport, the Buffalo Roadhouse in the Village, or, in Little Italy, Villa Pensa."

At the mention of this latter establishment the mayor veers off into a rhapsody on a particular favorite garlicky appetizer they serve there.

"If there's one single food I like as an appetizer," he says, "it's zucchini deep fried with olive oil, garlic, and onions. Served cold. It's the best appetizer and anyone who sends a note to me at City Hall, I'll send him the recipe."

If you were to get the idea by now that Koch is as opinionated about food as he is about everything else in the world, you would be right. The mayor is one of those people who is given to telling others what the best food of each and every category and subcategory is. With absolute certainty. I know the type well, being one myself. Koch manages to work in a "best this" or "best that" to punctuate every comment. When I ask him why he goes to the Bridge Café so often, for instance:

"For several reasons. It's my kind of restaurant. Informal, old, a lot of ambience, reminiscent of a Village bar . . . Most importantly, the food is superb. I've been on a diet now for fifty-nine and a half years, since the day after I was born; I have those fat cells, you know the kind that can expand and are always crying out for more food. So I have to stick with fish, and the fish here is the best in America."

Koch's second-favorite lunch spot, the Buffalo Roadhouse on Seventh Avenue South in the Village, has "the best sidewalk café in the city. And the best salads. A marvelous chef's salad. I'm trying to get them to start doing a Caesar salad, I'm working on them," he grumbles.

The talk shifts from food to power in the city. And, in fact, Koch is an acute, if occasionally cruel, observer of the way power and status relationships are revealed in the nuances of food rituals. There is a particularly memorable story in his book about the moment when Koch, newly elected mayor, recognized exactly how his status had shifted in the inner councils of the city's power brokers. It was at a labor-management breakfast jointly sponsored by David Rockefeller and Harry Van Arsdale. He notes that:

When I walked into the room, every one of them stood up. They sat me between Rockefeller and Van Arsdale. Rockefeller said, "Can I get you some coffee?" and he went up and got me a cup of coffee. Van Arsdale ran to get me a Danish. It was extraordinary treatment. And the reason it was so extraordinary is that neither one of these guys likes me. . . . So it is the office. Now, how do I know? Because half an hour later Senator Javits

walked into that room. And over the course of one of
the longest careers in the history of the U.S. Senate . . .
he worked his ass off for [these people]. And when *he*
came in, only six people stood up and they sent a waiter
to get him a roll.

I remind the mayor of this anecdote and ask him what
other surprising insights into the nature of power in New
York he's come up with since then.

The most surprising thing about power, says Koch, "is
how little I have. I mean it. First thing there is something
we have here that's comparable to the so-called French civil
service. It's called the American civil service. They're gonna
be there forever. They'll never die. They live to a hundred
twenty. They go through mayors like Ex-Lax goes through
the system."

The mayor's food enthusiasm tends frequently to flavor
even un-food-related discussions with rather colorful digestive metaphors.

There is a story he tells me, for instance, about the power
lunch he had here at this table with Leon Hess, the chairman of Amerada Hess Corporation and owner of the Jets,
formerly of New York. Actually it was a kind of reconcil-
iation lunch. The mayor and Hess had traded shots publicly
over Hess's decision to abandon Shea Stadium for New
Jersey's Meadowlands. The mayor had called Hess, if I
remember correctly, "peculiarly obsessed with the state of
the sanitation facilities" in Shea Stadium.

I ask the mayor if the lunch went well. They didn't get
into the bathroom question, he says. "Neither of us wanted
to vomit."

It occurs to me that the mayor's predilection for these,
uh, forceful digestive metaphors—don't forget "I give ulcers," and so on—may reflect a deeply food-influenced way
of looking at the governing process: government as the

digestive organ of the body politic, consuming tax money, churning out waste and "services." The budget then is a restrictive diet with its metaphors of belt-tightening and trimming fat, and the ever-hungry dieting mayor an organic embodiment of the city's physical/fiscal condition.

If so, there is cause for concern in the nature of the mayor's diet. Because at this point our food arrives, and frankly it isn't much. The soft-shell crabs are golden brown and buttery, their light and delicate breading laced with garlic that is assertive but not overpowering.

"They're good, the crabs," I tell the mayor.

"They're good," he agrees. "But they're small."

They are small. Three little creatures, each of which could fit comfortably within the palm of a dainty hand. They look a bit lonely on the otherwise empty plate. The only thing served with them is a side dish of coleslaw vinaigrette, an elaborately multicolored and tasty dish, but not much nourishment. That's all Koch eats.

But as we eat this Spartan fare, the talk is of Lucullan feasts. I get the mayor going on the game of best and worst food experiences.

"My supreme eating experience was at Maxim's in Paris," the mayor says. "The fresh *foie* there—you don't say *foie gras*, just fresh *foie*—is the most sublime of foods. I've had the new American *foie* they're doing, and it's just not equivalent. I don't want to get into whether they're torturing the goose or not. I hope the goose is enjoying the experience."

What about his ultimate American eating experience?

"Well, let me give you my most disappointing experience here. It was the first time I was to Lutèce. I was taken by someone obviously quite wealthy—it was before I was mayor; I was that person's guest. I'd been looking forward to it, looked at it as the epitome. So when the maître d' said, 'Allow me to order for you,' I said, 'Splendid.' Then it was brought over and I tasted it. It was Swedish meatballs!

And I thought, how could I have been euchred into coming to Lutèce and allowing this maître d' to shove Swedish meatballs at me?"

When I persist in asking for his most pleasant American eating experience, the mayor gets deeply into his whole duck thing.

"I am an expert on duck. All kinds of duck. The best duck is Peking duck—made in America, not Peking. The best duck in America, non-Peking, is made at The Four Seasons, and the Peking duck at the Peking Duck House, Twenty-two Mott Street, is the best in the world."

He goes into a long disquisition on the carving of Peking duck. How the American Peking duck places are superior to mainland Chinese Peking duck places because they carve the whole duck for the customer—all the juicy meat—and don't just serve slivers of skin. And how no one does duck better than that place at 22 Mott Street.

So what are we doing here then? I wondered to myself. Ah, the diet. The one he's been on for fifty-nine and a half years (when he says it that way, you sense he's suffered through every single self-denying minute of it).

Perhaps the mayor's famed irascibility could be traced to the pain of this constant self-denial. Here is a man whose expandable fat cells are crying out for rich, juicy, greasy, fatty Peking duck rolled in a pancake with scallions and that tasty plum sauce, the skin crackling and sublime. And yet he's feeding himself these three tiny soft-shell crabs and some shredded cabbage.

It was, after all, right before lunch, at the very hungriest moment of the day, that the mayor had called an unscheduled press conference to denounce the unions for a "raid on the treasury in the middle of the night." Could the rage of his rhetoric have been fueled by the anger he suffers from denying himself a midnight raid on the Gracie Mansion refrigerator? If I can practice self-denial, he seems to be saying, why can't these special interest groups? Would the city be governed with fewer ulcers all around if the mayor permitted himself Peking duck at lunch? Let him have those tiny garlicked crabs as a midnight snack. Or at least heavy up on the breakfast. Mr. Mayor, I have the feeling you're one of those deluded dieters who thinks skipping breakfast is a shrewd move. Wrong!

More evidence for the suffering-dieter theory of the Koch style surfaces in our discussion about newspaper editorial-board lunches. The mayor makes a point of using these lunches to get powerful opinion-molders to come around to his positions. But he has strong opinions about the relative merits of the food served by the three major dailies.

"The *News* does it much more expansively than the *Times* or the *Post*," he tells me. "Those two use their own kitchens to supply the food. The *News* does it at Paone's, out of the office. It's extraordinary!" he exclaims. "They take a private room. They really have the best desserts in the whole world. But of all those fabulous desserts there, the very best of the best is the chocolate cake." Chocolate seems to hold a place second only to duck in the mayor's pantheon, and at Paone's he says they have "a wonderful chocolate cake. A special chocolate-flake cake. That's *the* best place for chocolate."

But this chocolate reverie turns out once again to be a story of deprivation because the time has come to order dessert. And the mayor is raving about the chocolate cake here at the Bridge Café, a special double-chocolate fudge cake. In fact, the mayor orders it for me. "With whipped cream," he tells the waitress.

"You're not having any?" I ask him.

"My diet," he says glumly. There is a tragic intensity in this litany of renunciation. It is a side of the mayor I had not glimpsed before. The frustrated lover. He wants the chocolate cake. He speaks of it with longing, but he denies himself the pleasure. And genuinely suffers. You get the feeling this man suffers passionately every day for the desserts he denies himself.

And he does more than merely suffer for his passion for food. Once he nearly died for it, and he's not sure he won't go to hell for it, too.

As I am eating the genuinely, astonishingly intense chocolate cake he ordered for me, the mayor is telling me about the time he almost choked to death in a Chinese restaurant until a friend saved him with the Heimlich maneuver.

It was "either a sparerib or a spear of watercress that caused it," he says.

This hedge on the actual cause of the choking reflects the difficult political consequences of the story when it first appeared in the press. Most of the stories said the mayor choked on a sparerib. Now a sparerib in a Chinese restaurant is not going to be a beef rib. It's going to be a pork rib. *Trayf.* Unkosher. The mayor had not gone out of his way to make his sparerib habit a clandestine affair, but here it was suddenly all over the papers to the surprise of many of his Orthodox Jewish supporters.

The mayor is passionate and guilt ridden on the subject of pork. "I love Chinese food. Pork in particular. I always had guilt. But my feeling was, I'm not sure if I'm going to heaven, but I'm going to take a chance. I figure if that's my only sin, God will forgive me. The Orthodox Jews, I believe, in the beginning were a little offended, but then they decided: That should be his only sin. Isn't it nice he's not hypocritical?

"I think that's what they think," the mayor adds pensively. "But I want them to know," he concludes, "that I feel a little guilty. Not so guilty as to stop . . ."

The bill arrives. The mayor picks it up and starts adding and dividing.

"I never let anyone take me out to eat and I don't like

to pay for another man's food," he declares. "So we divide equally. I usually serve as the treasurer. Let's see." The mayor mumbles some figures. "That comes to fifty-six dollars with tip, or fourteen dollars each."

"But I was the only one who had dessert," I say. "Shouldn't mine be more?"

"We don't get that picky," he says.

Oh yes. I promised to tell you the story about the mayor and the garlic on the strawberries. Wolf told it to me. It seems that the mayor was having a dinner at Gracie Mansion for a German-American group, and kept emphasizing to the kitchen that he wanted garlic on everything. Somehow this got misinterpreted, or an accident happened. The massive amounts of garlic got too close to the dessert strawberries, and gave them a garlicky bouquet.

This was discovered at the last minute and reported to the mayor. "I guess we'll have to throw them away," the kitchen staffer said to Koch.

"No, don't throw them away," the mayor said.

"They weren't served at the dinner, were they?" I asked Wolf.

"Only to Ed," he said.

BATTLE TALES FROM BLACK ROCK

—————•—————

A Briefing from CBS News President Van Gordon Sauter

Ron,
  At one point in our conversation . . . relating to Tet and whether it was a military victory, etc. . . . I mentioned a conversation between an American colonel and a North Vietnamese colonel. It took place in 1975. The American said, "You know you never defeated us on the battlefield." The Vietnamese answered: "That may be so . . . but it is also irrelevant."
                    —Note from Van Gordon Sauter

The breakfast is at the Dorset, the gentlemanly, clublike dining room where the top executives of the three networks like to ease their way into the broadcasting day before heading off for Black Rock, 30 Rock, and—as they ought to call ABC now—Cap Rock.

And so, yes, the setting has been genteel and subdued. But the talk has been of war. Jungle wars. Plains wars. Wars of perception. Wars of deception. And hot-breathing, jugular-slashing hand-to-hand combat.

Talking with Van Gordon Sauter, the CBS executive vice-president in charge of its besieged and embattled news division, is a bit like getting a battlefront briefing from a Napoleonic marshal at the height of the death struggle with the Third Coalition.

Sauter is the media general who took command of CBS News back in 1981 when it was reeling from post-Cronkite demoralization and ratings decline. He swiftly whipped the troops into line behind Dan Rather and recovered the ratings points the *CBS Evening News* had lost to his rival Roone Arledge of ABC.

But just a few months into Sauter's tenure, General Westmoreland launched his attack, and Sauter's been at war ever since. No sooner does CBS win a decisive victory in the War over the War in the Westmoreland suit than Jesse Helms's troops hit it on the right flank and Ted Turner makes an assault from the Sun Belt. All the while, the nonstop ratings war among the news divisions of the three networks never deescalates, with ABC fading, but NBC suddenly looking like it's ready to make an assault on CBS's evening news superiority. I ask Sauter, an amateur medievalist and student of the Crusades, whether he sees any military analogy between the assault on Black Rock and, say, the siege of the Crusaders' castles by the infidels.

No, he says, it's more "like a plains war. Where you're in eastern Montana and you're moving across the plains and you're wide open and there's a lot of diversionary tactics . . ."

But not even the chaotic savagery of a plains war can capture the intensity of the hand-to-hand, face-to-face combat that took place in the Westmoreland trial courtroom.

When Sauter talks about the climactic moments of the trial, his metaphors shift from those of military combat to something more primitive, something jungle-animal-like. I ask Sauter (who was a defendant in the case until just before trial) whether he was ever worried about the outcome.

"When Westmoreland was presenting his case, I didn't feel any breath on my jugular, if you will. You didn't get a sense that they were really at your throat. They were making it very uncomfortable, but they weren't at your throat. And then when we got up—you could feel their throat," he says with barely restrained satisfaction.

"How did CBS turn the whole Westmoreland war around?" I ask Sauter. For three years there had been nothing but criticism and setbacks for the network over the documentary: A *TV Guide* exposé called it a "smear"; CBS's internal investigation found fault with its methods; its producer, George Crile, was suspended for violating some rule about taping phone calls. A lot of Westmoreland's initial witnesses looked strong, particularly if you read the *Times* accounts of the trial. It even seemed possible that Westmoreland's attorney, Dan Burt, might be able to make good on his boast that he was going to use the Westmoreland case to "dismantle" the network.

And then the amazingly swift turnaround and capitulation. I ask Sauter if he could pinpoint a single moment in which the trial battle turned around.

He points to the dramatic decision by the general's lawyers to call George Crile to the stand as a "hostile" witness for the general's side.

"I think when Burt failed to damage Crile—you could begin at that point to see the shift," Sauter says. "To me that was the pivot, and from that point on, when CBS began to present its witnesses, there was a momentum developing that just could not be stopped. And in those last few days the plaintiffs saw that they were going to lose this case on malice and they were probably going to lose on truth. And that this mammoth exercise which involved the lives of so many people, with so many reputations hanging in the balance, was, from their point of view, heading toward a cataclysmic conclusion. And at that point they knew it was over and they left the field."

What was it about Crile's performance on the stand that made it so effective? Sauter makes Crile on the stand sound like some deadly computerized battlefield weapon.

"Crile had marshaled such a volume of information on the topic. Once you pressed the button, the computer could not be turned off. It's just a deluge. To discuss this topic with Crile at this stage is truly one of the great boring experiences of the eighties. Well, they pressed the button. And Crile is just unstoppable. And he just had fact, fact, fact, fact, fact. It was a classic performance."

I ask Sauter to tell me about the surrender negotiations with the general. There'd been a report that a year ago, before the trial opened, CBS had been willing to offer the general a statement affirming the network's belief in his patriotism and loyalty in return for dropping the suit. The actual settlement a year later added pointedly that the general had performed his duties patriotically and loyally "as he saw them."

"I wrote most of the original proposed statement," Sauter tells me. "It would have provided a better cover, if you will, for the general's withdrawal than the document that was eventually done."

Because?

"It [Sauter's original draft] was more gracious. It was a lot more respectful of the general. And, quite frankly, when I wrote it with [CBS general counsel] George Vradenburg, I said, 'Gosh, I'm wondering if this isn't too nice.' And, of course, they [the Westmoreland side] rejected it out of hand with certain scurrilous comments about it."

Scurrilous?

"Oh, they were scurrilous," he repeats, although he professes to forget the exact language the general's lawyers used in their rejection.

"And I was very relieved [that they rejected it]," Sauter tells me, "because I thought, 'What if I've been overly generous and given away the company store?' "

But what about that statement CBS finally made? Was it still too generous to the retreating general? After all, the documentary portrayed Westmoreland conspiring to deceive his military and civilian superiors on a grave issue, the strength of the enemy, during wartime when thousands of American lives were at stake. How could that in any way be described as "patriotic" and "loyal"?

Sauter offers what might be called the "stamina theory" of the general's conduct: "I think there was a conviction on the part of many Americans in the military and out of the military that, if we just had the stamina to stay with this war over a period of time, we could prevail, and that anything that could be done to keep that effort going would bring us closer to our goal."

In other words, he seems to be saying, the general was deceiving America's leaders and the American people but deceiving them for what he believed to be a "higher" patriotic goal.

"That war was, in effect, being conducted in the minds and the guts of the American people," Sauter says. "It was a war of perceptions."

At this point the waiter arrives for our orders. I ask for bacon and eggs.

"I'm fasting again," Sauter tells the waiter, "so I will not be eating here outside of my petrochemicals."

He points to a semicircle of Tab bottles arrayed in front of him—always a fixture wherever he eats, wherever he is.

"Are you fasting for spiritual renewal?" I ask Sauter.

"No, to get into my summer clothes," he says.

If the Westmoreland battle is behind him, the War over the War is not over. And there are indications it, too, is turning into a War Against CBS. In right-wing literature, in Richard Nixon's recent *No More Vietnams*, on the editorial page of *The Wall Street Journal*, a classic "stab in the back" theory is being developed that blames the media for the loss of Vietnam and singles out CBS for playing the most treacherous role in snatching victory from the United States.

In its purest form, the stab-in-the-back theory argues: Tet was a catastrophic defeat for the NLF guerrillas, but television portrayed it as their victory and shattered U.S. morale just when our boys were about to win the war, just as General Westmoreland was asking for the extra two hundred thousand troops that would have *really* guaranteed our victory. But CBS, and Walter Cronkite in particular, transformed our "victory" into an image of defeat, thus losing the war General Westmoreland could have won.

I ask Sauter about the most recent *Journal* editorial blaming CBS.

"I think it's inaccurate, and I fundamentally also think it's irrelevant. It looked to me as if somebody there got into a rage. A snit," he says, warming to the subject. "I almost thought that their commuter train had broken down, and by the time they got to the office, they were just absolutely furious with the world. And instead of taking it out on some underpaid, overworked secretary, they saw something about CBS News and that was it. There was an explosion."

Sauter has equally acerbic things to say about another CBS foe—Senator Jesse Helms. Sauter, who describes himself as "very conservative" politically, doesn't think Helms is a real conservative.

"I think he represents an unusual strain, if you will, of

conservative positioning in society, and I don't think it's shared by a lot of people," he says. "I don't see the conservatives—the thinking conservatives—in this society rallying around Jesse Helms and saying, 'Hey, [the CBS takeover] is a marvelous idea.' Because they're not. They don't think this is a good idea at all. . . ."

But what about these relentless attacks from the right? Won't they eventually, along with the Westmoreland trial, have a chilling effect on CBS? Could CBS's victories in the courtroom and the boardroom turn out—like American victories on the Vietnam battlefield—to be irrelevant? Have they already lost the war to the conservative guerrillas? "In other words," I ask Sauter, "if you have reporters down there in Central America who are saying critical things about the war, would they get something as strong on the air now?"

"I'd say two things. First, I don't think the Westmoreland trial has had a chilling effect on CBS News. You've got to keep one thing in mind about CBS News: It's only made up of fifteen hundred people and they have very strong convictions about their craft. I don't think there is any way to put a chill on them even if you were so perverted that you wanted to. . . ."

The consequence of the victory over Westmoreland, Sauter says, is that it will have "a chilling effect on some individuals who say, 'Hey, we can sustain a deception for a long period of time.' "

The real question, Sauter says, is whether televised coverage of war will make it impossible to conduct any Vietnam-style wars at all. He calls this the "large issue which I don't think anybody has really paid a great deal of attention to during the trial—which is, with television being what television is, is it feasible to conduct those kinds of wars? Immaterial whether the war is legitimate or illegitimate, efficiently handled or mishandled—can that kind of an effort be sustained with the degree of coverage which would inevitably and appropriately be brought to bear on it? Can you transcend those images of horror and destruction—that is a marvelously consequential issue. . . .

"The military," he says, "won't send us to wars if there is not a national resolve to support it. And I think that what has happened is that, through television, we, in a peculiar kind of way, have almost guaranteed that the portrayal of war on television *will* test the national resolve."

"Wouldn't you say that closing the Grenada invasion to TV cameras was an example of the Reagan administration realizing exactly what you're saying?"

"There's no doubt in my mind for any number of reasons they didn't want the media there. And it's not just an issue of the element of surprise."

"Has CBS entered into a protest of the Grenada precedent?"

"Oh, I think we were very strong on that issue."

It's time now to turn from the jungles of Vietnam to the jungles of Wall Street and Network Row. SEC rules forbid Sauter, as a CBS executive, from commenting on the Ted Turner bid, but he's not shy about commenting on the implications of the Capital Cities merger for his troubled rival at ABC, Roone Arledge.

"I thought it was an absolutely perfect marriage," he declares. "I thought it was great for both of them and great for the industry."

"I've heard people in the news business say that Capital Cities with its cost-cutting, bottom-line approach to everything will not tolerate ABC News's high-budget, high-salary structure and that other network news divisions will be affected. Maybe other networks like the idea because it'll bring salaries down. Is that why you like it?"

"Oh no," he says. "No, no, no," he adds. "That's a different issue. I just think if you look at it in a structural sense, the wedding of those two companies is very appropriate—Cap Cities has a great deal of management skill and ABC is an organization that's trying to build itself out of a serious problem. . . . I mean, you know, three years ago we got involved in CBS News in radically changing the cost circumstances. And made drastic cost reductions. 'Draconian!' were the cries from the people. We were going to disembowel the institution. As it turned out, it is probably one of the best things that ever happened to CBS News; we moved ourselves onto a very sound financial footing and developed cost control systems which will serve us for years. The greatest threat to editorial integrity and independence is red ink."

When you think about it, Sauter's reply to my Cap Cities cost-cutting question is a brilliant double-bank shot. One might almost call it Machiavellian in its cleverness. The message to corporate execs and stockholders of CBS and ABC: We at CBS have already made extreme cuts, but ABC News is really still living high off the hog and *needs* Draconian chopping down. Take that, Roone.

How serious is ABC's "serious problem"?

"This morning the ratings came out for last week," Sauter tells me. "[The *CBS Evening News*] was in an unusually—for this time of the year—unusually dominant first-place position. And ABC has really fallen back."

What's responsible for ABC's plunge? Sauter offers a Roone Arledge–kryptonite theory.

"Roone is the vital center of that institution," he says. "And I thought ABC News began to lose its vital center when Roone began to shift his attention to the Olympics. What's the stuff that Superman has? Kryptonite? Is that the good stuff for Superman or the bad stuff?"

"It's good and bad," I reply knowledgeably, from years of reading Superman comics. "The green is bad and the red is highly unpredictable."

"Well, whatever," says Sauter, showing surprisingly little interest in this important distinction. "Roone is the energy source in that institution. And for whatever reason, starting, I think, before the Olympics, I think they seemed to lose it for a period of time. I don't think they've gotten it back yet. ABC News needs Roone. And if Roone is diverted, there's trouble in River City."

Again, I'm diverted by what seems to be another subtle Machiavellian subtext in Sauter's comments on ABC. Was his rival and counterpart Roone actually diverted? Was there trouble in River City, or would Sauter like to *make* trouble in River City by making it seem that his rival Roone couldn't handle both Sports and News at the same time?

This leads me to wonder what Sauter *really* means when he suggests that ABC might replace Peter Jennings with Ted Koppel.

He raises the issue in another context by wondering out loud to me, "I don't know what's going to happen to *Nightline*. If Koppel goes and does the ABC *World News Tonight*, I don't know what will then happen to *Nightline* in terms of its unique contribution. . . ."

"Is Koppel going to go to *World News Tonight*?" I ask Sauter. It was the first I'd heard of it.

"I don't know what's going to happen there," he disclaims. "I am a Peter Jennings fan. But," he says, "nothing is forever, and they've obviously gone through a period now where they find themselves in third place. . . . And I would imagine at some point they're going to have to say. 'How do we make this better?' "

Is he floating this idea because he wants to *help* ABC? Or because the departure of Koppel from *Nightline* would make it commercially possible for CBS to field a *Nightline*-type show in that time slot? Perhaps for Diane Sawyer? I confess I can't untangle it.

What about NBC? I ask Sauter. What's been responsible for the resurgence of their nightly news?

"I have long contended that NBC was a sleeping giant," he says, "Some people said they weren't sleeping, they were brain dead. But I thought some strong leader with a keen sense of institutional promotion would come along and either wake them up, or if they were brain dead, resuscitate them. When [former PBS president Larry] Grossman was appointed there, I didn't think Grossman was the guy. But in a few months he certainly turned me around on that. And he has been remarkable in his ability to energize that institution. They've become very, very good."

It was time to turn our attention to Sauter's own operation, and the changes he's been bringing to CBS News.

Sauter's lasting legacy, the one he'll be judged by, is in the way he's reconceptualized the *Evening News with Dan Rather*.

When Sauter took over as head of CBS News late in 1981, Rather had just taken over from Cronkite, and both anchorman and broadcast were floundering without an identity. Without a clear notion of what they were doing. Meanwhile the newly energized ABC news had overtaken CBS in the ratings.

Sauter turned things around dramatically, but it's been a turnaround that's been largely misunderstood. Too much attention has been paid to the cosmetic aspects of the change, such as Rather's sweater-vest, the electronic graphics, and the like. And too little notice has been taken of the way the whole philosophy, the nature of the *CBS Evening News* has been altered.

"Correcting the cosmetics of the broadcast was very simple. A two-week endeavor," Sauter says dismissively. "We got rid of the opening animation. And we shot Rather larger. We put in bumpers [the coming-attraction shots for stories]. We changed the music. We changed the cutaway shots. That was all just broadcast mechanics and very easily achieved. The complex thing was to change the orientation of the broadcast."

"Could you sum up that change?"

"We moved the broadcast out of Washington. We emphasized stories from across the country where we could tell national stories through human experience and human perceptions more than through statements of bureaucrats and politicians. We tried to find the theme stories which responded to what the aspirations and apprehensions of the American people were. We emphasized storytelling, both verbally and visually."

The change in Dan Rather's wardrobe was less important, says Sauter, than the way he retailored Rather's behind-the-scenes role in the broadcast.

"We made a conscious effort to get him involved in many of the management decisions. He was the managing editor, and I said to him, 'Hey, one of the things the managing editor does is to deal with personnel issues and sometimes with budget issues; it's your job to be aware of these things.' And he embraced that. He's a very emotional person. He is an embracer," he says continuing his character study of his anchorman. "He reaches out to embrace people. Does he have a temper? He has a monumental temper. And does it occasionally come loose? Yes it does, and he can go into a monumental rage."

Emotion is the key to Sauter's reconceptualized vision of the *Evening News*. More than emotion. A special way of capturing emotional moments: Sauter's controversial Theory of Moments.

What is a Sauterian Moment? It's the ten seconds of tape within a three-minute *Evening News* segment that informs us how a news event *feels* to those affected by it. In its most clichéd form, it's a silent study of the emotions registering on a dispossessed farmer's face as his land is being auctioned off, the look on the face of a laid-off steelworker's wife when she gets in line for food stamps for the first time.

Cumulatively the Theory of Moments as articulated by

Sauter and Rather aims to take the *Evening News* beyond Cronkite's "That's the way it is," into the realm of "That's the way it *feels*."

When I first wrote about the way Sauter and Rather were pushing Moments on the *CBS Evening News* a couple of years ago in *Esquire*, it stirred up trouble both inside and outside the newsroom. George Will picked up on my story and attacked the Moment Theory as emotional propaganda posing as objectivity.

Inside CBS, a former staffer told me, "Rather came out looking like [a jerk] with his Moments buttons, so you didn't hear much talk about Moments for a long time after that."

I ask Sauter if Moment Theory still prevails at CBS News.

"I am always joyful when I see somebody use the visual medium effectively," he says. "That's really what Moments are about—using television and its cinematic revelation . . . to reveal . . . to share with our viewers. It allows them to share, to feel, to have a link."

What about George Will's objection that it's emotional manipulation?

"I find it nothing more than using the unique attributes of this medium. Obviously, in the hands of an ill-motivated person that can be very dangerous or very evil. But I don't think we hire those people."

"Can you recall certain favorite Moments from recent *Evening News* broadcasts that embody this?"

"You know what I'd like to do?" he asks me. "What if I sent you a cassette with some?"

When Sauter's cassette arrived a few days later, it proved to contain five recent *Evening News* segments. Three of them involved Vietnam or its legacy. All five of them were intensely emotional, a couple real tearjerkers. But there was one moment that transcended considerations of theory. It was one of the most stunning and brilliant pieces of TV journalism I'd ever seen.

The piece was put together by Charles Kuralt, and it was nearly Nabokovian in its structural complexity. Kuralt opened with a clip from a Vietnam battlefield piece he'd done twenty years ago called, appropriately enough, "One Moment in the War." It was about three soldiers in a platoon Kuralt had been covering. We see them first happy and healthy. Then, we watch them go out on a mine-detecting mission. We hear an explosion and we see them come back: one dead; one with his leg shattered, soon to be amputated; the third physically intact but torn apart by what he's witnessed.

Then Kuralt swiftly takes us twenty years forward to the present, tracks down the two survivors and the family of the dead soldier. There is a moment in the footage of the widow and children that is the central moment of the piece and one of the most genuinely shocking moments of TV I've ever seen. It happens when Kuralt shows to the family the clip of the father being blown up twenty years ago. We watch them watching him die. *Seeing the footage for the first time.* Not exactly seeing him die, but hearing it: There's a moment when Kuralt's 1985 camera gives us a close-up of the widow's face as she watches the 1965 clip—a moment when we hear the explosion and see her flinch as if hit by the sound of her husband being blown up.

The piece says more about television, the war, and memory than anything else about Vietnam I've ever seen. And it embodies the "marvelously consequential" point Sauter had made earlier about the shocking power of the TV image and how its very intensity inevitably will test the national resolve to conduct such wars.

Shortly after watching Sauter's Moment tape, I came across something in my reading that seemed to define more clearly the elusive meaning of a Moment. When I stopped by Sauter's office at Black Rock a few days later, I decided to try it out on him.

"It's from Lionel Trilling's introduction to the stories of Isaac Babel," I told him. "Trilling's trying to articulate the place of the epiphany in the fiction of Joyce and Babel, and this is how he defines an epiphany: 'Suddenly, almost miraculously, by a phrase or a gesture, a life would thrust itself through the veil of things and for an instant show itself forth, startling us by its existence. . . . To this end he concerns himself with the given moment—' "

"Jesus!" Sauter exclaimed, interrupting me. "Where has that been? What the fuck have you been doing with that? My God. That's incredible," he says. "That's it."

RESTAURANT SADNESS

———— ❧ ————

In Which *New York Times* Critic Bryan Miller Reveals the Dark Side of Restaurant Madness

A bizarre ten-thousand dollar bribe offer. The pervasive influence of the CIA. False identities. Threatening phone calls. The high-stakes, high-risk confluence of greed and intrigue. Needless to say, we're talking about the restaurant business in Manhattan.

We're talking about it with Bryan Miller, the new incumbent of the most powerful position in that frenzied industry: chief restaurant reviewer for *The New York Times*. You could think of him as the single most powerful luncher in the power lunch industry. We're having lunch with him at a place he's preparing to review, a traditional French restaurant in the Beekman Tower called La Petite Marmite.

Miller's position gives him nearly the same singular power over restaurant openings that the *Times* theater critic has over play openings. Perhaps not the same power to kill, but at least as much power to guarantee success for those he favors with a review.

Miller, who is only thirty-three, took over the *Times* post in October 1984, succeeding Marian Burros, who succeeded Mimi Sheraton. Many food followers have commented favorably on the combination of wry irreverence and down-to-earth enthusiasm he's brought to restaurant review prose, which is so often characterized by worshipful solemnity or gushing effusions.

Faced almost immediately with the full, cresting frenzy of Restaurant Madness, he managed to communicate in his reviews and his popular "Diner's Journal" columns the excitement of new and offbeat places (El Internacional, the Village Lobster, Arcadia) without swooning over places that are merely scenes.

Although he's written about food for the *Times* and a number of other publications for years, he's still new enough at the game to have maintained, for the most part, his anonymity. He pays cash at lunches and uses his wife's credit card to pay for dinners. He believes he's still not recognized at most establishments he visits.

"Mimi Sheraton was known in about ninety percent of the places she went to by the time she left," he says. "And Marian Burros is known almost everywhere she goes. So I hope to preserve my anonymity. You really try hard, but if you get caught, what are you going to do? If you're recognized, you can usually see through it."

"The smart thing for owners who recognize you," I suggest, "would be to do their best not to let you know they know and yet somehow raise the level of everything so you'd think it was always that way for everyone, right?"

"Most people don't do that. That's the smart thing. But they don't. They gush all over you. Here for instance," he says, lowering his voice and glancing at the attentive maître d', "he's being smart about it. I think he probably knows.

He's being pretty discreet. There's another whole school of restaurant reviewing, which is to tell them you're coming and say, 'I'm coming, do your best. . . .' "

"Is it true," I ask, "that some restaurants have photographs of prominent reviewers taped to their kitchen walls to make sure the help spots them?"

"People have told me that." He doesn't think there are any black-market photographs of him floating around, but he does think there's at least one group that's aware of his appearance.

"The restaurant community is a pretty tight group," he says, "at least among French people. I'm sure there are a few French restaurateurs who could describe me and say I have a French wife and I look like a rube passing plates all around the table. But to make a fetish of anonymity is more about showmanship than anything else."

Miller manages to keep a sense of humor about Restaurant Madness, but the mad competition for his attention and favor is deadly serious, with at least two restaurateurs allegedly making what seemed like crude bribe offers through a third party.

"I'll tell you something really bizarre," Miller confides to me. "I have a friend who is a good source I've cultivated, and this particular friend of mine gets around a lot among certain restaurateurs because of her business. There's a restaurant, I don't know exactly where it was—and I told her I didn't want to know—that offered her ten thousand dollars to get me to come down there and let them know in advance. She would get ten thousand bucks."

"That's amazing."

"But it was contingent on me going and giving them a certain number of stars, at least two stars. I was just blown away. And then someone else passed the word to her to pass the word to me that there was good money in it if I wanted to play ball."

"They actually used those words?"

"No, not 'play ball,' but 'if I would cooperate.' They were pretty crude approaches."

Most people in the business have been "very upstanding" he assures me. "Sometimes if they suspect who I am, they'll try to buy me wine—they don't know the ground rules. Many people, readers, think that I even get free meals at restaurants, which is incredible to me."

What's really incredible is the actual amount of *Times* expense money Miller spends on his assignment. He estimates he's now spending at the rate of sixty thousand dollars a year.

"It's expensive," he says. "I really give the *Times* credit. There's no other paper in America that would spend this money. Before taking the *Times* job, I was offered a job at the *Miami Herald* doing this, and they have tons of money, but they wanted me to do the reviews based on one visit, just two people. I told them I wouldn't do it. With the *Times*, I must go three times to each place, and they'll let me go as many times as I want, and I sometimes bring five or six people along. I don't think there's anybody that spends what I spend."

"You may spend more than any other reporter in America."

"I think so. They say it's a very important column for the readers and they want to do it right."

Spending all that money eating all those expensive meals can get pretty arduous, it seems. Already on the Thursday we met he seemed weary.

"This is a pretty heavy week," he sighs. "Last night I was at a place called One Hudson Café. You know that?"

"Pastel lighting and a triangular interior, TriBeCa—"

"It's a beautiful place. I wish there were something to recommend, but the guy just has one real flaw: He can't cook. Everything we had was bad. He had a nice aesthetic and the food *looked* great. It was terrible."

"It's amazing that the owner doesn't have a sense of what's going on."

"He *is* the owner."

He returns to recounting his heavy week.

"I just got back from California, where I did twenty-two restaurants in eleven days, and I'm a little behind on deadlines, so I've been doing a blitz. The night before was Felidia. Another overpriced Italian restaurant. Many people say it's the best in town."

"And what did you think of it?"

"I was very disappointed. Every time I go I'm disappointed. We had some real troubles with freshness and sent back some quails one night that tasted freezer burned and old and smelly. Really, they were just foul. Then I had these Adriatic shrimp that are like langoustines. Very expensive: It's twenty-six dollars for four of them, and they were just old. They just had a lot of mileage on them. And everybody told me Felidia is the greatest place. There are lines; there must be twenty-five people at the bar waiting to spend eighteen dollars on a bowl of pasta. We've hit the eighteen-dollar-pasta level."

"Is that a breakthrough?"

"It was fifteen. They're at eighteen and they're beating people away. The kitchen is overtaxed and the menu is too big. That's why you have all this old food. At that price range it's not common. Those are Côte Basque prices. You'll get ineptitude at those prices more than you'll get old food."

From the way he talks, it sounds as if he has to wade through a lot more ineptitude and bad food than a human being could bear.

"Not this place," he says, indicating the newly renovated, half-empty dining room of La Petite Marmite. "We came here one night because we had gone to another place that was such a disaster that we left. We ate half of a meal and came here."

"What was the place you walked out on?"

"Manhattan Market."

"Another overcrowded place."

"It's a very popular place. It was highly touted and it just didn't pan out. And I can't afford to have that many strikeouts with a deadline every week. So we've gotten to the point where if things look pretty bleak—the appetizers come and I start to think, well, if it's really this bad . . . It's like going out on a story and it's not panning out. You don't hang around for the whole thing if you can help it. So we politely paid our bill, mumbled something about a movie, and came here."

The more I talk to Miller, the more I discern a certain nightmarish subtext to what seems like a dream job. The man has suffered through a lot of bad meals.

"What was your worst nightmare meal?" I ask him.

"My nightmare meal? I've had some real dogs. I had one at Joanna's Place uptown. Boy. That was the time we had a bowl of pasta that, when the fork went into it, the entire pasta came up with it. There have been some disaster meals, I'd have to say."

"What are some others?"

"We had a funny incident once going to a restaurant. We were really starving, we couldn't wait to get some bread, and we all sort of attacked this loaf of bread at once, and when it opened up, there was this long-deceased fly baked right into the middle of it, looking up. And then the moral dilemma was, do you write about this or not? I decided that I wouldn't unless the place was so bad that you wanted to twist the knife at the end. So I never wrote about it."

(I think he really missed the boat there. That fly was probably not a *mistake*, but one of the chef's special *encroûtée* entrées, a Continental twist on an old American regional specialty.)

Miller doesn't believe in twisting the knife.

"When I took this job, Abe Rosenthal said two things: 'One, just remember you're not covering the Vietnam War. You're writing about something that's basically pleasurable; try and convey the pleasure where it fits.' And the second thing he said was 'Don't be mean; don't be cruel to people, don't hit below the belt.' "

"A food watcher I spoke to said that one thing she'd noticed about your column is that you tend to like places where people are having a lot of fun, with rolled-up sleeves, newspapers for tablecloths. Is that true?"

"Yes, I think I approach it that way. First of all, it's fun to write about people. I watch to see if people are having a good time. At the Village Lobster, for instance, people are drooling things down their ties and they're drinking beer. I think people really respond to the idea that you can get down and dirty eating lobster. I wrote about that rather than doing a very clinical review about these things being oversteamed and those a bit limp. It's not great, but you'll have fun going there, and fun is part of what it's all about. You don't go out just for sustenance. You go out for fun, especially in this town."

Fun. Are people actually having fun in Restaurant Madness restaurants? Granted, food is mostly beside the point; the purpose is to appear, to seem to *belong* wherever it is the madness is maddest. The food is mainly a fashion accessory, a prop in the performance-art concept of the place. But it has been my experience and the experience of many food-fashion victims I talk to that the food in such places can, with distressing frequency, be *so* bad, so aggressively awful, it threatens to intrude, in its overt bogusness, on the covert artifice of the whole experience. The food can be so inexcusably bad it threatens to puncture the whole illusion, the delicate gestalt of it all with a galling Emperor's-Nouvelle-Suit-of-Clothes feeling.

In fact, I think few Restaurant Madness types fail to

sense the disparity between the orgiastic promise of over-heated restaurant-review prose and the reality of what's served at most of these overheated new restaurants. Indeed, I think, not far beneath the surface of Restaurant Madness there lurks the melancholy pang of Restaurant Sadness. When a $120 dinner for two is that bad, it makes it all the more difficult to forget how many lives could be saved in East Africa for the price of four Adriatic shrimp with too much mileage on them. The recognition is, well, *sad*.

Restaurant Sadness. Miller and I discuss various theories explaining the often appalling difference between expectation and promise in so many new restaurants. He seems to lean toward fingering the CIA as the culprit.

"It frustrates me and makes me angry sometimes when you go three times in a row to some place that has a really classy look to it—they send a menu to me in the office and it really looks exciting, and you go running down there and it's a couple of lawyers who've hired an architect, and they make this boffo place, and the last thing they do is hire some kid out of the CIA, throw him into this huge kitchen, and say, 'Go ahead, do your thing.'"

The CIA, needless to say, is the Culinary Institute of America, the Hyde Park institution that turns out many chefs.

Miller doesn't sound as if he's a big fan of the CIA.

"They teach banquet cooking for the local bingo chapter," he says. "And then they come down here and it's '*Oh, CIA*,'" he says with mock reverence. "In France a good chef can spend half a century before he gets to that point."

I try out my theory of Restaurant Sadness on Miller: "Is there some kind of cognitive dissonance process going on that explains why people keep going back despite bad food? With a hot restaurant, they've waited hours beyond their reservation, everyone's told them it's great, the crowd is right, and they hate to admit the food—they have to say the food is great to justify the shallowness of the experience."

"That's funny," he says. "I was just saying that the other night when we were at Felidia. That you've expended all this energy and you've paid these very high prices and it was highly recommended. It would take a real independent spirit to say, 'This is garbage.' I'm not saying they always serve—they're capable of serving excellent food—but I do think that's it. I think to a large extent people psych themselves into believing it's better than it really is. There are some restaurants that are just near toxic and they're packed every night. I think the role of critic is to sort of run gastronomic interference for the reader—I'll waste my money so you shouldn't have to waste yours."

The cognitive dissonance effect can turn nasty, it seems, when a critic demotes a restaurant around which a cult of believers has formed. Miller recently demoted La Grenouille, a four-star place, to two stars. And he took Vienna 79, a onetime four-star restaurant that had already been demoted to two, down one painful peg further to a solitary star.

"Vienna 79 was the most controversial one I've done," he tells me. "I wrote a pretty tough review; I was treated just terribly there. I never experienced worse service in my life. And after the review came out, I got obnoxious phone calls, people threatening me and wanting to meet me in the parking lot. People who had been eating there for years. They took it personally. . . ."

How bad was the service?

"We were squeezed in between tables, and all night long these waiters were coming by and *hitting* us. I mean, one almost knocked my mother off her chair. And they never said excuse me. You think I'm making this up, but I'm not. We asked the maître d' to change our wine order, and he looked at me as if I'd asked him to borrow his car for the weekend. . . . And as for the waiters, well, I worked in the kitchen of a French restaurant for a year," he says, "but occasionally I'd wait tables, and there were two things I was told: One is, don't touch your face with your hands when you're on the floor. And two, don't stand around and chat with your colleagues. These guys [at Vienna 79] were sort of slumped in the back of the room laughing and telling jokes, and here we are looking at the silverware. That's certainly not four-star. It's not three-star. It's not even two-star service, that. But on top of that, the food was really bland. It was one-star food."

Let's get into the star system. I tell Miller the one failing of the *Times* four-star system is the meaninglessness of a one-star "Good" rating. Isn't the one-star category just a catchall for three-star places turning into disasters, for perky inexpensive places that serve solid food, and mediocre ethnic restaurants?

"I find the star system very restricting," Miller says. "I think that's the hardest part of this job. Sometimes I'll finish writing a review and then agonize over these stars. Because you're right: The leap from one to two is so much bigger than from two to three. And I'll often say, 'This is a one and a half,' or 'This is a half.' There's a place I did called Arcadia, which I thought was very innovative, a very good new restaurant. I was thinking, well, three stars? . . . Côte Basque has three stars . . . if that has three stars, how can I give this new place, kind of untested, three? I realize how much power these things have, so I go back and forth. You try hard, but then you criticize a place very severely and you have one star after it. And down below that translates as 'Good.' Still, say you have a three-star restaurant that's really gone downhill. Well, I can't see bringing it back from three to zero unless it was just horrible. I wish I didn't have any involvement with any stars."

"Wouldn't it be easier if you had half stars? Or would it just drive you crazy?"

"I think it *would* be better. I wonder whether it would

drive the reader crazy. I've spoken to some of my editors about it and they're not dead against it. Gault-Millau has a twenty-point system, and that would be great because the gradation could be there. I'd rather just have people read the review and get their own impressions. How's your salad?"

I had ordered a smoked-fish salad.

"The salmon's okay," I say, not too decisively.

"Could I have just a little? I'll swap," he says, offering me some of his salad. "This is part of the game."

"What's that you have?" I ask, eyeing his offering suspiciously.

"This is a little smoked duck breast with *mâche*," he says, indicating the expensive bitter lettuce, "which I love. Now what would you do," he asks, returning to the perplexities of the star system, "what would you do with a little hole-in-the wall Chinese restaurant with excellent food, really excellent food. It couldn't get three stars. But then if you gave it fewer stars, you'd feel you were cheating it. It just gets confusing."

He's also acutely aware of another problematic element in his position: the Heisenberg uncertainty principle as it applies to *Times* restaurant reviews. By focusing his attention on a place with a favorable review, he almost inevitably *transforms* it irrevocably into a different place from the pleasant one that inspired the review in the first place. The moment the review is out, the place becomes impossible to get into, the food often impossible to eat. Few kitchens can handle the transformation from leisurely dining into instant Restaurant Madness.

"I don't have to write a rave for it to happen," Miller says. "I can write a one-star and you won't be able to get into the place. Two-star will really have people down the block, and three-star, they'll need the National Guard. It's not because of me, it's the institution I write for, and the place that food has in people's—I wrote about a little place downtown called Manhattan South. This was only 'Diner's Journal,' but Thursday night at ten-thirty—the paper must have hit the streets at ten twenty-nine—their phone started ringing. People started running to the restaurant holding the first edition, making reservations for that weekend. And they told me the phone never stopped ringing all night long into the next day until they just pulled it off the hook. . . ."

Bad as the situation is for the reader of his reviews, there's a special sort of Restaurant Sadness about this process for Miller himself. Every time he enjoys a meal good enough to inspire him to write about it, he knows that doing so will forever destroy his ability to return and enjoy it again: *That which he enjoys, he destroys.*

"There's a lovely Parisian-style bistro I ran across down in the West Village," he says, "called Au Troquet. I'm preparing to write about it, and it's got excellent food, a wonderful family atmosphere. It's run by a father and son. It's just a perfect place now," he says wistfully. "But I'm afraid that if I go back a few weeks after the review comes out, there'll be nothing left but a smoking ruin after the crowd descends."

"Do you go back after a rave to see whether standards have fallen?"

"I should, but the truth is I just don't have the time all the time. Does the food deteriorate? Do the prices go up? I know prices *have* gone up. I've heard that. I wish I had time to go back purely for my personal taste. But I can't because I'm always looking for something new. So I never get to go out for fun."

"What about the health hazards of the job?"

"There *are* health hazards. I've always been congenitally skinny, twenty-five pounds underweight, and never gained weight. And now I've suddenly gained fifteen pounds since last September. So it's a killer. I've joined a health club. I was there at seven-fifteen this morning. Calaerobics. My wife, too. We bought a digital scale. What kills me, I think, is that I haven't learned the art of tasting. I'm an *eater*. I eat my whole dinner and I taste everybody else's. It's the desserts that got me."

"You eat the whole dessert and then you taste everyone else's?"

"Yeah. This can't go on."

THE PASSIONS OF MARIO CUOMO

❦

In Which the Governor Sends a Mickey Mouse Watch to Roy Cohn and Calls Ed Koch a Pelagian Heretic

Who is that tall, spectral figure haunting the gloomy halls of the state capitol building today? Who is that silver-haired, patrician wraith with the lines of a shattered past engraved on his face?

Could it be—yes—*it's John Lindsay.*

Once the Great White Hope of American liberalism, the shining paladin of urban progressivism—what's he doing here in the lobby of Mario Cuomo's statehouse office?

What Lindsay's doing in the lobby is, in fact, lobbying. The former mayor is here today as a lobbyist for Drexel Burnham Lambert. The high-flying "junk-bond" financiers have hired Lindsay to importune the governor to veto the antitakeover (some say anti–Ted Turner) legislation now on his desk.

Some might relish the ironic appropriateness of this apparition, this Ghost of the Fiscal Crisis Past. After all, here's Lindsay, whom many blame for turning New York City's credit obligations *into* junk bonds, now a paid hireling for the junk bond kings of the private sector.

Some might relish it, but I don't. Coming upon Lindsay on my way to sit down with Cuomo was like seeing a sad, cautionary specter. Once, in college, from a distance, I'd believed in the shining promise of the Lindsay crusade, believed that he might be the one to translate the ideals of the civil rights movement into workable realities on the streets of the cities of the North. And then, as a reporter during the dying days of the second Lindsay administration, I'd seen at close hand exactly why Lindsay came to be called the Man Who Gave Good Intentions a Bad Name.

Would it be different with Mario Cuomo? After his electrifying, impassioned keynote speech at the 1984 Democratic National Convention—the one he'd called "A Tale of Two Cities"—Cuomo succeeded to that place in the hearts of the hopeful that Lindsay once had. Only the thought was, the hope was, that Cuomo's different: He's not another Lindsay. He's got the passion for the old ideals, but he knows how to make them work. He's got a kind of passion for perfecting the mechanical details of governing that make the difference between mere good intention and successful results. Unlike Lindsay, he's got a way with people that turns them on rather than off to his ideals.

And there was something else about Cuomo that encouraged the hope he wouldn't end up like Lindsay: his reputation as a killer debater and a go-for-the jugular politician. This was the Cuomo who took apart first Ed Koch and then Lew Lehrman in the '82 campaign debates, the Cuomo who's not afraid to trade head shots with Reagan's designated hit man, Pat Buchanan. The guy who took on his own archbishop on theological grounds at Notre Dame.

If Reagan has adopted Rambo as his role model, Cuomo

makes you think of the Clint Eastwood character in *Pale Rider*: the mysterious stranger in the clerical collar folk call the Preacher. He speaks in parables of love, but when he runs into resistance from the greedy, land-raping federals, the Preacher's eyes gleam and he takes great pleasure in blowing the feds full of holes.

Has the phrase "linebacker's eyes" ever been applied to Mario Cuomo? It's used to describe the gleam of passionate intensity that certain souls on fire, like Jack Lambert and Jack "Hacksaw" Reynolds, evince in the anticipation of cutting halfbacks in half.

All I knew about Cuomo's brief career as a minor-league baseball prospect was something I read about a fistfight he'd had with a catcher in the Class B league. But I have the feeling he might have chosen the wrong sport: He could have been a linebacker.

This afternoon as he barrels into the conference room in which I've been waiting, he manifests the burly, aggressive physical presence of a crack linebacker. When he sits himself down, he doesn't really sit. He crouches over the table, shoulders hunched forward, elbows advanced, looking like a roverback hanging over the gap at scrimmage, eager to nail an errant ballcarrier behind the line.

And when he senses intellectual error Cuomo shows you those linebacker's eyes. They gleam with pleasure as he blows holes in arguments and demolishes confused lines of thought. I found Cuomo thoughtful, introspective, compassionate, all those things, and he's got a great stern-but-kind-teacher side to him. But when he spots a mistake he's more like Hacksaw Reynolds than Mr. Chips.

In fact the first thing he wanted to do in our conversation was correct a mistake I'd made about him some months ago. Actually it was a mistake Roy Cohn made.

"Cuomo's tough," Roy had told me during my lunch with him. "I saw one thing he did that *scared* me."

What was it that scared Roy, a guy who prides himself

on not scaring easily? It was a devastating debating move Cuomo pulled on his hapless gubernatorial opponent, Lew Lehrman, in the climactic debate of the '82 campaign—a one-line remark that shocked Lehrman out of his red suspenders and left him for dead in the debate.

But, Cuomo tells me, Roy Cohn's account of that particular Cuomo moment got it wrong.

"Roy is saying 'Cuomo is one guy I'm afraid of because he went charging over to Lehrman, grabbed his wrist— some bellicose gesture like that—and said to Lehrman, *'My, isn't that an expensive watch.'* Well that didn't occur at all."

What then did happen?

"What occurred was, we were standing side by side debating and Lew was trying to interrupt my answers. Apparently he had some kind of *strategy* in mind," says Cuomo, barely suppressing his evident contempt for the strategic genius behind this tactic, "and at one point he leaned right over in front of me while I was speaking and jammed his watch in my face. He said 'Look at the time.' And I never even touched him. I looked at the watch and I said, *'My, that's an expensive watch.'* And the place broke up.

"So it wasn't me going over to Lehrman," says Cuomo, intent on setting the record straight. "It was Lehrman coming over to me. It wasn't me grabbing his wrist. It was Lehrman thrusting his watch in my face."

He pauses and smiles with satisfaction. "It was, however, I who said, *'My, that's an expensive watch.'*"

The distinction seems important to Cuomo: He didn't hit Lehrman with a low blow—it was a counterpunch.

Not that Cuomo takes the whole thing *that* seriously. It was, after all, Mario Cuomo, he reminds me, who sent Roy Cohn a Mickey Mouse watch after reading Cohn's "Cuomo scares me" comments.

"Can you get the note to Roy Cohn about the Mickey Mouse watch?" the governor calls out to his secretary.

The note that Cuomo sent to Cohn along with the Mickey Mouse gift reads: "I would never be unwise enough to debate you as a politician. But when finally the public drives me back to the practice of the law and I find myself head to head against you, wearing this will protect you from the kind of attack I made on Lew."

Setting aside the exact circumstances of the expensive-watch attack, what is it with these tough-guy Republicans like Roy Cohn and Pat Buchanan, the most recent victim of a Cuomo counterpunch? Why, I ask the governor, are these GOP street fighters frightened of Mario Cuomo?

"Because they're making a mistake," he says. "Because they misperceive me. Because they don't know me. I'm the easiest opponent they could have, I'm sure. They just don't know me."

"And what is the misperception they have?"

"They're confused. They think because I stood up and spoke about family and speak about law and order without surrendering to the death penalty, because I can balance a budget and still give more money to people in wheelchairs—they're confused into thinking that because I can do all of these things, which is exactly what they say Republicans are supposed to do, that means I'm going to run for president and then for sure they'd lose."

"And why are they wrong in—"

"Because I'm not running for president," he says. "If they knew the truth, which is, all I'm planning is to run for governor, they could all be relieved. They wouldn't bother with me—they'd go beat up Gary Hart."

"Why have you decided not to run for president?"

"I haven't decided not to run for president," he says, correcting me. "I said I'm planning to run for governor. They think I'm planning to run for president."

And of course an answer like that will not do much to change their minds, if you ask me.

But rather than get into that game, there's someone I'd

like to introduce you to now. Someone you'll undoubtedly be hearing more about if Cuomo does run for president. Someone you probably need to know to understand Cuomo as a person and a politician.

Maybe you know about this guy already: the French paleontologist and Jesuit priest whose attempts to speak of spirituality in Darwinian and Einsteinian terms were suppressed by the church until after his death in 1955.

I'm speaking, of course, of Pierre Teilhard de Chardin, Mario Cuomo's spiritual mentor.

I'd been surprised to find that nothing I'd read about Cuomo had focused attention on the importance of Teilhard to him. There had been no mention of Teilhard's inspirational work *The Divine Milieu*, which, Cuomo told me, he'd read "a hundred times."

Cuomo's *Diaries* hint strongly at the centrality of Teilhard to him. In one typical passage from 1981 he finds himself worrying about money: His wife's unhappy with him for not having gotten bigger bucks out of his law practice, and he's unhappy that the political career he sacrificed the big bucks for isn't really doing much to make the world better.

"I wonder what Teilhard would say about this kind of thinking," Cuomo writes. "Is it a form of weakness? How do I deal with what he would call the diminishments of my own spirit and the diminishments imposed by the world?"

Before going up to Albany to sit down with Cuomo, I brushed up on Teilhard, having been impressed by his speculative evolutionary theory in *The Phenomenon of Man* in college, but being kind of rusty on the details. *The Divine Milieu* is far more explicitly devotional and Catholic: It's an impassioned, inspirational work that takes off from the thesis that the universe of matter and energy revealed by contemporary subatomic physics and astrophysics is not a challenge to faith, but rather further revelation of the glory of Created Being. Yes, we are living in a material world, Teilhard says, anticipating you know who. But the material world (including human nature) is interpenetrated with divine potential—it's a "divine milieu," the way energy is the "milieu" of matter in relativistic physics.

I was curious to find out just how important this vision was to the governor. And surprised at just how passionate he was about it.

Our conversation about Teilhard, which somewhat incongruously followed the one about Roy Cohn and the Mickey Mouse watch, began, nonetheless much like that one, with Cuomo correcting another mistake I made.

This time it was my misreading of a passage in *The Divine Milieu* that I had been certain was a key to Cuomo's character development.

The passage I got wrong comes from Teilhard's introduction, in which he's describing the particular kind of person *The Divine Milieu* will have the most meaning for: "A certain kind of human spirit known to every spiritual director."

What is it about this certain kind of spirit? He's the kind of person who has a taste for the life of this world but a "higher Will" to withdraw from what he sees as the sinful confusion of the fallen world in search for the purity of loving God alone. Someone, in other words, who might be drawn to the priesthood or the monastic life for reasons of self-sanctification but who would be better off, Teilhard wants him to know, embracing rather than rejecting the world.

Is that you? I asked Cuomo.

Right doctrine, wrong guy, he replied—in essence. But before refuting my conjecture about his character he reproved my obvious quick-study job on *The Divine Milieu*.

"If you read it only once, then you are missing all the joy of reading it a hundred times as I have," he told me, "because as you know, it's poetry, a kind of intelligent emoting."

Then he got down to the task of setting me straight on the nature of its importance to his personal development.

"First, let me tell you what I think Teilhard is saying," Cuomo begins. "He devotes the book 'to those who love the world.' What he really says is, God so loved the world that he made man. Now it's very important to remember the context. He was banned. The reason he was banned is that before Vatican II it was common to interpret the Catholic theology in this country as saying this world is an evil place. A series of moral obstacles. The best you can do is repair to the monastery and weave baskets. Monks weave baskets to give their hands something to do in the grim interval between birth and eternity. Teilhard was a reaction to all that. Teilhard was saying that *debases* God. That *demeans* God. God didn't make us to get ready for the next world. He made us to be involved in this world. What he is saying to people like me is: The world is good, involvement is good, pain is good, sorrow is good—Being is good. It's very important to somebody raised in the Jimmy Breslin era, when if girls wore patent-leather shoes the nuns got upset because boys would look under their skirts by the reflection. So what kind of spirit am I?" Cuomo asks, coming back, now that he has defined my terms more precisely, to my original question.

"I'm not a spirit, I'm a struggler, a confused human who knows way down deep that there's something immensely beautiful about this world and who, when he comes across a Teilhard, says, 'Hallelujah! Prayers have been answered,' because Teilhard is one who as a scientist, a paleontologist, was able to say to you with perfect theological probity, 'You're right, Mario. I don't understand it either and I'm smarter than you, but I know that it's beautiful and I know you ought to stay with it and I know the more deeply you get involved in it, the more deeply you become a part of it, the more beautiful it gets and we are building up.' We diminish physically to build up spiritually, and when it's all over it just begins, so it's—"

"So it wasn't that you were tempted by renunciation," I say, interrupting Cuomo as the distinction he is making finally dawns on me. "It's the opposite: You found in him a vindication for a temperamental preference for this world."

"This world has a significance better than the significance taught by the old—" He searches for a word for the anti-world Catholic thinkers. "They weren't theologians because they didn't understand the theology. They were good religious people," he says, finally coming up with a charitable formulation for the error he sees in their ways. "Good religious people who concentrated on sin instead of opportunity."

I hadn't planned to get as deeply into theological questions as we did, but I think you get a sense of Cuomo's thought process at its most unmediated—in every sense of the word—when he's talking about such questions as the nature of hell and the continuing mystery of the origin of evil.

We got into hell and evil when I once again strayed into error—this time in my interpretation of a particularly cryptic reference to Teilhard in Cuomo's *Diaries*. Amidst the chaos of his primary campaign against Ed Koch, Cuomo found himself "thinking through the Apostles' Creed in my mind, the old creed that said, 'He descended into hell.' Matching it up to Teilhard." I had a theory about what that passage was *really* about, which I tried out on the governor:

"I wondered whether you were comparing your entering New York State politics to Christ descending into hell?"

"Oh no. No, not really. No," Cuomo says, "because that's inconsistent with believing as I do that almost all of involvement is good. So all the pain of politics and all the disappointment of politics, all the imperfections of politics, that's part of living and experiencing."

What was it then that he was speculating about in that

passage when he talked about matching up the old Apostles' Creed with Teilhard?

The theology of hell is "still kind of bothersome" to him. Cuomo says. "If you look at the old Apostles' Creed and you compare it to what's said as a creed now—one of the principal differences is that they leave out of the present creed the portion that says Christ descended into hell."

So?

"I concluded from much analysis while jogging that what they're really saying in the new creed is, hell is the *void*. But the old creed suggested there was a *place*, an existence beneath us the way the world is a place. The new creed suggests that the real hell is a nothingness and a vacuum. And that's a colossal step forward. What Teilhard, I guess, would have said is there is a heaven but there is no hell in the sense of punishment."

Questions of hell and punishment lead him to leap to the theological controversy over the nature of evil.

"There is no explanation for evil, obviously, and Teilhard is very clear on that, too, but—"

"No explanation for evil in Teilhard?"

"I don't think anywhere really. There isn't sufficient understanding allowed us to be able to explain evil—I mean not sin, but unexplained pain to children sitting in Vietnamese villages who got their eyes blown out of their heads by explosions they didn't know were coming and that they had nothing to do with. The mother losing four children in a row, the apparently senseless tragedy. My brother's son freezing to death in the backyard at age five out in Copiague. How do you explain that? The apparent injustice. You can't. You read McBrien's two volumes on Catholicism, which is now all the rage theologically for Catholics—he says there's no point in giving a lot of pages to the subject of evil because we don't *have* an explanation."

Returning to Teilhard, I wondered if there might be

something more about him that Cuomo identified with. Perhaps the way his heretical tendencies got him in trouble with his religious superiors might have fortified Cuomo in his outspoken disagreement with Archbishop O'Connor over abortion rights.

"Teilhard was a heretic, right?" I began. "He was condemned for—"

"No, no, he was not," Cuomo corrects me heatedly. "No, sir, there was nothing heretical about Teilhard."

"What about pantheism?" I suggest. "Pelagianism?" (The translator's footnotes to my edition of *The Divine Milieu* are replete with cautionary explanations of certain passages of Teilhard that, he says protectively, might *sound* pantheist, or hint at Pelagian tendencies, but are really okay in context. Pelagianism is the early church heresy that suggests that Adam's original sin does not necessarily taint all succeeding generations of mankind—that human endeavor has a potential for good in this world.)

Cuomo is particularly sensitive to my imputation that his spiritual mentor was a Pelagian heretic.

"Oh no, no, no, no," he says, quadruply negative. "He wasn't a Pelagianist either."

If he seems particularly upset about the imputation of Pelagianism, it may be because it's a particularly intriguing heresy to Cuomo. And one he will soon accuse Ed Koch, of all people, of adhering to.

But meanwhile he wants to correct my misuse of the word "heretic" in its application to Teilhard:

"The harshest criticism he got from the church was not that he should stop believing what he believed—he was just told that he was to stop publishing. It was John XXIII, that magnificent contribution to our humanity, who freed him from that and allowed him to publish, but just to seminarians where they could control it with guidance and understanding. And then eventually to the world at large.

But he was never declared a heretic. He was to be read with caution."

"I guess what I was getting at is, you've had this public battle with your bishop. Do *you* feel at all like a heretic?"

"If you don't mind, my *cardinal*," he says.

"Your cardinal now. Do you feel at all like a heretic?"

"No. I will be precise on this subject, and it's a great relief to be able to be. I wrote the Notre Dame speech only because the archbishop in one of his early appearances was asked on a television show whether I should be excommunicated, and my wife and son were together with me watching the show at the time, and I have never had a more painful moment than the moment of the archbishop's hesitation in answer to that question."

He pauses, a pained expression on his brow. "The archbishop has since many times, not once or twice but many times, made clear that that wasn't his intent, et cetera. But too late. The damage was done and I felt it was time therefore to write my own apologia, which I did with the help of a number of theologians. When I say the help, I wrote it and then distributed it to theologians whom I trusted. I was absolutely certain that I was right theologically, and since then in *America* magazine a couple of the leading theologians, or at least one in the country, have written that my position, whether they agreed with it or not as a matter of prudential judgment, was perfectly sound theologically, so I have no doubt that my position is sound theologically. My difference with my archbishop, now cardinal, is on a political judgment, agreeing that in my own personal life I would instruct those who wished my instruction that abortion was undesirable. What do you do about that politically? Do you try to pass a constitutional amendment which won't pass and which wouldn't do any good if it passed, or do you try to work affirmatively to convince people that there's a better way than abortion? I chose the latter. That's purely a matter of politics and I said so in the speech, and I'm right and I'm sure I'm right."

An admittedly irreverent thought strikes me at this point. How does a guy so concerned with theological correctness react to being named by *Playgirl* as one of its "Ten Sexiest Men"? A bit later I ask him what he thought of the accolade.

"Thank God John Candy made the list too," he says laughing. "That way I won't take myself too seriously."

"What *is* your attitude toward sexual revolution or whatever you want to call what's gone on for the last twenty years? How traditional are you? Do you disapprove of permissiveness or—?"

"It's not for me to approve or disapprove," he says, criticizing my question before giving a surprisingly impassioned answer. "I don't judge people's conduct that way. I think from society's point of view it would be better if we were less open about sex. I believe we have profaned it. I believe sex is a beautiful gift of God, or whatever, fate, nature. It is a magnificent opportunity to express real feeling. It is God's device for regeneration. It is a lot of beautiful things. It is not improved by the way in which we as a society are dealing with it publicly. I think we fail to teach the reverence for it that we should. I think we have debased it and that's unfortunate. I think we're all losers as a result of that. It means less to this generation than it might have.

"It's a very personal thing. Some people are married and are frequently involved in sexual encounters, some people very infrequently. It's a personal thing. I do think from society's point of view it would have been better if we had not profaned it the way we have. But aside from that, I think as a people it would be better for us if we were more consistent in keeping violence out of our public exhibitions than sex, for all that I've said about the profaning of sex. Even worse is what we've done with violence, and popularizing violence is one of the great social sins of our time.

I think those societies, I guess like Scandinavian societies where they allowed people vast freedom when it came to sexual preferences but were assiduous about trying to keep violence out of movies and publications, et cetera, where they can—that was probably a more intelligent judgment than the one we've made as a society."

Moral seriousness of this sort can be a bit of a problem with some. Recently I had dinner with a college friend and his wife who confessed their Cuomo Problem to me. They weren't the first. I'd found a number of Big Chill types who'd opted for the fast lane a bit resentful, hostile to Cuomo for reminding them of ideals—or, they'd say, illusions—they'd left behind.

Whatever was behind it, the way my friend's wife expressed her Cuomo Problem to me was: "I'd be more comfortable with Cuomo if I knew he had some really human faults, you know, even if it was that he binged on cookies at three in the morning without transforming it into a spiritual lesson."

I ask Cuomo if he would help her out by confessing to me some cookie-binge-type faults. He isn't very forthcoming.

"I have all the faults that everybody has," he insists, "all the appetites that other people have. We control them, each of us, in various ways, but we each sin seven times a day."

Somehow I don't think that was the kind of answer she had in mind, so I try to approach the virtuousness problem from another direction.

"There was something Murray Kempton said—did you read his review of your book?"

"I never understand what he's saying but I love everything he writes," Cuomo avers.

"Well he was very admiring of you in the review, but he also seemed to suggest that in your diary entries you were putting forward your humility in a somewhat prideful way."

Cuomo laughs. "See. I told you I had faults."

"Would you say it's true though?"

"If Murray said it, I'll accept it."

I begin to shift the subject when Cuomo interrupts, not content to let Kempton have the last word on his pride/humility quotient.

"I'll say this about Murray: He has a little bit of pridefulness about the way he writes about *my* pridefulness."

Do I seem a bit captious about Cuomo here? Perhaps because we're coming to a subject upon which I find his views genuinely admirable, and I don't want to seem like an uncritical sensibility when discussing them. The subject is racial justice, and I admire Cuomo because I think he's one of the few powerful politicians in America who still takes the unfulfilled goals of the civil rights movement seriously. Not only takes them seriously but takes seriously the task of making them work in a society that wants to ignore the past by calling itself "postracist," as the fashionable neoconservative phrase goes.

You can hear how impassioned Cuomo is on the subject of race when I ask him how he would have handled racial relations in New York City differently from Ed Koch.

"There *is* a difference, I think, between the mayor and me," Cuomo says. "I think he uses the notion of *evenhandedness* where I would use the notion of *equity*. I have heard him say, 'I treat blacks and whites the same way.' That can be misunderstood at a time when disproportionate numbers of blacks are vulnerable. Then people might mishear you and think that what you're really saying is 'I don't care if you're in trouble, I'm going to treat you like the people who are not in trouble.' Now that doesn't make any sense. That's what Marie Antoinette said: Let them all eat cake. So he puts a greater stress on pure equality. I think more about trying to even up the competition. There are some who are left behind through no fault of their own, who need extra help, and I think we should give them the extra help. The analogy I have used is a family with two children, one in a wheelchair, one wins medals for track. That creates a whole series of situations where the one in the wheelchair should get a little more help than the one who can win medals at track. That's not evenhandedness. So there is that difference. And I think when the mayor talks about equality a lot of blacks like it, the ones who are making it, et cetera. But the ones who are at the bottom, who are vulnerable, who are out of work, who are dropouts, think, 'You oppressed us for a couple of hundred years, you enslaved us, you debased us, you tried to dehumanize us, and then you release us and say, "Now you're like everybody else. I'm going to treat you evenhandedly." But that's not right because for two hundred years you created a negative. Now you're going to have to do at least two hundred years of positive to make up for it.' I think that's the attitude that some have that the mayor doesn't successfully respond to."

Did you catch the shift Cuomo makes in the midst of this response? I could hear it in his voice, but you can see it on the printed page, too. He begins with semantic distinctions and argumentative analogies (Marie Antoinette, the family with the kid in the wheelchair) to make his point intellectually.

Then something happens to his voice. He stops speaking in his own first-person voice and begins speaking *in the voice of the victims* of racism ("You oppressed *us* for a couple of hundred years, you enslaved *us*, you debased *us* . . ."), a voice that takes on tones of genuine pain and anger, not just abstract empathy.

In that astonishing keynote address, Cuomo called on Americans not to cease "to feel one another's pain." That can be an empty rhetorical formulation. But in Cuomo's case, I get a feeling it's a *description* of a kind of spiritual discipline he practices in his approach to political problems.

There's a fascinating, characteristically Cuomo-esque postscript to our discussion of Koch and race, one that provides another revealing glimpse into the governor's thought process. And one that gives me an opportunity—at last—to correct an error Cuomo made, in theological reasoning no less.

I don't know whether or not it was prompted by my mention of Pelagianism in connection with his spiritual mentor, or whether Cuomo just has Pelagianism on his mind these days, but a week after our conversation in Albany a quote from Cuomo appeared in print that accused Ed Koch of "Pelagianism."

When I say "a quote from Cuomo" accused Koch of Pelagianism, I may be on shaky ground, because the quote wasn't directly attributed to the governor. The quote appeared in a Ken Auletta *Daily News* column on Koch and race; Auletta attributes the quote to "a thoughtful public official." Judge for yourself if you think I'm rash in concluding it's Cuomo speaking here:

"The core difference between Koch and, say, Governor Cuomo," the "thoughtful public official" says, "is that Koch is a Pelagian. . . . If a kid from the ghetto can't make it, the Pelagian says it's their responsibility. The fact that God placed that kid in the ghetto, gave him no father, and that he was raised poor, that's of no concern."

While I agree with Cuomo on the merits of the equality argument (if somebody can prove to me it wasn't Cuomo speaking, I promise to enter a Trappist monastery and take a vow of silence), nonetheless I think the "thoughtful public official" has made an error in the logic of his heresiology.

His comparison of Koch to the Pelagians does a disservice to the Pelagians, who were far more generous in their view of human nature than Cuomo's analogy would imply. After all, the heresy of the Pelagians was their rather optimistic belief that natural man was not inevitably corrupted by original sin and was capable, in fact, of moral good and spiritual improvement. It is the gloomy predestinarian Augustine (who believed natural man, as such, was beyond hope and who in fact was chief scourge of Pelagianism in the church) to whom Koch is more aptly compared.

And, in fact, I'd say that both Cuomo and his mentor, Teilhard, are closer in spirit—on the doctrinal spectrum that runs from Pelagius to Augustine—to the Pelagians, in their love of this world and belief in the possibility of spiritual evolution, than they are to Augustine. Indeed, there's a technical term Protestant theologian Paul Tillich uses that, although Cuomo would probably deny it, fits both Teilhard and Cuomo: "semi-crypto-Pelagians." (Here's an issue the newly Catholicized Lew Lehrman could really run with next time he debates Cuomo: Okay, it's an expensive watch, but my opponent is a semi-crypto-Pelagian.)

At this point I decided to see what Cuomo's views were on a different kind of heresy. A political heresy. About the lesson of the New York fiscal crisis. The orthodox establishment theology on this point, even among "responsible" New Yorkers, is that New York sinned, that New York and New Yorkers deserve the blame for our plight because our profligate bleeding-heart compassion was blind to hard-headed reality—and the rest of the country shouldn't be taxed to support our immorality.

The first hint I had that Cuomo didn't buy the self-hating logic of the Blame New York First crowd was that stinging "share the derelicts" wisecrack he had delivered down in Washington a week earlier.

The governor was testifying before a House committee on his opposition to the Reagan tax plan's elimination of state- and local-tax deductibility—a complex, eye-glazing issue no Democrat wanted to touch, but which Cuomo seized on and turned into a moral crusade. One he seems to be winning.

Anyway, an earnest Republican House member from New Hampshire somewhat patronizingly suggested to Cuomo that the committee might deign to offer New York and other high-tax states with large social-service budgets "a portion" of the deductibility they wanted.

Fine, said Cuomo, and we'll send New Hampshire "a portion of our derelicts, our homeless, our illegal aliens, and drug addicts."

I thought that raised an important question the Blame New York First crowd has ignored. "Isn't it true," I ask Cuomo, "that the plight of the northern cities is not due to their immorality but to the costs they incur caring for the victims of southern racism, the vast migration of southern blacks who have sought refuge here?"

"I put it a little differently," Cuomo says, "but I made the same point and that is, we bear burdens that are basically national in their genesis and in present responsibility. Welfare, everybody knows, is a national problem. It's not ours. Not all the welfare cases are indigenous. They can travel here from any part of the country. That's the Constitution."

"Don't you think that in the way the fiscal crisis has been written about, New Yorkers have been unfairly portrayed as immoral and wasteful . . .?"

"There is a regrettably prevalent view of us," Cuomo says, "as not just wasteful but as loud, even debauched, unpleasant, crude, indifferent to other people. I mean, it's a terribly harsh judgment. And again, it's not everybody of course, but too many people feel that way about New York. There may even be a little jealousy in it because of the spectacular quality of New York City, the bigness of it and the largeness; there may be a resentment about that. There is an intimidation factor as well. People are intimidated by the speed that they see here, the pace that they equate with frenzy. The president was aware of it, and the Republicans were aware of it and played to it by starting their whole campaign for this [tax plan] running against New York. In the president's first speech, he took the opportunity to refer to New York specifically. We're the only state he mentioned."

The talk turns to Forest Hills—and John Lindsay.

Cuomo says he met with Lindsay earlier today about the takeover bill, but sitting across the table from him, he couldn't help but think of Forest Hills.

"We didn't talk about Forest Hills," Cuomo says, "but I can't look at John without thinking of it."

Forest Hills was the beginning of the end for John Lindsay and the beginning of the beginning for Mario Cuomo.

Forest Hills—the revolt of the middle-class Queens community against the Lindsay administration plan to stick high-rise, low-income projects for ghetto dwellers in their midst—was, of course, what brought Cuomo into public life. His ability to "feel the pain" and fears of the angry white residents of Forest Hills enabled him to gain community acquiescence to a scaled-down integrated project that salvaged a workable reality from the blundering, self-destructive good intentions of the Lindsay administration.

"What's the Forest Hills project like now?" I ask Cuomo.

"It's beautiful," he says. "I went back there with Harry Reasoner a little bit ago to do *60 Minutes*. We walked the grounds. Every time I go home to Queens I go past it. I stopped by there the other day with somebody in the car just to show it to them."

"You wrote in the Forest Hills diary," I say, "that toward the end you thought it might be a turning point away from the attempt to integrate housing or, on the other hand, it might be a turning point for the better where communities are consulted, et cetera. Which do you think it has been?"

"It helped end housing programs," says Cuomo. "The Nixon impoundment was in '72, and we never had another large public-housing program. Forest Hills helped produce a political environment that allowed the federal government to walk away from its obligation for low-income housing, and they have ever since."

"Would you favor a return to some kind of attempt to . . . ?"

"I certainly would, but I'm not going to wait for it. That's why Mayor Koch and I have put together the biggest housing program in the history of the state. It would mean seventy-five thousand units if we could get the legislature to adopt the legislation we need to spend the Battery Park and Port Authority monies."

"You've been spending the day listening to lobbyists like Lindsay for and against the takeover bill. What's your thinking on it?" I ask Cuomo.

"I have not arrived at a conclusion yet. It's complex. I would like to protect my native businesses here, but I'm concerned that we shouldn't do it in such a way as to be out-and-out protectionist about it. I don't think that would be wise. I'm concerned, too, about what appears to be an unfairness to Ted Turner. Not because Ted Turner would be good for me personally if he took CBS, because I don't suspect he would be, and not because he would be good for New York, because I suspect he would take jobs out of New York if he took CBS, but because he got caught midstream, and we oughtn't, I don't think, to play the game that way. That's my present thinking. I may change my mind."

"You know Democrats have a reputation for being antibusiness. Are you antibusiness?"

"I couldn't be if I cared about those people in wheelchairs and the people out of work, because the place they're going to get a job is in the private sector. You can't make it with the public payroll. You just can't put enough people to work. It costs you too much. So if there's any hope for those eight hundred thousand or so AFDC [Aid for Dependent Children] people, it's in the private sector. That means business. So I'm not only not antibusiness, I am probusiness. Not so that they can all drive Rolls-Royces and wear pinky rings but so that we can create the base we need to do the things we need for people who aren't given the chance to work because they're too old or too weak or because there simply is no job. So yes, I'm very much pro–private sector strength."

By now time was running out, and so I tried to ask the governor one last question that had been on my mind. But first I had to go through one last corrective struggle:

"Last question," I begin.

"You said that already," Cuomo snaps.

"No, I said *two* more questions."

"No, you didn't, you said two more questions *two* questions ago."

"No, no, no."

"Yes, you did."

"We'll go back to the tape."

"When you play the tape you'll see what a good lawyer I am."

Okay, it turns out he was right. But I'm still right about his semi-crypto-Pelagianism. And he let me ask my final question anyway:

"I was struck as I arrived today," I begin, "seeing John Lindsay down there with some other lobbyists waiting in line. Here was the guy who was the great hope of American liberalism and now he's a high-paid lobbyist for Drexel Burnham. Do you think you'll ever end up as a high-paid lobbyist for corporations?"

"Hmm. I don't know. I kind of doubt it. The only reason I could possibly do that would be for the money, and I hate to say this, but money has never meant everything to me that it should have. If I were a little more careful about money, I would have had a lot more of it, and I would have had a lot more freedom and probably could have done a lot more things than I have. But now I have a son who I am sure is going to get rich if he keeps his health, and I've told him to go into the law practice. He wants public life. He never said that. He won't say it to me but I know it. He's my blood and he wants public life. But first, I told him, go and make money so they can't commandeer you. You see, if you come to this business needing the job then there is the temptation to do things you otherwise might not if you were secure. So I said, build yourself a secure niche. He'll be rich in no time. Honestly. My daughter, my first, is a doctor. My two girls after Andrea are so beautiful and so bright that they're going to make it.

"Money now means something because it keeps you free to be a public servant. I can settle for one hundred thousand dollars. I don't need two hundred fifty thousand. So I doubt very much that I would wind up that way. I'd like to wind up as a judge, a teacher maybe. Not with a lot of classes. That's too hard. I would like to wind up being free to read, being free to listen to music. So anyway, no, I don't want to be a lobbyist. No. I don't want to finish that way."

He pauses. Suddenly a new notion strikes him: "I want to die sliding into third base." Then his eyes light up: "No, throwing a hook shot. I think ideally I'd like to die with the ball just hitting the net, probably a left-hand hook shot off the back wall."

Cuomo gets up and demonstrates his form for that Final Shot.

"It just hits the net," he says with a smile of triumph. "The bell goes off. That's it."